I.C.C
TROPHY
Kuala Lumpur, Malaysia
1997

Edited by Peter Griffiths

Statistics by Darren Senior

Published by the Association of Cricket Statisticians and Historians, West Bridgford, Nottingham
1997
Typeset by Limlow Books
Printed by Tranters, Derby
ISBN: 0 947774 83 1

PREFACE

The Association of Cricket Statisticians and Historians (ACS) provides in this book a brief overview and full scorecoards of the 1997 ICC Trophy competition that took place in Kuala Lumpur, Malaysia in March and April. It also brings up to date the competition records and individual career figures for each country. Previous tournaments are covered in the two earlier volumes in this series – the first covering the 1979, 1982 and 1986 competitions in England and the second covering the 1990 competition in Holland and the 1996 competition in Kenya. Copies of these books are still available from the ACS shop for those wishing to possess a full record of the six competitions that have taken place so far.

The ICC Trophy has continued to grow in importance – once again more countries took part – Italy and Scotland being the newcomers in the 1997 competition. Scotland achieved the distinction of winning through to the 1999 World Cup at their first attempt.

We have managed to find more details for the previous tournaments and a list of amendments for the previous books is printed at the end of this volume. In particular, further research has shown the correct names of players. We have indicated in the brief biographies those players in this tournament who appeared in previous volumes in this series with a different name. The ACS will be grateful if anybody can fill in the gaps that remain or can provide any further corrections. These will be published in future editions as further tournaments are played.

For this tournament the I.C.C. registered all players to ensure they were eligible to take part and we are indebted to them for providing basic biographical data for the players and premission to reproduce it here. We also thank the I.C.C. for permission to reproduce the playing conditions. We are very much in the debt of CricInfo "The home of cricket on the internet" (http://www.cricket.org/) who provided live coverage of most of the matches on the internet and to Travis Basevi of CricInfo who whilst in Malaysia organising the internet coverage was able to answer questions on the scorecards as the matches progressed. This helped considerably and saved much agonising over scorecards long after the matches had taken place as had happened previously. Our thanks also go to the organising committee in Malaysia for providing Travis with facilities. The standard of scoring has improved considerably, but there are still a few gaps in the information. It is to be hoped that in the next tournament all information will be present.

We are grateful to Ralph Dellor for providing us with an independent overview of the tournament which he covered. As in the previous volumes, Darren Senior has compiled the statistics, most of which have not appeared anywhere else. Thanks also go to Travis Basevi and CricInfo for providing the photographs.

The ACS is also grateful to the following for their help with biographical information, corrections and other details: B.C.Roberts (Argentina), A.C.Douglas (Bermuda), T.Mathura (Canada), S.Nissen (Denmark), East and Central Africa Cricket Conference, P.I.Knight (Fiji), T.Finlayson (Gibraltar), R.D.Brewster, R.Mawhinney and C.Speak (Hong Kong), G.Byrne (Ireland), L.Bruno (Italy), R.Armstrong and Jasmer Singh (Kenya), V. Maha and W.Satchell (Papua New Guinea), N.Leitch and A.Ritchie (Scotland), J.Grimberg and P.C.Manoharan (Singapore), J.Ward (Zimbabwe), Philip Bailey, Vic Isaacs and N.T.Plews.

Peter Griffiths
August 1997

FOREWORD
by Ralph Dellor

Jagmohan Dalmiya, the new President of ICC, has been a fervent advocate of the globalisation of cricket. His contention has been that the game is too good to be confined to a select and elite group of countries. The pleasures of cricket are such that the game should be made accessible to everyone. While it might be thought that certain practical difficulties would prevent complete pursuance of this objective, there is scarcely a speck in the ocean on which some standard of cricket is not now played. The game is seen from Finland to The Falklands, even if the quality of performance needs to be considerably enhanced for cricket to become a truly world game.

This fact was evident at the 1997 ICC Trophy, held in Kuala Lumpur, Malaysia. At the top there were teams which could soon develop towards Test status; lower down there were national teams to which ordinary club players in England could aspire with the right nationality. Nevertheless, 22 nations were represented in what was claimed to be the largest international cricket tournament that the world has seen and that, in itself, represents a significant spread in the development of the game.

The final itself was a triumph for Bangladesh as a whole, for Steve Tikolo as a batsman and for the much-maligned Duckworth-Lewis formula. Several critics of the system for setting targets in a rain-affected match were forced to concede that the total calculated for a Bangladeshi victory was realistic, even if the successful charge was ultimately affected by a lack of communication. Could Kenyan captain Maurice Odumbe really have been the only person on the ground not to know that there could not be a tie? With one run needed for a Bangladeshi win, he set five fielders back to save two. Had that not been the case, Steve Tikolo's superb 147 would have surely claimed the prize. There can be no higher praise for Tikolo other than to say that, had be been wearing a maroon cap instead of the green of Kenya, nobody would have questioned that they were watching a high-class innings from a West Indian Test batsman.

Of course, tournaments such as these are not all about the final. It could be claimed that the 3rd/4th place play-off was more important in that this match provided one berth in the draw for the World Cup itself in England in 1999. It went to Scotland at the expense of Celtic neighbours Ireland. And then there were the Italys, Papua New Guineas, Fijis, Gibraltars and the rest which made the whole event so colourful and vibrant.

Next time round it is only the top twelve nations who will contest the ICC Trophy for places in the World Cup. The authorities must also learn that even artificial wickets need attention to prevent them deteriorating as the competition reaches its important stages. In addition, in a country with such a wet climate, some provision other than a few plastic sheets must be found to protect playing areas against the weather.

Nevertheless, the matches were completed, some marvellously dramatic cricket was played and the whole experience of world cricket was enriched by the 1997 ICC Trophy, broadcast to the world by TWI. Globalisation is well under way.

ICC TROPHY 1997 PLAYING CONDITIONS

1. LAWS OF CRICKET

Except as varied hereunder the Laws of Cricket (1980 Code) Second Edition – 1992 and subsequent amendments, ICC Standard Playing Conditions as printed in the ICC Code of Conduct and Regulations booklet (August 1996) shall apply.

2. DURATION OF MATCHES

All matches shall be of one day's scheduled duration. The matches will consist of one innings per side and each innings will be limited to 50 six-ball overs. A minimum of 20 overs per team shall constitute a match.

There shall also be a reserve day for the semi-finals, final and third place play-off on which an incomplete match will be continued.

3. COMPETITION FORMAT

3.1 First Round

Competing teams are divided into 4 groups (2 groups of 6 teams, 2 groups of 5 teams). In each group, the teams will play each other once. The position of the teams in each group after the completion of the preliminary round matches will be determined on the basis of maximum points secured by a team according to the table of points provided in Clause 14 below.

Each group is as follows:

Group A	Group B	Group C	Group D
Kenya	Bangladesh	Holland	Bermuda
U.S.A.	U.A.E.	Canada	Scotland
Ireland	Malaysia	Namibia	Hong Kong
Gibraltar	Denmark	Fiji	Papua New Guinea
Singapore	West Africa	E. & C. Africa	Italy
Israel	Argentina		

3.2 Second Round (top 8 teams)

The top 2 teams from each group will qualify for the second round. The 8 teams in the second round shall be divided into 2 groups, as follows:

Group E	Group F
Champion Group A (E1)	Champion Group B (F1)
Champion Group D (E2)	Champion Group C (F2)
Runner-up Group B (E3)	Runner-up Group A (F3)
Runner-up Group C (E4)	Runner-up Group D (F4)

Each team will play the other team in its Group once, and the position of the teams in each Group after the completion of the second round matches will be determined by points on the same basis as the first round matches (refer Clause 14.1 below).

The winner of Group E will play the runner-up of Group F in the 1st semi-final; the winner of Group F will play the runner-up of Group E in the 2nd semi-final (refer Clause 14.3 below).

The winner of the 1st semi-final will play the winner of the 2nd semi-final in the Final. The losing semi-finalists will play each other to determine which team finishes in third place (refer Clause 14.3 below).

Plate Competition

The teams that finish in third place and below in each group after the first round matches will play a 'Plate' competition on a knock-out basis to determine who finishes in places 9 to 22.

If a Plate match is tied or there is no result, the team that finishes higher in the first round matches as determined in Caluse 14.1 shall be declared the winner.

Refer also to Clause 14.

4. HOURS OF PLAY, INTERVALS AND MINIMUM OVERS IN THE DAY

4.1 Start and Cessation Times:

0900 – 1300 (first sesion)
1300 – 1345 (lunch)
1345 – 1715 (second session)

4.2 Interval Between Innings

The innings of the team batting second shall not commence before the scheduled time for commencement of the second session unless the team batting first has completed its innings at least 30 minutes prior to the scheduled interval, in which case a 10 minute break will occur and the team batting second will commence its innings and the interval will occur as scheduled.

Where play is delayed or interrupted the umpires will reduce the length of the interval as follows:

Time Lost	Interval
Up to 60 Minutes	30 Minutes
Between 60 and 120 Minutes	20 Minutes
More than 120 Minutes	10 Minutes

Note: Refer also to the provisions of Clause 7.2

4.3 Intervals for Drinks

Two drinks breaks per session shall be permitted, each 1 hour 10 minutes apart. The provision of Law 16.6 shall be strictly observed except that under conditions of extreme heat the umpires may permit extra intervals for drinks.

An individual player may be given a drink either on the boundary edge or at the fall of a wicket, on the field, provided that no playing time is wasted. No other drinks shall be taken onto the field without the permission of the umpires. Any player taking drinks onto the field shall be dressed in proper cricket attire.

5. APPOINTMENT OF UMPIRES

There shall be a panel of 22 umpires for on-field duties for the first and second round and Plate matches. For the semi-finals, final and third place play-off umpires from the National Grid International Panel will be appointed by ICC.

There shall also be a panel of 8 umpires, nominated by the Malaysian Cricket Association, for third umpire duties for the first and second round matches and Plate matches. These umpires will assist the on-field umpire when requested and whenever possible. They will also act as the replacement on-field umpire in the event that one of the on-field umpires is unable to continue.

Third Umpire/TV Replays for semi-finals; Final and Third place playoff

5.1 General

a) The Malaysian Cricket Association will ensure a separate room, or sectioned off area, is provided for the third umpire and that he has access to a television monitor and direct sound link with the television control unit director to facilitate as many replays as is necessary to assist him in making a decision.

b) The third umpire shall call for as many replays from any camera angle as is necessary to reach a decision. As a guide, a decision should be made within 30 seconds wherever possible, but the third umpire shall have discretion to take more time in order to finalise a decision.

c) The on-field umpire has the discretion whether to call for a TV replay or not and should take a common-sense approach. Players may not appeal to the umpire to use the replay system – breach of this provision would constitute dissent and the player could be liable for discipline under the Code of Conduct.

5.2 Run-out, Stumping and Hit Wicket Decisions

a) The on-field umpire shall be entitled to call for a TV replay to assist him in making a decision about a run-out, stumping or hit wicket appeal.

b) An on-field umpire wishing the assistance of a TV replay shall signal to the third umpire by making the shape of a TV screen with his hands.

c) If the third umpire decides the batsman is out a red light is displayed; a green light means not-out. Should the third umpire be temporarily unable to respond, a white light (where available) will remain illuminated throughout the period of interruption to signify to the on-field umpires that the TV replay system is temporarily unavailable, in which case the decision will be taken by the on-field umpire.

5.3 Boundary Decisions

a) The on-field umpire shall be entitled to call for a TV replay to assist him in making a decision about whether the fieldsman had any part of his person in contact with the ball when he touched or crossed the boundary line or whether a four or six had been scored.

b) An on-field umpire wishing the assistance of a TV replay shall signal to the third umpire by use of a two-way radio transceiver – the third umpire will convey his decision to the on-field umpire by this method.

c) The third umpire may initiate contact with the on-field umpire by two-way radio if TV coverage shows a boundary line infringement.

6. THE TOSS

The captains, dressed in on-field match clothing, shall toss for the choice of innings on the field of play 30 minutes before the scheduled or rescheduled time for the match to start. The referee will accompany the captains and supervise the toss.

7. LENGTH OF INNINGS

7.1 Uninterrupted matches

a) Each team shall bat for 50 (six ball) overs unless all out earlier. A team shall not be permitted to declare its innings closed.

b) If the team fielding first fails to bowl the required number of overs by the scheduled time for cessation of the first session, play shall continue until the required number of overs has been bowled.

Unless otherwise determined by the referee, the innings of the team batting second shall be limited to the same number of overs bowled by it, at the scheduled time for cessation of the first session. The over in progress at the scheduled cessation time shall count as a completed over.

The interval shall not be extended and the second session shall commence at the scheduled time.

The referee may increase the number of overs to be bowled by the team bowling second if, after consultation with the umpires he is of the opinion that events beyond the control of the bowling team prevented that team from bowling the required number of overs by the scheduled time for the cessation of the innings of the team battng first.

c) If the team batting first is all out and the last wicket falls at or after the scheduled time for the interval, the innings of the team batting second shall be limited to the same number of overs bowled to the team batting first at the scheduled time for the interval (the over in which the last wicket falls to count as a complete over).

d) If the team batting first is dismissed in less than 50 overs, the team batting second shall be entitled to bat for 50 overs except as provided in (c) above.

e) If the team fielding second fails to bowl 50 overs or the number of overs as provided in 7.1(b), (c) or (d) by the scheduled cessation time, the hours of play shall be extended until the required number of overs has been bowled or a result achieved.

7.2 Delayed or Interrupted Matches (First and Second Round and Plate matches only)

7.2.1 General

a) The object shall always be to rearrange the number of overs so that both teams have the opportunity of batting for the same number of overs. A team shall not be permitted to declare its innings closed.

A minimum 20 overs have to be bowled to the team batting second to constitute a match subject to the provisions of Clause 7.1(b).

The calculation of the number of overs to be bowled shall be based on an average rate of 15 overs per hour in the total time available for play. If a reduction of the number of overs is required, any recalculation must not cause the match to be rescheduled to finish earlier than the original cessation time. This time may be extended to allow for one extra over for both teams to be added if required.

b) If the team fielding second fails to bowl the required number of overs by the scheduled cessation time, the hours of play shall be extended until the overs have been bowled or a result achieved.

c) The team batting second shall not bat for a greater number of overs than the first team unless the latter has been all out in less than the agreed number of overs.

d) Fractions are to be ignored in all calculations re the number of overs.

7.2.2 Delay or Interruption to the Innings of the Team Batting First

a) If the number of overs of the team batting first is reduced, a fixed time will be specified for the completion of the first session, as calculated by applying the provisions of Clauses 4.2 and 7.2.1(a).

b) If the team fielding first fails to bowl the required number of overs by the scheduled time for cessation of the first session, play shall continue until the required number of overs has been bowled, and Clause 7.1(b) shall apply.

c) If the team batting first is all out and the last wicket falls at or after the scheduled time for the interval, Clause 7.1(c) shall apply.

7.2.3 Delay or Interruption to the Innings of the Team Batting Second

If it is not possible for the team batting second to have the opportunity of batting for the same number of overs as the team batting first, the overs to be bowled shall be reduced at the rate of 15 overs per hour for time lost.

7.3 Delayed or Interrupted Matches (semi-finals, etc.)

7.3.1 General

a) In matches for which a reserve day has been allocated, any rearrangement of the number of overs that may be necessary due to a delayed start or one or more interruptions in play as a result of adverse ground, weather or light conditions or any other reason, shall only be made on the second day. The timing and duration of all suspensions of play (including all intervals) or delays on any day will be taken into account when calculating the length of time available for either innings.

b) The object shall always be to rearrange the number of overs so that, if possible, both teams have the opportunity of batting for the same number of overs.

Except as provided for in Clause 7.3.3 below, the calculation of the number of overs to be bowled shall be based on a rate of 15 overs per hour in the total available for play up to 5.15pm on the last scheduled day of the match. If a reduction of the number of overs is required, any recalculation must not cause the match to be rescheduled to finish earlier than the original cessation time. This time may be extended to allow for one extra over for both teams to be added if required.

A minimum of 20 overs must be bowled to the team batting second (subject to it not being all out earlier) in order to constitute a match, unless the provisions for Clause 7.1 (b) apply (ie if the innings of the team batting second is reduced to less than 20 overs as a result of that team having earlier failed to bowl the required number of overs (minimum 20 overs) by the scheduled time for the completion of the first innings).

c) If the team fielding second fails to bowl the required number of overs by the scheduled cessation time, the hours of play shall, subject to conditions of ground, weather and light, be extended until the overs have been bowled or a result has been achieved.

d)   The team batting second shall not bat for a greater number of overs than the team batting first unless the latter has been all out in less than the agreed number of overs.

e)   Fractions are to be ignored in all calculations re the number of overs.

7.3.2 Delay or Interruption of the Innings of the Team Batting First

a)   If the number of overs of the team batting first is reduced, a fixed time will be specified for the completion of its innings, as calculated by applying the provisions of Clauses 4.2 and 4.3 (whichever versions apply depending on whether a reserve day has been allocated for the match or not). Clause 7.2.1 (a) (if appropriate) and Clause 7.2.1 (b).

b)   If the team fielding first fails to bowl the required number of overs by the scheduled time for the cessation of the first session, play shall continue until the required number of overs has been bowled, and Clauses 7.1 (b) and (c) shall apply.

c)   If the team batting first is all out and the last wicket falls at or after the scheduled time for the interval, Clause 7.1 (c) shall apply.

7.3.3 Delay or Interruption to the Innings of the Team Batting Second

It it is not possible for the team batting second to have the opportunity of batting for the same number of overs as the team batting first, the overs to be bowled shall be reduced at the rate of 15 overs per hour for playing time lost, bearing in mind the provisions of Clauses 7.2.1 (a) (if appropriate) and 7.2.1 (b).

Unless provided for in 7.1, 7.2, and 7.3 above, the number of overs to be bowled by either team will be decided by the Management Committee, whose decision will be final.

8.   RESTRICTIONS ON THE PLACEMENT OF FIELDSMEN

Two semi circles shall be drawn on the field of play. The semi circles have as their centre the middle stump at either end of the pitch. The radius of each semi circles (*sic*) is 30 yards (27.5m). The ends of each semi circle are joined to the other by a straight line drawn on the field on the same side of the pitch.

The field restriction area should be marked by continuous painted while lines or 'dots' at five yard (4.5m) intervals, each 'dot' to be covered by a white plastic or rubber (but not metal) disc measuring seven inches (18cm) in diameter.

At the instant of delivery, there may not be more than five fieldsmen on the leg side.

For the first 15 overs only two fieldsmen are permitted to be outside the field restriction marking at the instant of delivery. For the remaining overs only five fieldsmen are permitted to be outside the field restriction marking at the instant of delivery.

Where play is delayed or interrupted affecting the innings of the team batting first and the total number of overs available is reduced, the number of overs in regard to field restrictions shall be reduced proportionately. Fractions are to be ignored.

In the event of an infringement, the square leg umpire shall call and signal no ball.

9.   NUMBER OF OVERS PER BOWLER

No bowler shall bowl more than 10 (six ball) overs in an innings.

In a delayed or interrupted match where the overs are reduced for both teams or for the team bowling second, no bowler may bowl more than one-fifth of the total overs allowed. This restriction shall not apply to the team fielding second where the provisions of Clause 7.1(b) have been applied.

Where the total overs is not divisible by 5, one additional over shall be allowed to the maximum number per bowler necessary to make up the balance.

In the event of a bowler breaking down and being unable to complete an over, the remaining balls will be bowled by another bowler. Such part of an over will count as a full over only in so far as each bowler's limit is concerned.

The scoreboard shall show the total number of overs bowled and where possible, the number of overs bowled by each bowler.

10. NO BALL

Short Pitched Bowling – if the ball passes or would have passed above the shoulder height of the striker standing upright at the crease, either umpire shall call and signal no ball.

11. WIDE BOWLING – JUDGING A WIDE

Umpires are instructed to apply a very strict and consistent interpretation in regard to this Law in order to prevent negative bowling wide of the wicket.

Any offside or legside delivery which in the opionion of the umpire does not give the batsman a reasonable opportunity to score shall be called a wide. As a guide, on the leg side a ball landing clearly outside the leg stump going further away shall be called a wide.

12. THE BALL

The Malaysian Cricket Association shall provide "Kookaburra CB104 Regulation 4-piece" red cricket balls which will be used in all matches. Each fielding team shall have one new ball for its innings.

In the event of a ball becoming wet and soggy as a result of play continuing in inclement weather or it being affected by dew, or becoming significantly discoloured and in the opinion of the umpires being unfit for play, the ball may be replaced for a ball that has had a similar amount of wear, even though it has not gone out of shape.

Either bowler or batsman may raise the matter with the umpires and the umpires' decision as to a replacement or otherwise will be final.

Law 5

The fielding captain or his nominee may select the ball with which he wishes to bowl from the supply provided by the Malaysian Cricket Association. Such a selection must take place in the presence of the referee.

The umpire shall retain possession of the match ball(s) throughout the duration of the match when play is not actually taking place. During play umpires shall periodically and irregularly inspect the condition of the ball and shall retain possession of it at the fall of a wicket, a drinks interval, at the end of each over, or any other disruption in play.

Law 5.5 – Ball Lost or Becoming Unfit for Play

In the event of a ball during play being lost or, in the opinion of the umpires, being unfit for play through normal use, the umpires shall allow it to be replaced by one that in their opinion has had a similar amount of wear. If the ball is to be replaced, the umpires shall inform the batsman.

13. THE RESULT

13.1 A result can be achieved only if both teams have had the opportunity of batting for at least 20 overs, subject to the provision of Clauses 7.1(b) and 7.2.2(b) unless one team has been all out in less than 20 overs or unless the team batting second scores enough runs to win in less than 20 overs.

All matches in which both teams have not had an opportunity of batting for a minimum of 20 overs, shall be declared no result.

13.2 Tie

In matches in which both teams have had the opportunity of batting for the agreed number of overs, subject to the provisions of Clauses 7.1(b) and 7.2.2(b) the team scoring the higher number of runs shall be the winner. If the scores are equal, the result shall be a tie and no account shall be taken of the number of wickets which have fallen.

13.3 Delayed or Interrupted Matches – calculation of the Target Score

If the innings of the team batting second is delayed or interrupted and it is not able to receive its full quota of overs, the target score shall be calculated based on the percentage of the run scoring resources available during the innings which is lost due to the suspension in play. This percentage depends not only on the number of overs which are lost but also on the stage of the innings at which they are lost and the number of wickets that have fallen at the time of the suspension.

The percentage factors have been derived from a detailed mathematical analysis of a database of previous ICC Trophy matches with the object of establishing "normal" performance.

14. POINTS

The points system shall be as follows:

Win	2
Tie or No Result	1
Loss	0

14.1 First Round Matches

In the event of the teams finishing on equal points, the right to play in the second round will be decided by the most wins in the first round or, when teams have both equal wins and equal points, the team which was the winner of the first round match between them will be placed in the higher position or, if still equal, the higher net run rate in the first round matches. In a match declared no result, run rate is not applicable.

14.2 Second Round Matches

In the event of the teams finishing on equal points, the right to play in the semi-final will be decided by the most wins in the second round matches or, when teams have both equal wins and equal points, the team which was the winner of the second round match played between them will be placed in the higher position or, if still equal, the higher net run rate in the second round matches. In a match declared no result, run rate is not applicable.

14.3 Final Matches

Semi-final

If a semi-final is tied or there is no result, the team that finished higher in the second round matches as decided by Clause 14.2 shall proceed to the Final.

Third place playoff

If the third place playoff match is tied or there is no result, the team that finished higher in the second round matches as decided by Clause 14.2 shall be declared the winner. If both teams finished in the same position in their group after the second round matches the winner will be the team with the greater number of points in the second round matches or, when teams have both equal wins and equal points, the higher net run rate in the second round matches.

Final

In the event of a tied final or there is no result, the teams will be declared joint winners.

A team's net run rate is calculated by deducting from the average runs per over scored by that team throughout the competition, the average runs per over scored against that team throughout the competition.

In the event of a team being all out in less than its full quota of overs, the calculation of its net run rate shall be based on the full quota of overs to which it would have been entitled and not on the number of overs in which the team was dismissed.

15. SUBSTITUTES

15.1 Law 2.1 will apply as modified:

In normal circumstances, a sbstitute shall be allowed to field only for a player who satisfies the umpires that he has become injured or become ill during the match. However, in very exceptional circumstances, the umpires may use their discretion to allow a substitute for a player who has to leave the field or does not take the field for other wholly acceptable reasons, subject to consent being given by the opposing captain. If a player wishes to change his shirt, boots etc., he may leave the field to do so (no changing on the field) but no substitute will be allowed.

15.2 Law 2.6 (Runner's Equipment) will apply as modified:

The player acting as runner for an injured batsman shall at all times wear similar external clothing and protective equipment as the injured batsman.

15.3 Law 2.9 – Fieldsman Leaving the Field

In place of Law 2.8, the following will apply:

No fieldsman shall leave the field or return during a session of play without the consent of the umpire at the bowler's end. The umpire's consent is also necessary if a substitute is required for a fieldsman at the start of play or when his side returns to the field after an interval. If a member of the fielding side does not take the field at the start of play, leaves the field or fails to return after an interval and is absent from the field longer than 15 minutes:

i)   the player shall not be permitted to bowl in that innings after his return until he has been on the field for at least that length of playing time for which he was absent.

ii)   the player shall not be permitted to bat unless or until, in the aggregate, he has returned to the field and/or his side's innings has been in progress for at least that length of playing time for which he has been absent, or, if earlier, when his side has lost five wickets.

The restriction in (i) and (ii) above shall not apply if the player has sufferd an external blow (as opposed to an internal injury such as a pulled muscle) whilst participating eariler in the match and consequently been forced to leave the field. Nor shall it apply if the player has been absent for very exceptional and wholly acceptable reasons (other than injury or illness) and consent for a substitute has been granted by the opposing captain.

Note – in the event of a fieldsman already being off the field at the commencement of an interruption in play through ground, weather or light conditions, he shall be allowed to count any such stoppage time as playing time, provided that he personally informs the Umpires when he is fit enough to take the field had play been in progress.

16.   LAW 3.8 – FITNESS OF GROUND, WEATHER AND LIGHT

16.1 Add the following paragraph (a) and delete clause (i):

The umpires will suspend, or continue to suspend play for bad light when they consider that there is a risk of serious physical injury to the batsman. Amongst the facts to be considered are background, sight screens and the type of bowling. Before deciding to suspend play, or not to resume play after an interval on account of bad light (but for no other reason), the umpire shall establish whether the captain of the batting team (the batsmen at the wicket may deputise for their captain) wishes to continue in unfit conditions; if so, his wishes shall be met.

16.2 Add the following to the last sentence of 3.8 (a) (ii):

… or, as a consequence of a change of bowler, if batting conditions have become more dangerous.

16.3 The umpires shall disregard any shadow on the pitch from the stadium or from any permanent object on the ground.

17.   LAW 6- THE BAT

Law 6.1 will apply as modified:

The bat overall shall not be more than 38"/96.5 cm in length; the blade of the bat shall be made of wood, shall have a conventional "flat" face and shall not exceed 4¼"/10.8 cm at the widest part.

18.   LAW 7 – THE PITCH

In addition to the Law 7.2, the following will apply:

Captains, umpires, the referee and groundsmen should co-operate to ensure that, prior to the start of any day's play, no-one bounces the ball on the pitch or strikes it with a bat to assess its condition or for any other reason, or causes damage to the pitch in any other way.

Prior to the start of play on any day, only the captain and team coach may walk on the pitch to assess its condition. Spiked footwear is not permitted.

19. **LAW 10- THE PITCH**

19.1 Rolling of the Pitch

Law 10.1 will apply, but add the following sentence to the first paragraph:

In addition the umpires are empowered to authorise the groundsman to roll, sweep and otherwise treat the pitch by such manner and means which they, bearing in mind the advice of the groundsman, consider will return the state of the pitch as near as possible to that pertaining when the choice of innings was made.

20. **LAW 10.3 – MOWING OF THE OUTFIELD**

The outfield shall be mown after the conclusion of play, and/or prior to the start of the next match.

21. **COVERING THE PITCH – BEFORE AND DURING A MATCH**

In place of Law 11.1 and 11.2, the following shall apply:

In all matches, the pitch shall be entirely protected against rain up to the commencement of play and for the duration of the period of the match. It shall be wholly covered at the termination of each day's play or providing the weather is fine, within a period of two hours thereafter.

The covers shall be removed no later than 8.00am on the morning of the match provided it is not raining at the time, but they will be replaced if rain falls prior to the commencement of play.

Attention is drawn to Law 3 Note (c) and Law 11.3.

22. **DRYING OF PITCH AND GROUND**

The umpires may instruct the groundsman to use any available equipment, including any roller for the purpose of drying the pitch and making it fit for play.

Note – an absorbent roller may be used to remove water from the covers including the cover on the match pitch.

23. **LAW 15.2 – PRACTICE ON THE FIELD**

At no time on any day of the match shall there be any bowling or batting practice on the pitch or the square, except in official netted practice pitch areas. In addition there shall be no bowling or batting practice on any part of the square or the area immediately parallel to the match pitch after the commencement of play on any day. Any fieldsman contravening this Law may not bowl his next over.

No practice may take place on the field if, in the opinion of the umpires, it could result in a waste of time.

24. **BOUNDARIES**

The boundary shall be the fence or a rope inside the fence. The pitch shall be a minimum 60 yards from one boundary square of the pitch. The straight boundary at both ends of the pitch shall be a minimum of 60 yards. Distances shall be measured from the centre of the pitch to be used. Whenever possible the boundary shall be 70 yards from the centre of the match pitch, provided than no boundary be less than 60 yards.

If an unauthorised person enters the playing arena and handles the ball, the umpire at the bowler's end shall be the sole judge of whether the boundary allowance should be scored or the ball be treated as still in play or called dead ball if a batsman is liable to be out as a result of the unauthorised person handling the ball.

24.1 Sight Screens

Sight screens shall be provided at both ends of all grounds. Advertising shall be permitted on the sight screen end behind the striker, providing it is removed for the subsequent over from that end without delaying the match.

25. LAW 22.7 – BOWLER INCAPACITATED OR SUSPENDED DURING AN OVER

The following shall apply in place of Law 22.7:

If for any reason, a bowler is incapacitated while running up to bowl the first ball of an over, or is incapacitated or suspended during an over, the umpire shall call and signal "dead ball" and another bowler shall bowl or complete the over from the same end, provided only that he shall not bowl two overs, or part thereof, consecutively in one innings.

26. LAW 24.1 THE BALL – MODE OF DELIVERY

Law 24.1 will apply except that the bowler may not deliver the ball underarm. If a bowler bowls a ball underarm the umpire shall call and signal dead ball.

In addition, the umpire at the bowler's end shall call and signal no ball if a ball which the umpire considers to have been delivered:

i)   bounces more than twice or
ii)   rolls along the ground or
iii)   comes to rest

before it reaches the striker or, if not otherwise played by the striker, before it reaches the popping crease. If the ball comes to rest in such circumstances, the umpire will call No Ball and Law 25.3 shall apply.

27. LAW 24.2 – FAIR DELIVERY – THE ARM

Law 24.2 shall apply with the following:

The umpire shall also adopt the procedures of caution, final warning, action against the Bowler and reporting as set out in Law 42.8

28. LAW 24.8 AND 25.6

In addition, the following shall apply:

No balls and wide balls not scored from shall be included in the bowling analysis of the bowler responsible.

29. LAW 30 – BOWLED

The following shall apply in place of Law 30.1(b):

He plays the ball, or if it touches his person, then hits or kicks it into and breaks his wicket and in the umpire's judgement an attempt to protect the wicket has been made, the striker will be given out on appeal - bowled. Completion of the stroke will not be considered if an attempt is made to protect the wicket. See Law 34.1 (Out – Hit the Ball Twice)

30. HELMETS (AND PROTECTIVE EQUIPMENT)

In addition to Laws 23.1 (e), 32.2 (e), 38 Note (c) and 41.4 the following shall apply:

The striker is out under this Law if the ball is deflected from his bat onto his own protective helmet and he is subsequently caught. Runs may be scored off deflections from the batsman's or fielder's helmet.

A batsman may call for a helmet to be brought out to him at any time. He must then wear or carry it personally all the time while play is in progress, or can have it taken off the field at the fall of a wicket, or at the end of an over, or at any drinks interval.

In all cases, no actions involving helmets are to waste playing time. Umpires are not to hold helmets.

The exchanging of protective equipment between members of the fielding side on the field shall be permitted provided that the umpires do not consider that it constitutes a waste of playing time. A batsman may only change other items of protective equipment (e.g. batting gloves, etc.) provided that there is no waste of playing time.

31. FOOTWEAR

Spiked footwear is permitted, except for batsmen, bowlers and wicketkeepers.

32. LAW 42.4 – (LIFTING THE SEAM) AND 42.5 – (CHANGING THE CONDITION OF THE BALL)

In the event that a ball has been interfered with and requires replacement the batsman at the wicket shall choose the replacement ball from a selection of six other balls of various degrees of usage (including a new ball) and of the same brand as the ball in use prior to the contravention.

33. LAW 42.9 – THE BOWLING OF FAST, HIGH, FULL PITCHED BALLS

Law 42.9 shall be replaced by the following:

The bowling of fast high full pitched balls is unfair.

A fast high full pitched ball shall be defined as a ball that passes, or would have passed, on the full above waist height of a batsman standing upright at the crease. Should a bowler bowl a fast high pitched ball, either umpire shall call and signal no ball.

In the event of such unfair bowler the umpire at the bowler's end shall adopt the procedures of caution, final warning, action against the bowler and reporting as set out in Law 42.8

34. "HITTING UP"

Teams are required to observe Ground Authority regulations and to exercise the utmost care and caution when engaging in practice and pre-match warm-up and "hitting-up" activities so as to avoid the risk of injury to members of the public, damage to the centre wicket region and to perimeter fencing.

34. GENERAL

Any queries or disputes not covered in the above playing conditions should be referred to the Management Committee. The Management Committee has the power to make a decision on any query or dispute of the playing conditions and their decision shall be final.

Bangladesh captain Akram Khan holds aloft the ICC Trophy

GIBRALTAR v IRELAND   (First Round, Group A)
Played at Victoria Institute, Kuala Lumpur, March 24, 1997.

Ireland won by 192 runs

IRELAND				GIBRALTAR		
J.D.Curry	b Johnson	52		D.Robeson	c M.W.Patterson b Doak	5
D.A.Lewis	not out	127		N.Churaman	c Lewis b Doak	13
*J.D.R.Benson	c Churaman b Cary	73		*C.Rocca	c Eagleson b M.W.Patterson	8
A.R.Dunlop	not out	4		T.Buzaglo	c A.D.Patterson b M.W.Patterson	0
N.G.Doak				R.Buzaglo	c Benson b M.W.Patterson	0
†A.D.Patterson				D.Johnson	c Doak b McCrum	4
P.G.Gillespie				G.De'Ath	run out	8
R.L.Eagleson				C.Clinton	c A.D.Patterson b M.W.Patterson	0
M.W.Patterson				†S.Shephard	b McCrum	5
P.McCrum				T.Garcia	c McCrum b Eagleson	5
G.L.Molins				S.Cary	not out	7
Extras	b 1, lb 7, w 12, nb 2	22		Extras	lb 9, w 21, nb 1	31
Total	(2 wickets, 50 overs)	278		Total	(all out, 32.2 overs)	86

1-86(1), 2-248(3)

1-22(2), 2-32(1), 3-35(4), 4-39(3), 5-47(5), 6-54(6),
7-61(8), 8-69(9), 9-73(7), 10-86(10)

Gibraltar Bowling	O	M	R	W		Ireland Bowling	O	M	R	W	
Churaman	10	0	53	0	(4w,1nb)	Doak	10	3	12	2	(1w)
Cary	10	0	65	1	(3w)	Molins	10	5	16	0	(2w)
Johnson	10	0	53	1	(2w,2nb)	M.W.Patterson	6	1	22	4	(9w)
De'Ath	10	1	48	0	(2w)	McCrum	4	0	20	2	(8w,1nb)
Garcia	10	1	51	0	(1w)	Gillespie	2	0	7	0	(1w)
						Eagleson	0.2	0	0	1	

Umpires: J.K.Kruger (Namibia) and J.Luther (Denmark)   Man of the Match: D.A.Lewis

Lewis's 127 took 142 balls and lasted 205 minutes.

ISRAEL v KENYA   (First Round, Group A)
Played at Kelab Aman, Kuala Lumpur, March 24, 1997.

Kenya won by 7 wickets

Toss: Israel

ISRAEL				KENYA		
S.B.Perlman	b Odoyo	16		A.Y.Karim	run out	1
Y.Nagavkar	c and b Odoyo	6		S.K.Gupta	c sub (A.Vard) b Ashton	27
L.Hall	c Patel b Odoyo	14		†K.Otieno	run out	22
D.Silver	c and b Odumbe	36		S.O.Tikolo	not out	71
A.Talkar	c and b L.O.Tikolo	7		*M.O.Odumbe	not out	27
*H.Awasker	c and b Odumbe	17		H.S.Modi		
R.Ashton	not out	23		T.Odoyo		
A.Moss	c sub (J.Angara) b Karim	4		L.O.Tikolo		
B.Kehimkar	lbw b Karim	6		A.Suji		
†P.Smith	not out	1		M.A.Suji		
V.E.Worrell				B.Patel		
Extras	b 1, lb 6, w 13, nb 4	24		Extras	lb 1, w 7, nb 1	9
Total	(8 wickets, 50 overs)	154		Total	(3 wickets, 31.2 overs)	157

1-33(2), 2-34(1), 3-59(3), 4-83(5), 5-108(6),
6-123(4), 7-138(8), 8-151(9)

1-14(1), 2-54(2), 3-45(3)

Kenya Bowling	O	M	R	W		Israel Bowling	O	M	R	W	
M.A.Suji	6	1	19	0	(1w,2nb)	Moss	6	1	25	0	(3w,1nb)
S.O.Tikolo	10	3	24	0	(6w)	Worrell	3	0	20	0	(1w)
Odoyo	8	0	22	3	(3nb)	Ashton	6.2	0	39	1	(2w)
A.Suji	4	2	10	0		Hall	5	1	16	0	
Karim	7	0	22	2		Awasker	6	0	31	0	
L.O.Tikolo	5	0	20	1	(4w)	Nagavkar	5	0	25	0	(1w)
Odumbe	10	1	30	2	(1w)						

Umpires: G.F.Malik (U.A.E.) and W.Smith (Scotland)   Man of the Match: S.O.Tikolo

SINGAPORE v UNITED STATES OF AMERICA (First Round, Group A)

Played at Perbadanan Kemajuan Negari Selangor, Kuala Lumpur, March 24, 1997.

United States of America won by 106 runs

Toss: Singapore

U.S.A.		
E.A.Lewis	c Stone b Martens	9
M.C.Adams	c Stone b Martens	8
†R.Denny	c Sithawalla b Wilson	20
A.D.Texeira	run out	27
*S.F.A.F.Bacchus	c David b Deshpande	36
Aijaz Ali	b Muruthi	4
D.I.Kallicharran	not out	60
Z.Amin	run out	2
K.Dennis	run out	40
R.Benjamin		
E.Grant		
Extras	b 5, lb 10, w 8	23
Total	(8 wickets, 50 overs)	229

1-23(2), 2-42(1), 3-58(3), 4-113(5), 5-125(6),
6-131(8), 7-212(9), 8-229(4)

SINGAPORE		
A.Dass	c Bacchus b Grant	3
M.H.Sithawalla	c and b Dennis	0
K.M.Deshpande	b Grant	11
A.J.Ranggi	st Denny b Amin	19
*R.T.Y.Mohamed	c Amin b Kallicharran	15
G.S.Wilson	st Denny b Kallicharran	2
R.Chandran	b Amin	0
R.David	c Denny b Bacchus	6
R.S.R.Martens	c Denny b Kallicharran	9
†J.H.Stone	not out	10
S.Muruthi	not out	8
Extras	lb 7, w 30, nb 3	40
Total	(9 wickets, 50 overs)	123

1-2(2), 2-29(1), 3-40(3), 4-74(4), 5-78(5), 6-79(7),
7-79(6), 8-95(9), 9-108(8)

Singapore Bowling

	O	M	R	W	
Wilson	10	0	35	1	(4w)
Martens	9	0	58	2	(2w)
Mohamed	10	1	37	0	
Muruthi	10	0	30	1	
Deshpande	10	1	30	1	(1w)
David	1	0	24	0	(1w)

U.S.A. Bowling

	O	M	R	W	
Dennis	7	4	8	1	(2w)
Benjamin	7	0	21	0	(14w,1nb)
Grant	5	1	22	2	(6w,1nb)
Amin	10	1	24	2	
Kallicharran	10	3	22	2	(5w)
Bacchus	8	2	16	1	(3w)
Lewis	3	1	3	0	

Umpires: Khoo Chai Huat (Malaysia) and E.D.Ohm (Netherlands)   Man of the Match: D.I.Kallicharran

Texiera retired hurt on 29 with the score at 113-3 and returned at the fall of the 7th wicket.

GIBRALTAR v UNITED STATES OF AMERICA (First Round, Group A)

Played at Rubber Research Institute, Kuala Lumpur, March 25, 1997.

United States of America won by 189 runs

Toss: United States of America

U.S.A.		
E.A.Lewis	c Garcia b Churaman	14
P.Singh	c Robeson b Churaman	69
†R.Denny	lbw b Johnson	34
A.D.Texeira	retired ill	44
*S.F.A.F.Bacchus	not out	100
Aijaz Ali	c De'Ath b Johnson	10
Nazir Islam	c De'Ath b Churaman	9
D.I.Kallicharran	not out	19
Z.Amin		
K.Dennis		
E.Grant		
Extras	b 2, lb 3, w 8	13
Total	(5 wickets, 50 overs)	312

1-22(1), 2-105(3), 3-144(2), 4-245(6), 5-271(7)

GIBRALTAR		
D.Robeson	c Texeira b Grant	1
T.Buzaglo	lbw b Grant	1
*C.Rocca	c Kallicharran b Bacchus	34
G.De'Ath	b Kallicharran	6
N.Churaman	lbw b Amin	14
R.Buzaglo	not out	20
D.Johnson	c Denny b Amin	0
†S.Shepherd	lbw b Kallicharran	1
T.Garcia	c Texeira b Kallicharran	5
A.Hewitt	b Nazir Islam	10
S.Cary		
Extras	b 7, lb 4, w 19, nb 1	31
Total	(9 wickets, 50 overs)	123

1-3(2), 2-7(1), 3-39(4), 4-73(3), 5-80(5), 6-80(7),
7-84(8), 8-104(9), 9-123(10)

Gibraltar Bowling

	O	M	R	W	
Churaman	10	0	64	3	(1w)
Cary	10	0	57	0	(1w,1nb)
De'Ath	10	1	60	0	
Johnson	10	0	52	2	(4w)
Garcia	10	0	74	0	(2w)

U.S.A. Bowling

	O	M	R	W	
Dennis	5	2	5	0	(1w)
Grant	5	0	8	2	(3w)
Aijaz Ali	6	1	16	0	(2w,1nb)
Nazir Islam	4	0	14	1	(9w)
Kallicharran	10	3	24	3	(3w)
Amin	10	1	27	2	(1w)
Bacchus	10	1	18	1	

Umpires: T.Cooper (Fiji) and W.Maha (Papua New Guinea)   Man of the Match: S.F.A.F.Bacchus

Texiera retired ill at 209-3.

KENYA v SINGAPORE   (First Round, Group A)

Played at Royal Selangor Club, Bukit Kiara, Kuala Lumpur, March 25, 1997.

Kenya won by 2 wickets   Toss: Singapore

SINGAPORE			KENYA		
†J.H.Stone	b M.A.Suji	0	A.Y.Karim	lbw b Wilson	8
M.H.Sithawalla	c Otieno b S.O.Tikolo	3	†K.Otieno	c Stone b Wilson	0
C.J.F.Gunningham	c L.O.Tikolo b Karim	13	S.O.Tikolo	c Stone b Martens	10
*R.T.Y.Mohamed	c S.O.Tikolo b Odoyo	9	*M.O.Odumbe	c Swee Heng b Martens	8
Goh Swee Heng	c S.O.Tikolo b A.Suji	3	A.Suji	lbw b Wilson	10
G.S.Wilson	c Karim b Odoyo	1	T.Odoyo	lbw b Martens	2
R.Chandran	b L.O.Tikolo	26	L.O.Tikolo	b Wilson	2
R.S.R.Martens	lbw b Karim	1	E.O.Odumbe	lbw b Mohamed	5
D.J.Chelvathurai	not out	9	M.Suji	not out	14
M.Patil	b M.A.Suji	2	L.Onyango	not out	9
R.P.Ramadas	b M.A.Suji	0	B.Patel		
Extras	b 1, lb 1, w 18, nb 2	22	Extras	lb 2, w 20	22
Total	(all out, 44.4 overs)	89	Total	(8 wickets, 30 overs)	90

1-2(1), 2-11(2), 3-34(4), 4-34(3), 5-37(6), 6-47(5),
7-53(8), 8-80(7), 9-87(10), 10-89(11)

1-1(2), 2-15(1), 3-30(4), 4-40(3), 5-47(6), 6-48(5),
7-52(7), 8-80(8)

Kenya Bowling	O	M	R	W		Singapore Bowling	O	M	R	W	
M.A.Suji	6.4	1	9	3	(5w)	Wilson	10	1	25	4	(8w)
S.O.Tikolo	6	3	11	1	(3w)	Martens	10	0	30	3	(1w)
Karim	10	2	25	2	(3w)	Mohamed	5	2	11	1	
Odoyo	6	2	8	2	(1w,1nb)	Patil	2	0	12	0	(9w)
A.Suji	5	1	10	1	(1w,1nb)	Ramadas	3	0	10	0	(2w)
Patel	5	1	8	0	(1w)						
M.O.Odumbe	5	0	12	0	(1w)						
L.O.Tikolo	1	0	4	1	(3w)						

Umpires: A.O.D.George (West Africa) and C.Hoare (Canada)   Man of the Match: M.A.Suji

IRELAND v ISRAEL   (First Round, Group A)

Played at Royal Military College, Kuala Lumpur, March 26, 1997.

Ireland won by 10 wickets   Toss: Ireland

ISRAEL			IRELAND		
Y.Nagavkar	c McCrum b Harrison	18	J.D.Curry	not out	51
A.Vard	lbw b Patterson	3	D.A.Lewis	not out	28
L.Hall	c Heasley b Patterson	4	*J.D.R.Benson		
D.Silver	c Curry b Heasley	13	A.R.Dunlop		
R.Ashton	c Benson b Doak	9	N.G.Doak		
*H.Awasker	b Doak	0	D.Heasley		
M.Talker	lbw b Harrison	7	G.D.Harrison		
A.Moss	not out	6	R.L.Eagleson		
M.Wadavakar	c Rutherford b Harrison	2	†A.T.Rutherford		
†P.Smith	c Benson b Doak	0	M.W.Patterson		
V.E.Worrell	b Doak	0	P.McCrum		
Extras	b 1, w 24, nb 1	26	Extras	lb 3, w 7	10
Total	(all out, 31.5 overs)	88	Total	(no wicket, 17.2 overs)	89

1-10(2), 2-21(3), 3-53(4), 4-70(1), 5-70(6), 6-77(7),
7-82(5), 8-85(9), 9-88(10), 10-88(10)

Ireland Bowling	O	M	R	W		Israel Bowling	O	M	R	W	
Patterson	4	0	14	2	(9w,1nb)	Moss	3	1	10	0	(2w)
McCrum	7	0	17	0	(2w)	Worrell	4	0	20	0	
Eagleson	4	1	9	0	(6w)	Hall	2	0	13	0	(1w)
Heasley	4	0	19	1	(3w)	Awasker	3	0	13	0	(1w)
Harrison	8	1	19	3		Ashton	2	0	7	0	(2w)
Doak	4.5	1	9	4	(1w)	Wadavakar	2	0	15	0	
						Nagavkar	1.2	0	8	0	

Umpires: Khoo Chai Huat (Malaysia) and D.Ker (Argentina)   Man of the Match: N.G.Doak

GIBRALTAR v KENYA   (First Round, Group A)

Played at Royal Military College, Kuala Lumpur, March 27, 1997.

Kenya won by 7 wickets   Toss: Kenya

GIBRALTAR				KENYA		
D.Robeson	c Otieno b S.O.Tikolo	1		A.Y.Karim	b Churaman	8
N.Churaman	c Karim b S.O.Tikolo	7		†K.Otieno	c R.Buzaglo b Churaman	0
*C.Rocca	c Otieno b S.O.Tikolo	0		S.O.Tikolo	c T.Buzaglo b Cary	3
D.Johnson	c Odumbe b S.O.Tikolo	1		*M.O.Odumbe	not out	16
T.Buzaglo	lbw b Karim	9		S.K.Gupta	not out	13
R.Buzaglo	c Odumbe b Karim	6		T.Odoyo		
G.De'Ath	c Otieno b Odoyo	1		L.O.Tikolo		
†S.Shephard	c S.O.Tikolo b Karim	0		A.Suji		
T.Garcia	run out	1		M.A.Suji		
A.Hewitt	c Odumbe b Karim	1		L.Onyango		
S.Cary	not out	0		B.Patel		
Extras	b 2, lb 1, w 9, nb 5	17		Extras	(b 1, w 5)	6
Total	(all out, 27.1 overs)	44		Total	(3 wickets, 12.4 overs)	46

1-10(1), 2-10(3), 3-13(2), 4-15(4), 5-36(6), 6-42(5),
7-42(8), 8-42(7), 9-44(9), 10-44(10)

1-5(2), 2-12(3), 3-16(1)

Kenya Bowling

	O	M	R	W	
M.A.Suji	7	2	9	0	(3w,4nb)
S.O.Tikolo	7	3	10	4	(2w)
Odoyo	7	0	15	1	(4w,1nb)
Karim	6.1	2	7	4	

Gibraltar Bowling

	O	M	R	W	
Churaman	6	2	9	2	(2w)
Cary	4	0	23	1	(1w)
Johnson	2	0	7	0	(2w,1nb)
Robeson	0.4	0	6	0	

Umpires: I.Massey (Italy) and H.Whitlock (Hong Kong)   Man of the Match: A.Y.Karim

IRELAND v UNITED STATES OF AMERICA   (First Round, Group A)

Played at Tenaga Nasional Sports Complex (Kilat Kelab), Kuala Lumpur, March 27, 1997.

Ireland won by 2 wickets   Toss: Ireland

U.S.A.				IRELAND		
E.A.Lewis	c Rutherford b Harrison	16		J.D.Curry	c Grant b Bacchus	25
P.Singh	lbw b Gillespie	4		D.A.Lewis	lbw b Amin	37
†R.Denny	c Benson b Doak	44		*J.D.R.Benson	c Amin b Lewis	31
A.D.Texeira	c Eagleson b Doak	40		A.R.Dunlop	c Dennis b Bacchus	12
*S.F.A.F.Bacchus	b Doak	0		N.G.Doak	lbw b Lewis	18
Aijaz Ali	c Lewis b Harrison	32		P.G.Gillespie	st Denny b Kallicharran	15
D.I.Kallicharran	c sub (S.Graham)			R.L.Eagleson	c Denny b Kallicharran	1
	b Molins	28				
K.Dennis	c Gillespie b Curry	2		G.D.Harrison	run out	18
Z.Amin	b Curry	12		M.W.Patterson	not out	27
Nazir Islam	c Molins b Curry	0		G.L.Molins	not out	5
E.Grant	not out	17		†A.T.Rutherford		
Extras	b 1, lb 1, w 15	17		Extras	b 4, lb 5, w 16, nb 1	26
Total	(all out, 50 overs)	212		Total	(8 wickets, 49.1 overs)	215

1-9(2), 2-61(1), 3-83(3), 4-85(5), 5-152(4),
6-152(6), 7-158(8), 8-185(9), 9-186(10), 10-212(7)

1-43(1), 2-92(2), 3-122(4), 4-133(3), 5-156(5),
6-158(7), 7-159(6), 8-206(8)

Ireland Bowling

	O	M	R	W	
Gillespie	4	0	21	1	(1w)
Patterson	3	0	15	0	(8w)
Eagleson	3	0	18	0	(1w)
Harrison	10	0	56	2	
Doak	10	3	27	3	(1w)
Molins	10	0	45	1	(2w)
Curry	10	1	28	3	(1w)

U.S.A. Bowling

	O	M	R	W	
Dennis	5	0	26	0	(2w,2nb)
Grant	4.1	0	22	0	(2w)
Aijaz Ali	5	0	16	0	(3w)
Bacchus	10	1	33	2	(1w)
Amin	8	0	40	1	(1w)
Kallicharran	9	0	34	2	(3w)
Lewis	8	1	35	2	(1w)

Umpires: R.Butler (Bermuda) and W.Smith (Scotland)   Man of the Match: J.D.Curry

M.W.Patterson's 3rd over was one ball short.

ISRAEL v SINGAPORE   (First Round, Group A)

Played at Victoria Institute, Kuala Lumpur, March 27, 1997.

Singapore won by 65 runs

Toss: Singapore

SINGAPORE

†C.J.F.Gunningham	b Moss	2
M.H.Sithawalla	c Vard b Kehimkar	4
A.J.Ranggi	c and b Awasker	38
K.M.Deshpande	c Ashton b Hall	29
*R.T.Y.Mohamed	c Smith b Ashton	33
Goh Swee Heng	c Vard b Awasker	12
G.S.Wilson	c Nagavkar b Ashton	50
R.Chandran	run out	2
R.David	c Smith b Ashton	5
R.S.R.Martens	c Silver b Ashton	2
S.Muruthi	not out	4
Extras	lb 4, w 18, nb 1	23
Total	(all out, 49.5 overs)	204

1-6(1), 2-6(2), 3-88(4), 4-89(3), 5-106(6), 6-161(5), 7-165(8), 8-189(9), 9-191(10), 10-204(7)

ISRAEL

Y.Nagavkar	c Gunningham b Wilson	12
A.Vard	b Wilson	2
*H.Awasker	b Wilson	15
D.Silver	run out	40
A.Talkar	c Martens b Deshpande	3
L.Hall	c Deshpande b Mohamed	0
R.Ashton	b Muruthi	11
A.Moss	c Wilson b Martens	23
M.Jawalekar	c Chandran b Muruthi	1
B.Kehimkar	c Martens b Muruthi	12
†P.Smith	not out	6
Extras	b 3, lb 1, w 10	14
Total	(all out, 43.4 overs)	139

1-12(2), 2-34(3), 3-44(1), 4-56(5), 5-57(6), 6-89(4), 7-105(7), 8-108(9), 9-121(8), 10-139(10)

Israel Bowling

	O	M	R	W	
Moss	10	2	40	1	(4w,1nb)
Kehimkar	10	0	29	1	(2w)
Ashton	9.5	0	54	4	(7w)
Awasker	10	1	34	2	(1w)
Hall	7	0	25	1	(2w)
Silver	3	0	18	0	(1w)

Singapore Bowling

	O	M	R	W	
Wilson	7	1	17	3	(3w)
Martens	10	0	37	1	(6w)
Mohamed	8	0	20	1	(1w)
Deshpande	8	2	33	1	
Muruthi	7.4	2	22	3	
David	3	0	6	0	

Umpires: A.F.M.Akhtaruddin (Bangladesh)and J.Luther (Denmark)   Man of the Match: G.S.Wilson

GIBRALTAR v SINGAPORE (First Round, Group A)

Played at Tenaga Nasional Sports Complex (Kilat Kelab), March 28, 1997.

Singapore won on a higher comparative score

Toss: Gibraltar

SINGAPORE

†J.H.Stone	lbw b Cary	4
A.Dass	b Churaman	6
A.J.Ranggi	lbw b De'Ath	13
K.M.Deshpande	st Shephard b Clinton	60
*R.T.Y.Mohamed	c Cary b Johnson	65
G.S.Wilson	c Johnson b Churaman	5
R.Chandran	run out	4
Goh Swee Heng	c Rocca b Churaman	1
R.David	not out	11
R.S.R.Martens	c R.Buzaglo b De'Ath	1
S.Muruthi	b Garcia	14
Extras	lb 8, w 6	14
Total	(all out, 49.3 overs)	198

1-8(2), 2-27(3), 3-31(1), 4-155(5), 5-163(4), 6-168(7), 7-170(6), 8-170(8), 9-174(10), 10-198(11)

GIBRALTAR

T.Buzaglo	run out	20
R.Buzaglo	lbw b Wilson	7
N.Churaman	c Stone b Martens	5
D.Johnson	c Stone b David	28
†S.Shephard	b Muruthi	21
*C.Rocca	c Deshpande b Muruthi	58
G.De'Ath	not out	9
C.Clinton	not out	0
S.Cary		
T.Garcia		
G.Mills		
Extras	lb 6, w 8	14
Total	(6 wickets, 44.4 overs)	162

1-16(2), 2-25(3), 3-67(1), 4-70(4), 5-148(5), 6-153(6)

Gibraltar Bowling

	O	M	R	W	
Mills	9	3	21	0	(1nb)
Churaman	10	2	38	3	
Cary	5	1	17	1	(2w)
De'Ath	10	3	29	2	
Johnson	6	0	38	1	(2w)
Garcia	4.3	0	27	1	
Clinton	5	0	20	1	(1w)

Singapore Bowling

	O	M	R	W	
Wilson	8.4	3	20	1	(2w)
Martens	10	2	23	1	(5w)
Mohamed	7	1	24	0	(1w)
Deshpande	8	0	34	0	
David	7	0	41	1	(1nb)
Muruthi	4	0	14	2	

Umpires: C.Sen and R.Valimahomed   Man of the Match: K.M.Deshpande

Rain stopped play at 5.10pm and the captains agreed to abandon the match at 6.15pm. Under the Duckworth-Lewis method Gibraltar needed to have scored 168 to have won.

IRELAND v KENYA   (First Round, Group A)

Played at Rubber Research Institute, Kuala Lumpur, March 29, 1997.

Kenya won by 119 runs   Toss: Ireland

KENYA			IRELAND		
A.Y.Karim	c Lewis b Patterson	6	J.D.Curry	b S.O.Tikolo	4
S.K.Gupta	c Dunlop b Gillespie	0	D.A.Lewis	b M.A.Suji	2
†K.Otieno	run out (Harrison)	12	*J.D.R.Benson	c and b S.O.Tikolo	8
S.O.Tikolo	lbw b Harrison	31	A.R.Dunlop	b M.A.Suji	0
*M.O.Odumbe	not out	99	N.G.Doak	c L.O.Tikolo b Karim	35
H.S.Modi	c Harrison b Molins	49	P.G.Gillespie	c L.O.Tikolo b S.O.Tikolo	4
T.Odoyo	b Doak	18	R.L.Eagleson	b Karim	4
L.O.Tikolo	b Curry	11	G.D.Harrison	run out (Odumbe)	11
A.Suji			†A.T.Rutherford	not out	25
M.A.Suji			M.W.Patterson	c sub (J.Angara)	13
				b L.O.Tikolo	
B.Patel			G.L.Molins	not out	0
Extras	b 3, lb 6, w 12	21	Extras	b 3, lb 3, w 14, nb 2	22
Total	(7 wickets, 50 overs)	247	Total	(9 wickets, 50 overs)	128

1-2(2), 2-25(1), 3-26(3), 4-98(4), 5-174(6), 6-204(7), 7-235(8)

1-8(1), 2-11(2), 3-11(4), 4-24(3), 5-39(6), 6-53(7), 7-77(5), 8-88(8), 9-126(10)

Ireland Bowling	O	M	R	W		Kenya Bowling	O	M	R	W	
Gillespie	6	1	19	1	(1w)	M.A.Suji	10	5	11	2	(4w)
Patterson	5	1	17	1	(5w)	S.O.Tikolo	10	1	28	3	(1w,2nb)
Eagleson	2	0	10	0	(3w,1nb)	Karim	10	4	11	2	(1nb)
Doak	10	0	61	1		Odoyo	6	0	18	0	(2w)
Molins	7	0	33	1		Odumbe	4	2	9	0	(2w)
Curry	10	0	60	1	(1w)	Patel	5	1	17	0	(1w)
Harrison	10	1	38	1	(2w)	L.O.Tikolo	5	0	28	1	(4w)

Umpires: E.D.Ohm (Netherlands) and A.A.Shaheen (Bangladesh)   Man of the Match: M.O.Odumbe

ISRAEL v UNITED STATES OF AMERICA   (First Round, Group A)

Played at Royal Military College, Kuala Lumpur, March 29, 1997.

United States of America won by 7 wickets   Toss: Israel

ISRAEL			U.S.A.		
Y.Nagavkar	b Grant	0	E.A.Lewis	c Wadavakar	16
				b Kehimkar	
A.Talkar	c Adams b Nazir Islam	10	P.Singh	c Smith b Moss	2
M.Jawalekar	c Amin b Aijaz Ali	8	†R.Denny	not out	44
D.Silver	b Nazir Islam	10	M.C.Adams	c Ashton b Moss	5
*H.Awasker	c Grant b Amin	4	*S.F.A.F.Bacchus	not out	33
R.Ashton	c Bacchus b Kallicharran	14	D.I.Kallicharran		
B.Kehimkar	run out	5	Z.Amin		
A.Moss	b Nazir Islam	21	Aijaz Ali		
M.Wadavakar	c Bacchus b Kallicharran	1	Nazir Islam		
†P.Smith	not out	7	E.Grant		
V.E.Worrell	b Abdul Nazir	4	Abdul Nazir		
Extras	b 2, lb 3, w 14, nb 2	21	Extras	b 3, lb 2, w 3	8
Total	(all out, 47 overs)	105	Total	(3 wickets, 24 overs)	108

1-0(1), 2-19(3), 3-32(2), 4-47(4), 5-47(5), 6-71(6), 7-74(7), 8-75(8), 9-99(9), 10-105(11)

1-21(2), 2-22(1), 3-27(4)

U.S.A. Bowling	O	M	R	W		Israel Bowling	O	M	R	W	
Grant	9	3	18	1		Moss	5	0	26	2	(1w)
Abdul Nazir	4	0	12	1	(3w,1nb)	Kehimkar	5	0	18	1	
Aijaz Ali	4	1	9	1	(4w)	Worrell	4	0	22	0	
Nazir Islam	10	1	15	3	(3w,1nb)	Awasker	3	0	9	0	
Kallicharran	10	3	19	2		Ashton	3	0	6	0	(1w)
Amin	10	1	27	1	(3w)	Wadavakar	3	0	11	0	(1w)
						Nagavkar	1	0	11	0	

Umpires: G.F.Malik (U.A.E.) and J.K.Kruger (Namibia)   Man of the Match: R.Denny

GIBRALTAR v ISRAEL   (First Round, Group A)
Played at Rubber Research Institute, Kuala Lumpur, March 30, 1997.

Gibraltar won by 2 wickets   Toss: Gibraltar

ISRAEL			GIBRALTAR		
Y.Nagavkar	b Churaman	0	R.Buzaglo	b Moss	19
M.Talker	b Churaman	0	A.Hewitt	b Moss	0
S.B.Perlman	lbw b Mills	3	*C.Rocca	lbw b Kehimkar	1
D.Silver	c Cary b De'Ath	12	N.Churaman	run out	3
†P.Smith	c and b Churaman	11	T.Buzaglo	lbw b Awasker	2
L.Hall	c Cary b De'Ath	5	†S.Shephard	c and b Ashton	10
R.Ashton	lbw b De'Ath	9	D.Johnson	c Awasker b Worrell	18
*H.Awasker	c Shephard b Churaman	23	G.De'Ath	not out	15
A.Moss	b Hewitt	7	G.Mills	c Smith b Worrell	0
B.Kehimkar	not out	0	T.Garcia	not out	3
V.E.Worrell	b Churaman	0	S.Cary		
Extras	b 5, lb 1, w 11	17	Extras	b 2, lb 3, w 11, nb 1	17
Total	(all out, 41 overs)	87	Total	(8 wickets, 34.2 overs)	88

1-0(1), 2-3(2), 3-8(3), 4-22(4), 5-28(6), 6-39(7),
7-73(8), 8-83(9), 9-87(5), 10-87(11)

1-5(2), 2-12(3), 3-28(4), 4-32(5), 5-33(1), 6-45(6),
7-83(7), 8-83(9)

Gibraltar Bowling	O	M	R	W		Israel Bowling	O	M	R	W	
Churaman	10	4	14	5		Moss	9	0	29	2	(6w,1nb)
Mills	7	0	16	1	(6w)	Kehimkar	9	3	18	1	(3w)
De'Ath	10	5	12	3	(1w)	Awasker	10	5	11	1	
Cary	6	1	17	0	(1w)	Ashton	4	0	18	1	(2w)
Garcia	7	1	22	0	(3w)	Worrell	2.2	1	7	2	
Hewitt	1	1	0	1							

Umpires: R.Butler (Bermuda) and A.O.D.George (West Africa)   Man of the Match: N.Churaman

IRELAND v SINGAPORE   (First Round, Group A)
Played at Kelab Aman, Kuala Lumpur, March 30, 1997.

Ireland won by 10 wickets   Toss: Singapore

SINGAPORE			IRELAND		
A.J.Ranggi	c A.D.Patterson b M.W.Patterson	2	J.D.Curry	not out	65
R.Chandran	lbw b M.W.Patterson	0	†A.D.Patterson	not out	44
K.M.Deshpande	c Gillespie b Curry	3	A.R.Dunlop		
C.J.F.Gunningham	c Benson b McCrum	3	*J.D.R.Benson		
*R.T.Y.Mohamed	c A.D.Patterson b M.W.Patterson	0	N.G.Doak		
G.S.Wilson	c Lewis b Graham	31	D.A.Lewis		
†J.H.Stone	lbw b McCrum	2	P.G.Gillespie		
S.Muruthi	run out	10	M.W.Patterson		
D.J.Chelvathurai	not out	23	G.D.Harrison		
R.S.R.Martens	b Doak	4	S.Graham		
R.P.Ramadas	st A.D.Patterson b Doak	3	P.McCrum		
Extras	lb 9, w 19, nb 1	29	Extras	b 3, w 1	4
Total	(all out, 46.5 overs)	110	Total	(no wicket, 10.2 overs)	113

1-3(2), 2-8(1), 3-8(5), 4-37(4), 5-48(7), 6-63(6),
7-80(8), 8-89(10), 9-93(11), 10-110(3)

Ireland Bowling	O	M	R	W		Singapore Bowling	O	M	R	W	
Gillespie	10	3	21	0	(4w)	Wilson	4	0	36	0	(1w)
M.W.Patterson	10	2	27	3	(9w)	Martens	2	0	38	0	
McCrum	9	5	11	2	(1w)	Mohamed	2	0	18	0	
Graham	7	2	20	1	(1w,1nb)	Ramadas	1.2	0	10	0	
Doak	6	1	17	2		Ranggi	1	0	8	0	
Harrison	3	0	3	0							
Curry	1.5	0	5	1							

Umpires: T.Cooper (Fiji) and G.F.Malik (U.A.E.)   Man of the Match: J.D.Curry

K.M.Deshpande retired hurt on 0 at 2/1 and returned at the fall of the 9th wicket.

KENYA v UNITED STATES OF AMERICA (First Round, Group A)

Played at University of Malaya, Kuala Lumpur, March 30, 1997.

Kenya won by 211 runs   Toss: Kenya

KENYA			U.S.A.		
A.Y.Karim	c and b Nazir Islam	34	E.A.Lewis	b M.A.Suji	0
S.K.Gupta	lbw b Dennis	3	P.Singh	lbw b S.O.Tikolo	3
†K.Otieno	st Denny b Bacchus	50	†R.Denny	c S.O.Tikolo b M.A.Suji	2
S.O.Tikolo	b Amin	10	A.D.Texeira	c Otieno b S.O.Tikolo	4
*M.O.Odumbe	st Denny b Lewis	83	*S.F.A.F.Bacchus	c Otieno b S.O.Tikolo	2
H.S.Modi	b Lewis	7	Aijaz Ali	c and b S.O.Tikolo	0
T.Odoyo	lbw b Bacchus	4	D.I.Kallicharran	c Modi b M.A.Suji	1
A.Suji	not out	20	Z.Amin	b M.A.Suji	3
L.O.Tikolo	not out	12	K.Dennis	run out (Karim)	1
M.A.Suji			Nazir Islam	c S.O.Tikolo b M.A.Suji	4
B.Patel			E.Grant	not out	0
Extras	b 4, lb 1, w 15	20	Extras	lb 8, w 4	12
Total	(7 wickets, 50 overs)	243	Total	(all out, 19 overs)	32

1-33(2), 2-63(1), 3-88(4), 4-162(3), 5-175(6),
6-186(7), 7-214(5)

1-0(1), 2-2(3), 3-5(2), 4-7(5), 5-15(4), 6-16(6),
7-21(8), 8-22(9), 9-32(7), 10-32(10)

U.S.A. Bowling	O	M	R	W		Kenya Bowling	O	M	R	W	
Dennis	7	0	25	1	(5w)	M.A.Suji	10	3	7	5	(1w)
Grant	7	0	34	0	(5w)	S.O.Tikolo	9	3	17	4	(3w)
Aijaz Ali	3	0	16	0	(1w)						
Nazir Islam	4	0	26	1	(1nb)						
Amin	7	1	24	1							
Kallicharran	7	1	37	0	(4w)						
Bacchus	8	1	50	2	(1nb)						
Lewis	7	0	26	2							

Umpires: D.Ker (Argentina) and J.Luther (Denmark)   Man of the Match: S.O.Tikolo

ARGENTINA v BANGLADESH (First Round, Group B)

Played at University of Malaya, Kuala Lumpur, March 24, 1997.

Bangladesh won by 5 wickets   Toss: Argentina

ARGENTINA			BANGLADESH		
M.J.Paterlini	lbw b Enamul Hoque	14	Athar Ali Khan	not out	39
B.C.Roberts	b Enamul Hoque	15	Naimur Rahman	run out	53
D.Forrester	st Khaled Mashud b Naimur Rahman	4	Sanvar Hossain	c Kirschbaum b Tunon	1
*G.P.Kirschbaum	st Khaled Mashud b Naimur Rahman	9	Aminul Islam	b Irigoyan	4
M.D.Morris	b Enamul Hoque	18	*Akram Khan	c Perez Rivero b Tunon	11
A.Perez Rivero	c Enamul Hoque b Mohammed Rafique	6	Minhajul Abedin	c Riveros b Tunon	5
†M.O.Juarez	lbw b Naimur Rahman	7	Mohammed Rafique	not out	15
B.I.Irigoyan	not out	30	Enamul Hoque		
C.T.Tunon	run out	1	Saiful Islam		
H.P.Pereyra	c Khaled Mashud b Hasibul Hussain	10	†Khaled Mashud		
M.J.Riveros	b Hasibul Hussain	4	Hasibul Hussain		
Extras	b 1, lb 10, w 9	20	Extras	w 11, nb 3	14
Total	(all out, 48.3 overs)	138	Total	(5 wickets, 24 overs)	142

1-31(2), 2-39(3), 3-45(1), 4-54(4), 5-69(6), 6-82(7),
7-98(5), 8-109(9), 9-131(10), 10-138(11)

1-78(2), 2-83(3), 3-89(4), 4-115(5), 5-124(6)

Bangladesh Bowling	O	M	R	W		Argentina Bowling	O	M	R	W	
Saiful Islam	10	2	24	0		Pereyra	6	0	21	0	(3w,2nb)
Hasibul Hussain	5.3	1	9	2	(3w)	Forrester	2	0	16	0	
Enamul Hoque	10	4	18	3		Perez Rivero	2	0	15	0	
Naimur Rahman	10	0	21	3	(2w)	Riveros	2	0	24	0	(5w)
Mohammed Rafique	9	0	36	1	(4w)	Tunon	8	0	42	3	(1w,1nb)
Minhajul Abedin	4	1	19	0		Irigoyan	4	0	24	1	

Umpires: C.Hoare (Canada) and L.Nelon   Man of the Match: Naimur Rahman

MALAYSIA v DENMARK   (First Round, Group B)

Played at Rubber Research Institute, Kuala Lumpur, March 24, 1997.

Denmark won by 31 runs

Toss: Denmark

DENMARK

S.A.Nielsen	lbw b Muniandy	12
M.Lund	c Menon b Jeevandran	43
†B.Singh	lbw b Selvaratnam	0
L.H.Andersen	lbw b Menon	15
P.Jensen	c K.Ramadas b D.Ramadas	18
*S.Henriksen	lbw b Jeevandran	13
M.H.Andersen	lbw b D.Ramadas	9
S.Vestergaard	c Selvaratnam b Jeevandran	13
T.M.Hansen	run out	5
S.K.Kristenson	not out	5
S.R.M.Sorensen	c K.Ramadas b Jeevandran	0
Extras	lb 4, w 6	10
Total	(all out, 47.2 overs)	143

1-35(1), 2-36(3), 3-62(4), 4-94(2), 5-98(5),
6-114(7), 7-122(6), 8-138(9), 9-139(8), 10-143(11)

MALAYSIA

S.V.Segeran	c Vestergaard b M.H.Andersen	23
Suresh Singh	lbw b Verstergaard	1
S.Navaratnam	lbw b M.H.Andersen	17
*R.Menon	b Hansen	0
Tan Kim Hing	c Lund b M.H.Andersen	2
†K.Ramadas	b M.H.Andersen	0
M.A.Williams	c Singh b Sorensen	19
S.N.Jeevandran	lbw b M.H.Andersen	0
D.Ramadas	lbw b Vestergaard	3
R.M.Selvaratnam	not out	14
M.A.Muniandy	b Sorensen	0
Extras	b 6, lb 5, w 16, nb 6	33
Total	(all out, 41.5 overs)	112

1-9(2), 2-60(3), 3-61(1), 4-63(5), 5-63(6), 6-64(4),
7-69(8), 8-77(9), 9-112(10), 10-112(11)

Malaysia Bowling

	O	M	R	W	
Muniandy	7	3	18	1	(4w)
Selvaratnam	9	1	33	1	(2w)
Menon	9	2	24	1	
Navaratnam	5	1	11	0	
Tan Kim Hing	2	0	11	0	
D.Ramadas	6	0	20	2	
Jeevandran	9.2	1	22	4	

Denmark Bowling

	O	M	R	W	
Vestergaard	8	1	14	2	(2w,2nb)
Sorensen	5.5	0	19	2	(2w)
M.H.Andersen	10	1	19	5	(5w,4nb)
Jensen	5	1	16	0	(1w)
Hansen	6	1	14	1	(2w)
Kristenson	5	1	13	0	(1w)
L.H.Andersen	2	0	6	0	

Umpires: R.Butler (Bermuda) and H.Whitlock (Hong Kong)

Man of the Match: M.H.Andersen

UNITED ARAB EMIRATES v WEST AFRICA   (First Round, Group B)

Played at Royal Selangor Club, Bukit Kiara, Kuala Lumpur, March 24, 1997.

United Arab Emirates won by 7 wickets

Toss: West Africa

WEST AFRICA

K.Sagoe	lbw b Arshad Laeeq	8
A.Crooks	run out	0
O.Ukpong	lbw b Shahzad Altaf	1
G.I.Wiltshire	run out	13
J.Omoigui	lbw b Arshad Laeeq	4
U.Ntinu	b Arshad Laeeq	0
*†O.O.Agodo	c Ali Akbar Rana b Asim Saeed	4
E.Nutsugah	b Arshad Laeeq	0
A.Kpundeh	c Ali Akbar Rana b Saeed-al-Saffar	9
S.Fadahunsi	not out	6
P.D.Vanderpuje-Orgle	b Salim Raza	1
Extras	b 2, lb 3, w 15, nb 6	26
Total	(all out, 40.2 overs)	72

1-6(2), 2-9(3), 3-35(4), 4-38(1), 5-40(6), 6-42(5),
7-45(8), 8-54(7), 9-69(9), 10-72(11)

U.A.E.

Asim Saeed	b Fadahunsi	17
Salim Raza	c Agodo b Vanderpuje-Orgle	15
Azhar Saeed	c Agodo b Fadahunsi	8
†Ali Akbar Rana	not out	8
Arshad Laeeq	not out	16
*Saeed-al-Saffar		
Shahzad Altaf		
Mohammad Atif		
Ahmed Nadeem		
Mehmood Pir Baksh		
Mohammed Tauqeer		
Extras	lb 2, w 7	9
Total	(3 wickets, 14.1 overs)	73

1-27(2), 2-46(3), 3-47(1)

U.A.E. Bowling

	O	M	R	W	
Shahzad Altaf	10	2	15	1	(3w,1nb)
Ahmed Nadeem	5	0	11	0	(4w,2nb)
Salim Raza	4.2	2	3	1	(1w)
Arshad Laeeq	10	2	14	4	(2w)
Mohammad Atif	7	1	11	0	(4w)
Asim Saeed	2	0	8	1	(2nb)
Saeed-al-Saffar	2	0	5	1	

West Africa Bowling

	O	M	R	W	
Fadahunsi	7.1	0	39	2	(5w)
Vanderpuje-Orgle	7	2	32	1	(2w)

Umpires: D.Beltran (Gibraltar) and I.Massey (Italy)

Man of the Match: Arshad Laeeq

Asim Saeed's first over was 1 ball short.

MALAYSIA v ARGENTINA   (First Round, Group B)

Played at Royal Military College, Kuala Lumpur, March 25, 1997.

Malaysia won by 81 runs — Toss: Argentina

MALAYSIA				ARGENTINA		
S.V.Segeran	c Paterlini b Lord	8		M.J.Paterlini	c K.Ramadas b Muniandy	5
V.R.Rajah	c Perez Rivero b Irigoyan	25		B.C.Roberts	b Navaratnam	15
S.Navaratnam	lbw b Irigoyan	22		D.Forrester	b Navaratnam	13
*R.Menon	c Juarez b Irigoyan	6		*G.P.Kirschbaum	c K.Ramadas b Tan Kim Hing	29
Tan Kim Hing	c Perez Rivero b Irigoyan	6		M.D.Morris	c and b Tan Kim Hing	18
†K.Ramadas	c Lord b Pereyra	2		A.R.Perez Rivero	run out	1
M.A.Williams	not out	56		†M.O.Juarez	run out	1
R.M.Selvaratnam	c Forrester b Perez Rivero	3		C.J.Tunon	c Navaratnam b Menon	1
D.Ramadas	c and b Perez Rivero	19		B.I.Irigoyan	not out	5
S.N.Jeevandran	c Juarez b Perez Rivero	16		H.P.Pereyra	run out	3
M.A.Muniandy	c Irigoyan b Perez Rivero	1		D.M.Lord	c Muniandy b Menon	0
Extras	lb 5, w 18, nb 2	25		Extras	lb 1, w 16	17
Total	(all out, 50 overs)	189		Total	(all out, 40.5 overs)	108

1-11(1), 2-64(2), 3-67(3), 4-82(5), 5-82(4), 6-84(6), 7-99(8), 8-143(9), 9-187(10), 10-189(11)

1-10(1), 2-34(3), 3-46(2), 4-95(4), 5-97(6), 6-99(5), 7-100(8), 8-100(7), 9-105(10), 10-108(11)

Argentina Bowling	O	M	R	W	
Tunon	10	0	37	0	(8w)
Lord	8	0	38	1	(1w,2nb)
Irigoyan	10	1	27	4	(7w)
Pereyra	10	2	17	1	
Perez Rivero	9	0	47	4	(1w)
Forrester	3	0	18	0	(1w)

Malaysia Bowling	O	M	R	W	
Muniandy	6	1	15	1	(2w)
Selvaratnam	5	0	15	0	(4w)
Menon	8.5	2	20	2	
Navaratnam	5	2	13	2	(6w)
Jeevandran	3	0	10	0	
D.Ramadas	5	2	14	0	(1w)
Tan Kim Hing	8	1	20	2	

Umpires: I.Massey (Italy) and V.M.Rafik (East & Central Africa)   Man of the Match: M.A.Williams

BANGLADESH v WEST AFRICA   (First Round, Group B)

Played at Perbadanan Kemajuan Negari Selangor, Kuala Lumpur, March 25, 1997.

Bangladesh won by 9 wickets — Toss: Bangladesh

WEST AFRICA				BANGLADESH		
K.Sagoe	c Khaled Mashud b Akram Khan	12		Athar Ali Khan	c Ntinu b Ukpong	17
A.Kpundeh	c Khaled Mashud b Hasibul Hussain	0		Naimur Rahman	not out	42
G.I.Wiltshire	c Naimur Rahman b Saiful Islam	1		Sanvar Hossain	not out	13
J.Omoigui	c Minhajul Abedin b Mohammed Rafique	10		Saiful Islam		
U.Ntinu	c Akram Khan b Minhajul Abedin	8		Hasibul Hussain		
*†O.O.Agodo	c and b Akram Khan	2		Mohammed Rafique		
O.E.Ukpong	c and b Minhajul Abedin	1		*Akram Khan		
E.Nutsugah	st Khaled Mashud b Minhajul Abedin	5		Minhajul Abedin		
S.Kpundeh	c Enamul Hoque b Naimur Rahman	14		Enamul Hoque		
S.Turay	not out	9		†Khaled Mashud		
S.Fadahunsi	c Khaled Mashud b Hasibul Hossain	4		Aminul Islam		
Extras	lb 4, w 12	16		Extras	lb1, w 10	11
Total	(all out, 39.1 overs)	82		Total	(1 wicket, 19.4 overs)	83

1-3(2), 2-10(3), 3-33(1), 4-33(4), 5-40(6), 6-41(7), 7-50(5), 8-65(8), 9-69(9), 10-82(11)

1-38(1)

Bangladesh Bowling	O	M	R	W	
Saiful Islam	7	0	13	1	(2w)
Hasibul Hussain	8.1	3	11	2	(3w)
Mohammed Rafique	5	1	8	1	
Akram Khan	6	2	14	2	(5w)
Minhajul Abedin	5	2	8	3	(1w)
Athar Ali Khan	3	0	13	1	(1w)
Naimur Rahman	2	0	4	1	
Enamul Hoque	3	0	7	0	

West Africa Bowling	O	M	R	W	
Fadahunsi	7	3	19	0	(4w)
Ntinu	3	0	20	0	(3w)
Ukpong	6.4	0	35	1	(2w)
S.Kpundeh	3	1	8	0	(1w)

Umpires: Makbul Jaffer (Kenya) and H.Whitlock (Hong Kong)   Man of the Match: Minhajul Abedin

DENMARK v UNITED ARAB EMIRATES   (First Round, Group B)

Played at University of Malaya, Kuala Lumpur, March 26, 1997.

Denmark won by 1 wicket
Toss: United Arab Emirates

U.A.E.			DENMARK		
Salim Raza	b Vestergaard	0	S.A.Nielsen	c Ali Akbar Rana b Arshad Laeeq	9
*Saeed-al-Saffar	c Henriksen b Sorensen	1	M.Lund	c Ali Akbar Rana b Ahmed Nadeem	11
Azhar Saeed	c Singh b Hansen	20	C.R.Pedersen	b Shahzad Altaf	1
Mehmood Pir Baksh	c Henriksen b Sorensen	2	P.Jensen	c Ali Akbar Rana b Arshad Laeeq	7
†Ali Akbar Rana	lbw b Jensen	6	*S.Henriksen	c Saeed-al-Saffar b Mohammad Atif	23
Arshad Laeeq	c Nielsen b Kristenson	46	†B.Singh	c sub (B.Jayawardene) b Azhar Saeed	6
Asim Saeed	c Sorensen b Kristenson	21	M.H.Andersen	c Ali Akbar Rana b Saeed-al-Saffar	30
Mohammed Tauqeer	c Nielsen b Vestergaard	8	S.Vestergaard	c Ahmed Nadeem b Saeed-al-Saffar	24
Ahmed Nadeem	c Andersen b Sorensen	6	S.K.Kristenson	st Ali Akbar Rana b Salim Raza	2
Shahzad Altaf	c Jensen b Vestergaard	7	S.R.M.Sorensen	not out	3
Mohammad Atif	not out	1	T.M.Hansen	not out	1
Extras	lb 2, w 22, nb 5	29	Extras	b 7, lb 5, w 16, nb 3	31
Total	(all out, 46.2 overs)	147	Total	(9 wickets, 50 overs)	148

1-0(1), 2-4(2), 3-17(4), 4-36(3), 5-46(5), 6-118(7),
7-118(6), 8-138(8), 9-147(9), 10-147(10)

1-25(2), 2-26(3), 3-37(1), 4-45(4), 5-69(6), 6-88(5),
7-134(8), 8-143(7), 9-143(9)

Denmark Bowling	O	M	R	W	
Vestergaard	6.2	2	16	3	(2w)
Sorensen	8	2	19	3	(8w)
Andersen	10	1	29	0	(5w,6nb)
Hansen	2.2	0	10	1	(5w)
Jensen	9	2	35	1	(4nb)
Kristenson	10	1	32	2	(2w)
Nielsen	0.4	0	4	0	(1nb)

U.A.E. Bowling	O	M	R	W	
Shahzad Altaf	10	2	15	1	(3w)
Ahmed Nadeem	10	1	21	1	(3w,3nb)
Arshad Laeeq	10	4	16	2	(6w)
Salim Raza	9	0	32	1	(3w)
Azhar Saeed	4	0	20	1	(2nb)
Mohammad Atif	4	0	19	1	(1w)
Saeed-al-Saffar	3	1	13	2	(2nb)

Umpires: N.T.Plews (England) and V.M.Rafik (East & Central Africa).   Man of the Match: S.Vestergaard
T.M.Hansen split the webbing of his hand while bowling his 3rd over (the 16th of the innings). The over was completed
by S.A.Nielsen. Hansen was replaced in the Denmark squad by O.H.Mortensen, the coach.

ARGENTINA v WEST AFRICA   (First Round, Group B)

Played at Rubber Research Institute, Kuala Lumpur, March 27, 1997.

West Africa won by 5 wickets
Toss: Argentina

ARGENTINA			WEST AFRICA		
M.J.Paterlini	c Agodo b Fadahunsi	15	K.Sagoe	c Arizaga b Irigoyan	18
B.I.Irigoyan	c Omoigui b Fadahunsi	7	O.E.Ukpong	lbw b Perez Rivero	0
M.D.Morris	lbw b Vanderpuje-Orgle	2	S.Turay	c Juarez b Irigoyan	0
*G.P.Kirschbaum	lbw b Vanderpuje-Orgle	4	*†O.O.Agodo	c Juarez b Perez Rivero	2
†M.O.Juarez	c Sagoe b Idowu	0	J.Omoigui	b Irigoyan	5
A.R.Perez Rivero	lbw b Idowu	4	G.I.Wiltshire	not out	29
M.K.van Steeden	b Idowu	4	S.Kpundeh	not out	17
H.P.Pereyra	c and b Kpundeh	10	S.Fadahunsi		
C.J.Tunon	run out	0	U.Ntinu		
G.F.Arizaga	b Idowu	7	P.D.Vanderpuje-Orgle		
D.M.Lord	not out	0	O.Idowu		
Extras	b 4, lb 2, w 18	24	Extras	lb 2, w 6	8
Total	(all out, 38.1 overs)	77	Total	(5 wickets, 20.1 overs)	79

1-17(2), 2-20(3), 3-39(1), 4-40(4), 5-40(5), 6-47(7),
7-51(6), 8-53(9), 9-77(8), 10-77(10)

1-13(2), 2-19(1), 3-19(3), 4-21(4), 5-29(5)

West Africa Bowling	O	M	R	W	
Fadahunsi	10	1	20	2	(5w)
Vanderpuje-Orgle	10	2	17	2	(4w)
Idowu	9.1	1	14	4	(5w)
Ukpong	6	1	15	0	(3w)
Kpundeh	3	1	5	1	(1w)

Argentina Bowling	O	M	R	W	
Irigoyan	7	1	35	3	(3w)
Perez Rivero	8	1	27	2	(1w)
Pereyra	3.1	0	11	0	
Tunon	2	0	4	0	(2w)

Umpires: T.Cooper (Fiji) and J.K.Kruger (Namibia).   Man of the match: O.Idowu

BANGLADESH v DENMARK (First Round, Group B)

Played at Royal Selangor Club, Bukit Kiara, Kuala Lumpur, March 27, 1997.
Bangladesh won by 5 wickets.   Toss: Denmark

DENMARK		
S.A.Nielsen	lbw b Akram Khan	23
M.Lund	lbw b Hasibul Hussain	0
C.R.Pedersen	lbw b Saiful Islam	2
J.S.Jensen	b Saiful Islam	0
*S.Henriksen	c Khaled Mashud b Akram Khan	15
†B.Singh	run out	4
M.H.Andersen	c and b Hasibul Hussain	1
S.Vestergaard	c Khaled Mashud b Mohammed Rafique	8
A.Rasmussen	st Khaled Mashud b Enamul Hoque	14
S.K.Kristenson	run out	5
S.R.M.Sorensen	not out	2
Extras	b 1, lb 4, w 16, nb 3	24
Total	(all out, 47.4 overs)	98

1-5(2), 2-12(3), 3-12(4), 4-54(5), 5-64(1), 6-65(6),
7-74(7), 8-80(8), 9-95(9), 10-98(10)

BANGLADESH		
Athar Ali Khan	c Henriksen b Jensen	32
Naimur Rahman	b Vestergaard	3
Sanvar Hossain	b Kristenson	10
Aminul Islam	c and b Henriksen	33
Mohammed Rafique	c Pedersen b Jensen	4
Minhajul Abedin	not out	1
*Akram Khan	not out	3
†Khaled Mashud		
Saiful Islam		
Enamul Hoque		
Hasibul Hussain		
Extras	lb 2, w 11	13
Total	(5 wickets, 33.5 overs)	99

1-6(2), 2-42(3), 3-74(1), 4-88(5), 5-95(4)

Bangladesh Bowling

	O	M	R	W	
Saiful Islam	8	1	12	2	(7w)
Hasibul Hussain	8.4	0	25	2	(7w,3nb)
Athar Ali Khan	3	0	18	0	(1w)
Akram Khan	10	3	10	2	(1w)
Enamul Hoque	10	2	13	1	
Mohammed Rafique	8	3	15	1	

Denmark Bowling

	O	M	R	W	
Vestergaard	5	0	17	1	(1w)
Sorensen	5	2	15	0	(2w)
Andersen	5	0	14	0	(7w)
Kristenson	6	2	14	1	(1w)
Jensen	7.5	3	18	2	
Rasmussen	4	0	18	0	
Henriksen	1	0	1	1	

Umpires: E.D.Ohm (Netherlands) and H.Reid (U.S.A.)   Man of the Match: Aminul Islam

MALAYSIA v UNITED ARAB EMIRATES (First Round, Group B)

Played at Perbadanan Kemajuan Negari Selangor, Kuala Lumpur, March 27, 1997.
United Arab Emirates won by 2 wickets.   Toss: Malaysia

MALAYSIA		
S.V.Segeran	c Ali Akbar Rana b Salim Raza	12
Suresh Singh	c Ali Akbar Rana b Ahmed Nadeem	2
V.R.Rajah	b Salim Raza	11
S.Navaratnam	b Arshad Laeeq	6
*R.Menon	c Ali Akbar Rana b Perera	18
M.A.Williams	run out	4
R.M.Selvaratnam	b Ahmed Nadeem	30
D.Ramadas	c Adnan Mushtaq b Arshad Laeeq	12
†K.Ramadas	run out	17
S.N.Jeevandran	run out	3
M.A.Muniandy	not out	0
Extras	b 2, lb 8, w 14, nb 1	25
Total	(all out, 49.3 overs)	140

1-14(2), 2-27(1), 3-37(4), 4-42(3), 5-62(6), 6-68(5),
7-101(8), 8-135(7), 9-140(10), 10-140(9)

U.A.E.		
Asim Saeed	b Muniandy	0
Azhar Saeed	c Navaratnam b Jeevandran	33
M.V.Perera	b Menon	26
Adnan Mushtaq	c K.Ramadas b Menon	2
†Ali Akbar Rana	c Suresh Singh b Navaratnam	28
Arshad Laeeq	c K.Ramadas b Navaratnam	2
Salim Raza	b Navaratnam	3
*Saeed-al-Saffar	not out	24
Mohammed Tauqeer	run out	6
Ahmed Nadeem	not out	1
Mohammad Atif		
Extras	b 1, lb 1, w 14	16
Total	(8 wickets, 47.5 overs)	141

1-1(1), 2-68(3), 3-70(4), 4-84(2), 5-87(6), 6-95(7),
7-127(5), 8-138(9)

U.A.E. Bowling

	O	M	R	W	
Ahmed Nadeem	7	0	27	2	(2w)
Asim Saeed	5	1	10	0	(3w,1nb)
Salim Raza	10	2	18	2	
Arshad Laeeq	9.3	3	28	2	(5w)
Saeed-al-Saffar	10	0	24	0	(3w)
Perera	8	1	23	1	(1w)

Malaysia Bowling

	O	M	R	W	
Muniandy	9	0	29	1	(2w)
Selvaratnam	5	0	9	0	(4w)
Menon	10	4	23	2	
Navaratnam	8.5	0	41	3	
Suresh Singh	2	0	7	0	(3w,4nb)
Jeevandran	8	1	16	1	(2w)
D.Ramadas	5	1	14	0	

Umpires: L.P.Hogan (Ireland) and Makbul Jaffer (Kenya)   Man of the Match: Ali Akbar Rana

MALAYSIA v WEST AFRICA   (First Round, Group B)

Played at Kelab Aman, Kuala Lumpur, March 28, 1997.
Malaysia won on higher comparative scoring rate

MALAYSIA				WEST AFRICA		
				Toss: Malaysia		
S.V.Segeran	c Idowu			K.Sagoe	c K.Ramadas	9
	b Vanderpuje-Orgle	25			b Navaratnam	
Suresh Singh	c Crooks b Fadahunsi	1		A.Crooks	b Selvaratnam	0
V.R.Rajah	lbw b Vanderpuje-Orgle	21		O.E.Ukpong	c Rajah b D.Ramadas	24
S.Navaratnam	c Sagoe b Idowu	0		S.Fadahunsi	c K.Ramadas	
					b Navaratnam	3
*R.Menon	not out	49		G.I.Wiltshire	run out	25
M.A.Williams	run out	15		A.Kpundeh	run out	14
R.M.Selvaratnam	c Ukpong b Omoigui	4		U.Ntinu	run out	17
D.Ramadas	c Crooks b Ntinu	1		J.Omoigui	not out	8
†K.Ramadas	c Ukpong b Ntinu	19		O.Idowu	c K.Ramadas b Muniandy	9
S.N.Jeevandran	c Crooks b Idowu	0		*†O.O.Agodo	not out	4
M.A.Muniandy	b Ntinu	2		P.D.Vanderpuje-Orgle		
Extras	lb 2, w 29, nb 2	33		Extras	b 2, lb 1, w 7	10
Total	(all out, 48.1 overs)	170		Total	(8 wickets, 44 overs)	123

1-11(2), 2-60(3), 3-61(4), 4-61(1), 5-97(6), 6-113(7),
7-116(8), 8-158(9), 9-167(10), 10-170(11)

1-3(2), 2-39(1), 3-39(3), 4-43(4), 5-66(6), 6-95(7),
7-101(5), 8-117(9)

West Africa Bowling	O	M	R	W		Malaysia Bowling	O	M	R	W	
Fadahunsi	10	0	45	1	(11w)	Muniandy	7	0	17	1	(2w)
Vanderpuje-Orgle	10	2	24	2	(4w)	Selvaratnam	2	0	18	1	(3w)
Idowu	10	3	24	2	(2w,1nb)	Menon	10	1	28	0	
Ukpong	6	0	25	0	(5w)	Navaratnam	5	1	9	2	(1w)
Kpundeh	7	0	27	0		D.Ramadas	10	3	23	1	
Omoigui	1	0	4	1	(2w)	Jeevandran	10	1	25	0	(1w)
Ntinu	4.1	0	19	3	(4w,1nb)						

Umpires: N.Gudker (Israel) and W.Maha (Papua New Guinea)   Man of the Match: R.Menon

Play stopped at 4.34pm due to rain and restarted at 4.58pm with no reduction in overs. Play was again stopped by rain at 5.12pm and finally abandoned. Under the Duckworth-Lewis method, West Africa needed to have scored 148 to win the match.

ARGENTINA v DENMARK   (First Round, Group B)

Played at Perbadanan Kemajuan Negari Selangor, Kuala Lumpur, March 29, 1997.
Denmark won by 150 runs

DENMARK				ARGENTINA		
				Toss: Argentina		
†S.A.Nielsen	c van Steeden b Lord	6		M.J.Paterlini	c Henriksen b Vestergaard	1
M.Lund	c Roberts b Perez Rivero	19		B.C.Roberts	c J.S.Jensen b Sorensen	7
C.R.Pedersen	b Irigoyan	1		*G.P.Kirschbaum	lbw b Vestergaard	4
*S.Henriksen	lbw b Arizaga	3		A.R.Perez Rivero	b J.S.Jensen	4
J.S.Jensen	lbw b Arizaga	43		B.I.Irigoyan	lbw b P.Jensen	5
P.Jensen	c Roberts b Arizaga	10		M.K.van Steeden	c Nielsen b Sorensen	0
B.Singh	st Jarez b Pereyra	57		†M.O.Juarez	c Vestergaard b Pedersen	9
M.H.Andersen	not out	52		H.P.Pereyra	st Nielsen b Kristenson	16
S.Vestergaard	b Lord	1		G.F.Arizaga	b Kristenson	0
S.K.Kristenson	not out	1		S.J.Ciaburri	st Nielsen b Kristenson	0
S.R.M.Sorensen				D.M.Lord	not out	0
Extras	lb 3, w 29, nb 1	33		Extras	b 4, w 25, nb 1	30
Total	(8 wickets, 50 overs)	226		Total	(all out, 35.1 overs)	76

1-24(1), 2-30(3), 3-49(4), 4-63(1), 5-94(6),
6-111(5), 7-222(7), 8-225(9)

1-5(1), 2-19(3), 3-39(4), 4-39(2), 5-48(5), 6-48(6),
7-68(7), 8-71(9), 9-75(10), 10-76(8)

Argentina Bowling	O	M	R	W		Denmark Bowling	O	M	R	W	
Lord	8	0	41	2	(11w,1nb)	Vestergaard	4	1	15	2	(6w,1nb)
Irigoyan	10	0	31	1	(11w)	Sorensen	10	2	15	2	(7w)
Arizaga	10	0	46	3	(4w)	J.S.Jensen	2	0	15	1	(6w)
Perez Rivero	10	0	42	1	(1w)	P.Jensen	9	5	7	1	
Pereyra	10	0	43	1	(1w)	Kristenson	7.1	1	16	3	
Ciaburri	2	0	20	0	(1w)	Pedersen	3	1	1	1	

Umpires: W.Maha (Papua new Guinea) and W.Smith (Scotland)   Man of the Match: B.Singh

BANGLADESH v UNITED ARAB EMIRATES   (First Round, Group B)

Played at Kelab Aman, Kuala Lumpur, March 29, 1997.

Bangladesh won by 110 runs

Toss: United Arab Emirates

BANGLADESH		
Athar Ali Khan	c and b Salim Raza	26
Naimur Rahman	c Perera b Salim Raza	19
Sanvar Hossain	b Arshad Laeeq	6
Aminul Islam	c Azhar Saeed b Saeed-al-Saffar	8
*Akram Khan	c Ali Akbar Rana b Azhar Saeed	13
Minhajul Abedin	b Salim Raza	37
Enamul Hoque	run out	37
Saiful Islam	c Mehmood Pir Baksh b Salim Raza	19
Mohammed Rafique	b Ahmed Nadeem	15
Hasibul Hussain	c Asim Saeed b Perera	2
†Khaled Mashud	not out	1
Extras	b 2, lb 5, w 12, nb 3	22
Total	(all out, 49.3 overs)	205

1-46(2), 2-56(3), 3-69(1), 4-76(4), 5-113(5),
6-152(6), 7-176(8), 8-192(7), 9-201(10), 10-205(9)

U.A.E. Bowling	O	M	R	W	
Ahmed Nadeem	6.3	0	29	1	(3w)
Asim Saeed	4	1	22	0	(2w)
Salim Raza	10	2	23	4	(1w)
Arshad Laeeq	10	1	48	1	(3w)
Saeed-al-Saffar	10	0	41	1	(3nb)
Azhar Saeed	8	0	29	1	
Perera	1	0	6	1	

U.A.E.		
Salim Raza	c Khaled Mashud b Saiful Islam	0
Azhar Saeed	c Aminul Islam b Saiful Islam	25
Adnan Mushtaq	c Sanvar Hossain b Athar Ali Khan	22
M.V.Perera	lbw b Akram Khan	1
†Ali Akbar Rana	c and b Mohammed Rafique	17
Arshad Laeeq	c Mohammed Rafique b Akram Khan	4
Mehmood Pir Baksh	c and b Enamul Hoque	6
Asim Saeed	lbw b Enamul Hoque	7
*Saeed-al-Saffar	run out	6
Mohammed Tauqeer	not out	0
Ahmed Nadeem	c Minhajul Abedin b Mohammed Rafique	0
Extras	lb 2, w 4, nb 1	7
Total	(all out, 34.2 overs)	95

1-0(1), 2-43(2), 3-46(4), 4-58(3), 5-64(6), 6-74(7),
7-84(8), 8-95(9), 9-95(5), 10-95(11)

Bangladesh Bowling	O	M	R	W	
Saiful Islam	7	0	17	2	(2w)
Hasibul Hussain	5	0	27	0	(1w,4nb)
Athar Ali Khan	7	0	16	1	(1w)
Akram Khan	8	0	22	2	
Enamul Hoque	6	2	9	2	
Mohammed Rafique	1.2	0	2	2	

Umpires: R.Butler (Bermuda) and H.Reid (U.S.A.)

Man of the Match: Enamul Hoque

ARGENTINA v UNITED ARAB EMIRATES   (First Round, Group B)

Played at Victoria Institute, Kuala Lumpur, March 30, 1997.

United Arab Emirates won by 8 wickets

Toss: Argentina

ARGENTINA		
*G.P.Kirschbaum	st Perera b Mohammad Atif	18
M.J.Paterlini	not out	77
B.I.Irigoyan	c and b Mohammad Atif	2
M.D.Morris	lbw b Arshad Laeeq	28
A.R.Perez Rivero	c sub (Mehmood Pir Baksh) b Mohammed Tauqeer	0
H.P.Pereyra	b Ahmed Nadeem	13
†M.K.van Steeden	run out	2
C.J.Tunon	b Arshad Laeeq	9
G.F.Arizaga	not out	8
M.J.Riveros		
A.M.Rowe		
Extras	lb 9, w 23	32
Total	(7 wickets, 50 overs)	189

1-39(1), 2-42(3), 3-94(4), 4-95(5), 5-150(6),
6-153(7), 7-175(8)

U.A.E. Bowling	O	M	R	W	
Ahmed Nadeem	10	1	31	1	(7w)
Jayawardena	6	1	26	0	(6w)
Arshad Laeeq	10	1	38	2	(6w)
Saeed-al-Saffar	4	1	16	0	
Mohammad Atif	8	1	31	2	(2w)
Hyder	6	1	12	0	(1w)
Mohammed Tauqeer	4	0	11	1	
Azhar Saeed	2	0	15	0	

U.A.E.		
Asim Saeed	b Tunon	0
Azhar Saeed	not out	66
Arshad Laeeq	c sub (D.M.Lord) b Pereyra	66
†M.V.Perera	not out	32
*Saeed-al-Saffar		
B.Jayawardena		
M.Hyder		
Mohammed Tauqeer		
Arif Yousuf		
Ahmed Nadeem		
Mohammad Atif		
Extras	lb 5, w 20, nb 1	26
Total	(2 wickets, 31.3 overs)	190

1-0(1), 2-134(3)

Argentina Bowling	O	M	R	W	
Tunon	7	0	25	1	(7w)
Irigoyan	8	0	33	0	(1w,1nb)
Riveros	3	0	10	0	(6w)
Pereyra	4	0	34	1	(1w)
Perez Rivero	4	0	26	0	(1nb)
Arizaga	3.3	0	40	0	(5w)
Rowe	2	0	17	0	(1nb)

Umpires: E.D.Ohm (Netherlands) and H.Whitlock (Hong Kong)   Man of the Match: Arshad Laeeq

MALAYSIA v BANGLADESH   (First Round, Group B)

Played at Tenaga Nasional Sports Complex (Kilat Kelab), Kuala Lumpur, March 30, 1997.

Bangladesh won by 59 runs   Toss: Bangladesh

BANGLADESH

Athar Ali Khan	c K.Ramadas b Selvaratnam	10
Naimur Rahman	c Rajah b Menon	17
Minhajul Abedin	c Navaratnam b D.Ramadas	42
*Aminul Islam	c Rajah b Jeevandran	21
Akram Khan	b Navaratnam	39
Jahangir Alam	run out	8
Enamul Hoque	c D.Ramadas b Menon	0
Khaled Mahmud	b Menon	33
Saiful Islam	b Navaratnam	12
Hasibul Hussain	not out	7
†Khaled Mashud	not out	6
Extras	lb 1, w 15	16
Total	(9 wickets, 50 overs)	211

1-26(1), 2-55(2), 3-89(4), 4-110(3), 5-126(6),
6-126(7), 7-186(8), 8-188(5), 9-205(9)

MALAYSIA

S.V.Segeran	c and b Minhajul Abedin	9
R.M.Selvaratnam	c and b Hasibul Hussain	5
V.R.Rajah	b Khaled Mahmud	2
*R.Menon	b Naimur Rahman	16
M.A.Williams	st Jahangir Alam b Enamul Hoque	58
S.Navaratnam	run out	12
†K.Ramadas	b Naimur Rahman	6
D.Ramadas	b Saiful Islam	23
S.N.Jeevandran	not out	3
Saat Jalil	not out	0
M.A.Muniandy		
Extras	b 1, lb 8, w 9	18
Total	(8 wickets, 50 overs)	152

1-12(2), 2-17(3), 3-35(1), 4-57(4), 5-79(6),
6-91(7), 7-142(5), 8-150(8)

Malaysia Bowling

	O	M	R	W	
Muniandy	9	0	41	0	(3w)
Selvaratnam	4	0	22	1	(8w)
Menon	10	2	43	3	(1w)
Navaratnam	9	2	36	2	(1w)
D.Ramadas	8	0	31	1	(1w)
Jeevandran	10	0	37	1	

Bangladesh Bowling

	O	M	R	W	
Saiful Islam	5	1	15	1	(2w)
Hasibul Hussain	7	2	10	1	(5w)
Khaled Mahmud	10	4	27	1	(2w)
Minhajul Abedin	8	1	29	1	
Naimur Rahman	10	3	30	2	
Enamul Hoque	10	1	32	1	

Umpires: S.Bachitar (Singapore) and W.Smith (Scotland)   Man of the Match: Minhajul Abedin

DENMARK v WEST AFRICA   (First Round, Group B)

Played at Royal Military College, Kuala Lumpur, March 30, 1997.

Denmark won by 8 wickets   Toss: West Africa

WEST AFRICA

K.Sagoe	c Henriksen b Sorensen	0
O.Ukpong	c and b Sorensen	6
†A.Kpundeh	lbw b Kristenson	30
S.Kpundeh	c Vestergaard b Kristenson	2
*E.Nutsugah	b Andersen	1
J.Omoigui	lbw b Kristenson	20
G.I.Wiltshire	c Singh b Andersen	25
K.Asiedu	lbw b Vestergaard	2
S.Fadahunsi	b Vestergaard	0
O.Idowu	b Vestergaard	2
C.Ahuchogu	not out	4
Extras	w 7, nb 6	13
Total	(all out, 45.5 overs)	105

1-1(1), 2-17(2), 3-27(4), 4-35(5), 5-58(3), 6-84(6),
7-99(8), 8-99(9), 9-99(7), 10-105(10)

DENMARK

M.Lund	lbw b Ahuchogu	1
†B.Singh	c A.Kpundeh b Fadahunsi	6
J.S.Jensen	not out	46
C.R.Pedersen	not out	34
S.R.M.Sorensen		
S.A.Nielsen		
M.H.Andersen		
S.Vestergaard		
A.Rasmussen		
*S.Henriksen		
S.K.Kristenson		
Extras	b 2, lb 5, w 9, nb 3	19
Total	(2 wickets, 22.5 overs)	106

1-13(2), 2-14(1)

Denmark Bowling

	O	M	R	W	
Sorensen	7	0	13	2	(2w,2nb)
Vestergaard	8.5	3	15	3	(2w)
Andersen	10	4	15	2	(4nb)
Kristenson	10	2	24	3	(1w)
Rasmussen	8	0	32	0	(2w)
Mielsen	2	1	6	0	

West Africa Bowling

	O	M	R	W	
Fadahunsi	8	1	23	1	(4w)
Ahuchogu	7	0	30	1	(3w,1nb)
Idowu	4	0	26	0	(2w,1nb)
Ukpong	3.5	0	20	0	(1nb)

Umpires: C.Hoare (Canada) and L.P.Hogan (Ireland)   Man of the Match:

EAST & CENTRAL AFRICA v NETHERLANDS   (First Round, Group C)
Played at Royal Military College, Kuala Lumpur, March 24, 1997.

Netherlands won by 8 wickets

Toss: Netherlands

EAST & CENTRAL AFIRCA			NETHERLANDS		
A.Ebrahim	c Cantrell b Lefebvre	0	*T.B.M.de Leede	c Nsubuka b Gomm	6
M.B.Musoke	c Cantrell b Khan	2	R.P.Lefebvre	not out	10
H.Bags	c van Oosterom b Khan	0	P.E.Cantrell	c Imran Brohi b Gomm	7
J.Lubya	lbw b Lefebvre	2	S.van Dijk	not out	1
*Imran Brohi	c de Leede b Khan	0	K-J.J.van Noortwijk		
C.M.Gomm	c Cantrell b Khan	0	†R.H.Scholte		
Y.S.Patel	c Zuiderent b Khan	5	M.A.C.Nota		
†J.Komakech	c Scholte b Khan	1	B.Zuiderent		
T.L.Mbazzi	b Khan	0	K.A.Khan		
A.N.Paliwala	c Scholte b van Dijk	3	Zulfiqar Ahmed		
F.Nsubuka	not out	0	R.F.van Oosterom		
Extras	lb 2, w 11	13	Extras	w 3	3
Total	(all out, 15.2 overs)	26	Total	(2 wickets, 5.3 overs)	27

1-1(1), 2-4(3), 3-10(4), 4-12(2), 5-12(6), 6-13(5), 7-17(8), 8-20(7), 9-26(10), 10-26(9)

1-8(1) 2-20(3)

Netherlands Bowling	O	M	R	W	
Lefebvre	6	0	9	2	(5w)
Khan	7.2	1	9	7	(3w)
van Dijk	2	0	6	1	(3w)

East & Central Africa Bowling	O	M	R	W	
Gomm	3	0	17	2	(3w)
Patel	2.3	1	10	0	

Umpires: A.O.D.George (West Africa) and Makbul Jaffer (Kenya)   Man of the Match: K.A.Khan

CANADA v FIJI   (First Round, Group C)
Played at University of Malaya, Kuala Lumpur, March 25, 1997.

Canada won by 4 wickets

Toss: Fiji

FIJI			CANADA		
J.Rouse	b Rana	10	*I.Liburd	b Maxwell	27
T.Batina	st Ramnarais b Seebaran	30	L.Bhansingh	not out	40
J.Sorovakatini	c Maxwell b Rana	1	M.Diwan	c Tadu b Maxwell	1
N.D.Maxwell	lbw b Rana	0	B.E.A.Rajadurai	c and b Tukana	8
*L.Sorovakatini	lbw b Rana	0	S.Seeram	c Cakacaka b Maxwell	2
†I.Cakacaka	c Johnson b Seebaran	17	D.Maxwell	run out	0
E.Tadu	lbw b Maxwell	3	M.Johnson	lbw b L.Sorovakatini	34
J.Mateyawa	c Diwan b Rajadurai	6	B.Seebaran	not out	1
W.Tukana	not out	17	†D.Ramnarais		
J.Seuvou	c Maxwell b Rajadurai	6	D.Joseph		
A.Tawatatau	c Ramnarais b Rana	16	S.Rana		
Extras	b 1, lb 6, w 15	22	Extras	lb 5, w 11, nb 1	17
Total	(all out, 41.1 overs)	128	Total	(6 wickets, 38.2 overs)	130

1-23(1), 2-41(3), 3-41(4), 4-41(5), 5-59(2), 6-74(7), 7-84(6), 8-86(8), 9-96(10), 10-128(11)

1-34(1), 2-47(3), 3-67(4), 4-70(5), 5-72(6), 6-121(7)

Canada Bowling	O	M	R	W	
Joseph	8	1	31	0	(7w)
Rana	9.1	2	29	5	(5w)
Maxwell	6	0	20	1	(1w)
Seebaran	9	1	18	2	(1w)
Rajadurai	6	1	7	2	
Bhansingh	3	0	16	0	(1w)

Fiji Bowling	O	M	R	W	
Tawatatau	5	0	34	0	(2w)
Seuvou	6	1	24	0	(2w)
Maxwell	7	2	16	3	(2w,1nb)
Batina	8	1	29	0	(3w)
Tukana	4	0	12	1	(1w)
Mateyawa	4.2	2	6	0	
L.Sorovakatini	4	1	4	1	(1w)

Umpires: D.Ker (Argentina) and W.Smith (Scotland)   Man of the Match: S.Rana

S.Rana took a hat trick (J.Sorovakatini, N.D.Maxwell and L.Sorovakatini) with the 3rd, 4th and 5th balls of his 5th over.

NAMIBIA v NETHERLANDS (First Round, Group C)

Played at Tenaga Nasional Sports Complex (Kilat Kelab), Kuala Lumpur, March 25, 1997.

Netherlands won by 10 wickets

Toss: Namibia

NAMIBIA

M.R.Barnard	c de Leede b Khan	4
*I.J.Stevenson	lbw b Khan	0
D.Keulder	c Zulfiqar Ahmed b Khan	3
B.G.Murgatroyd	run out	8
B.Kotze	lbw b Lefebvre	0
M.Karg	c Scholte b Lefebvre	0
†M.van Schoor	c Scholte b van Dijk	4
B.W.Ackerman	not out	36
I.van Schoor	c Scholte b Khan	7
D.Coetzee	run out	12
R.van Vuuren	b Lefebvre	0
Extras	lb 5, w 8, nb 3	16
Total	(all out, 48.5 overs)	90

1-5(1), 2-9(2), 3-17(3), 4-18(5), 5-18(6), 6-26(4), 7-29(7), 8-55(9), 9-89(10), 10-90(11)

NETHERLANDS

*T.B.M.de Leede	not out	46
R.P.Lefebvre	not out	35
P.E.Cantrell		
B.Zuiderent		
K-J.J.Noortwijk		
K.A.Khan		
S.van Dijk		
Zulfiqar Ahmed		
M.A.C.Nota		
R.F.van Oosterom		
†R.H.Scholte		
Extras	b 2, w 6, nb 2	10
Total	(no wicket, 23.5 overs)	91

Netherlands Bowling

	O	M	R	W	
Lefebvre	9.5	2	14	3	(1w,1nb)
Khan	10	2	24	4	(4w,2nb)
van Dijk	7	4	7	1	
Cantrell	10	5	12	0	(2w)
Nota	8	3	15	0	
Zulfiqar Ahmed	4	0	13	0	

Namibia Bowling

	O	M	R	W	
van Vuuren	5	1	14	0	
Ackerman	1	0	10	0	(1w,2nb)
Coetzee	1	0	6	0	(2w)
I.van Schoor	4	0	21	0	(1w)
Barnard	7	0	13	0	
Kotze	4	0	18	0	
Keulder	1.5	0	7	0	

Umpires: S.Bachitar (Singapore) and J.Luther (Denmark)

Man of the Match: R.P.Lefebvre

CANADA v NAMIBIA (First Round, Group C)

Played at Kelab Aman, Kuala Lumpur, March 26, 1997.

Canada won by 60 runs

Toss: Namibia

CANADA

*I.Liburd	c Coetzee b I.van Schoor	53
D.Chumney	c Keulder b Ackerman	0
M.Diwan	c Ackerman b van Vuuren	125
B.E.A.Rajadurai	c Coetzee b Kotze	62
D.Maxwell	c Seager b I.van Schoor	2
M.Johnson	c Ackerman b I.van Schoor	0
S.Seeram	c M.van Schoor b van Vuuren	0
B.Seebaran	b van Vuuren	0
D.Joseph	not out	8
†D.Ramnarais	not out	2
S.Rana		
Extras	lb 3, w 9	12
Total	(8 wickets, 50 overs)	264

1-3(2), 2-126(4), 3-246(3), 4-249(5), 5-250(6), 6-251(7), 7-252(8), 8-254(1)

NAMIBIA

M.R.Barnard	c Chumney b Joseph	2
*I.J.Stevenson	c sub (D.Etwaroo) b Maxwell	25
D.Keulder	c Johnson b Seebaran	41
B.G.Murgatroyd	c Chumney b Seeram	37
B.W.Ackerman	c Ramnarais b Seebaran	2
D.Kotze	lbw b Seeram	25
†M.van Schoor	not out	25
D.Seager	c sub (D.Etwaroo) b Seeram	8
I.van Schoor	run out	6
D.Coetzee	b Seeram	0
R.van Vuuren	lbw b Rajadurai	8
Extras	b 3, lb 8, w 14	25
Total	(all out, 43.2 overs)	204

1-2(1), 2-83(4), 3-98(3), 4-104(5), 5-143(2), 6-159(6), 7-174(8), 8-193(9), 9-193(10), 10-204(11)

Namibia Bowling

	O	M	R	W	
van Vuuren	10	2	55	3	(1w)
Ackerman	8	1	20	1	(2w)
Coetzee	5	0	34	0	(4w)
Barnard	7	1	39	0	
I.van Schoor	10	0	44	3	
Keulder	4	0	25	0	
Kotze	6	0	44	1	(1w)

Canada Bowling

	O	M	R	W	
Joseph	6	0	20	1	(3w)
Rana	5	0	23	0	(6w)
Seeram	10	1	50	4	(1nb)
Maxwell	6	0	32	1	(3w)
Seebaran	10	0	34	2	
Rajadurai	6.2	0	34	1	(1w)

Umpires: D.Beltran (Gibraltar) and N.Gudker (Israel)

Man of the Match: M.Diwan

I.Liburd retired hurt on 6 with the score at 6/1 and returned at the fall of the 2nd wicket. I.J.Stevenson retired hurt on 6 with the score at 22/1 and returned at the fall of the 2nd wicket. M.Diwan's 125 took 145 balls and included 8 fours and 5 sixes.

EAST AND CENTRAL AFRICA v FIJI   (First Round, Group C)

Played at Royal Selangor Club, Bukit Kiara, Kuala Lumpur, March 26, 1997.

Fiji won by 35 runs

Toss: East and Central Africa

FIJI

J.Rouse	lbw b Gomm	0
T.Batina	c Dudhia b Jivraj	0
J.Sorovakatini	c Nsubuka b Gomm	6
N.D.Maxwell	lbw b Mbazzi	33
*L.Sorovakatini	c Mbazzi b Jivraj	0
W.Tukana	c Dudhia b Lubya	17
A.Sorovakatini	b Lubya	0
J.Bulabalavu	c Komakech b Patel	1
†T.Cakacaka	b Patel	2
J.Mateyawa	lbw b Paliwala	20
A.Tawatatau	not out	9
Extras	b 1, lb 6, w 15, nb 1	23
Total	(all out, 40.3 overs)	111

1-0(1), 2-6(3), 3-6(2), 4-7(5), 5-48(6), 6-48(7),
7-49(8), 8-57(9), 9-74(4), 10-111(10)

EAST AND CENTRAL AFRICA

F.M.Sarigat	lbw b Batina	2
A.A.Dudhia	b Batina	3
C.M.Gomm	c Cakacaka b Tawatatau	0
†J.Komakech	lbw b Mateyawa	20
*Imran Brohi	c L.Sorovakatini b Tawatatau	1
J.Lubya	lbw b Tawatatau	0
Y.S.Patel	c Cakacaka b Maxwell	16
M.I.A.Jivraj	c J.Sorovakatini b Tukana	6
T.L.Mbazzi	run out	5
A.N.Paliwala	not out	4
F.Nsubuka	lbw b Batina	2
Extras	b 3, lb 5, w 7, nb 2	17
Total	(all out, 44 overs)	76

1-4(2), 2-5(3), 3-8(1), 4-9(5), 5-9(6), 6-44(7),
7-60(4), 8-64(8), 9-68(9), 10-76(11)

East and Central Africa Bowling

	O	M	R	W	
Gomm	6	1	19	2	(2w)
Jivraj	7	1	12	2	(3w,1nb)
Nsubuka	4	0	12	0	
Lubya	8	1	26	2	(1w)
Patel	7	1	12	2	(6w)
Paliwala	4.3	1	13	1	(1w)
Mbazzi	4	1	10	1	(1w)

Fiji Bowling

	O	M	R	W	
Tawatatau	10	6	8	3	(1w)
Batina	7	2	7	3	(1w,1nb)
Tukana	8	0	21	1	(2w)
L.Sorovakatini	6	1	10	0	(1w,1nb)
Mateyawa	10	1	21	1	(2w)
Maxwell	3	2	1	1	

Umpires: R.Butler (Bermuda) and W.Maha (Papua New Guinea)   Man of the Match: N.D.Maxwell

EAST AND CENTRAL AFRICA v NAMIBIA   (First Round, Group C)

Played at Perbadanan Kemajuan Negari Selangor, Kuala Lumpur, March 28, 1997.

Namibia won by 1 wicket

Toss: Namibia

EAST AND CENTRAL AFRICA

A.Ebrahim	c M.van Schoor b Ackerman	2
A.A.Dudhia	c Keulder b Barnard	14
M.B.Musoke	run out	30
*Imran Brohi	c B.Kotze b Keulder	17
J.Lubya	c van Vuuren b Keulder	0
C.M.Gomm	run out	29
H.Bags	c Karg b van Vuuren	7
Y.S.Patel	c Keulder b D.Kotze	10
M.I.A.Jivraj	run out	2
†J.Komakech	c M.van Schoor b van Vuuren	3
T.L.Mbazzi	not out	0
Extras	b 1, lb 6, w 21, nb 1	29
Total	(all out, 48.1 overs)	143

1-10(1), 2-60(3), 3-69(2), 4-71(5), 5-83(4),
6-107(7), 7-135(6), 8-138(8), 9-141(9), 10-143(10)

NAMIBIA

M.Karg	c Dudhia b Gomm	4
*I.J.Stevenson	c Mbazzi b Gomm	0
D.Keulder	c Imran Brohi b Lubya	15
B.G.Murgatroyd	c Mbazzi b Jivraj	14
D.Kotze	run out	37
B.W.Ackerman	lbw b Patel	4
†M.van Schoor	not out	32
M.R.Barnard	c Komakech b Patel	2
I.van Schoor	lbw b Mbazzi	6
B.Kotze	c Komakech b Patel	1
R.van Vuuren	not out	2
Extras	lb 4, w 22, nb 1	27
Total	(9 wickets, 46.5 overs)	144

1-2(2), 2-9(1), 3-33(4), 4-41(3), 5-59(6), 6-106(5),
7—110(8), 8-123(9), 9-131(10)

Namibia Bowling

	O	M	R	W	
van Vuuren	9.1	2	13	2	(4w,1nb)
Ackerman	7	1	28	1	(6w)
B.Kotze	2	0	8	0	(4w)
Barnard	10	2	21	1	(1w)
I.van Schoor	4	0	24	0	(5w)
Keulder	10	3	22	2	(1w)
D.Kotze	6	0	20	1	

East and Central Africa Bowling

	O	M	R	W	
Gomm	9	0	36	2	(7w,1nb)
Jivraj	10	0	30	1	(3w)
Lubya	5	1	14	1	(2w)
Patel	10	0	28	3	(6w,1nb)
Bags	3	0	10	0	(1w)
Mbazzi	9.5	1	22	1	(3w)

Umpires: A.O.D.George (West Africa) and D.Ker (Argentina)   Man of the Match: M.van Schoor

FIJI v NETHERLANDS   (First Round, Group C)

Played at Royal Military College, Kuala Lumpur, March 28, 1997.

Netherlands won by 6 wickets   Toss: Fiji

FIJI

J.Rouse	c de Leede b Cantrell	30
T.Batina	lbw b Edwards	18
J.Sorovakatini	c Scholte b Lefebvre	1
N.D.Maxwell	c Zulfiqar Ahmed b Cantrell	14
*L.Sorovakatini	c Zuiderent b Cantrell	4
W.Tukana	st Scholte b Cantrell	0
†I.Cakacaka	c Cantrell b Lefebvre	4
E.Tadu	c Cantrell b Lefebvre	1
A.Sorovakatini	not out	7
J.Mateyawa	lbw b Lefebvre	4
A.Trawatatau	c de Leede b Nota	0
Extras	lb1 , w 10, nb 2	13
Total	(all out, 41.2 overs)	96

1-27(2), 2-28(3), 3-56(4), 4-79(5), 5-79(1), 6-83(6), 7-84(7), 8-85(8), 9-91(10), 10-96(11)

NETHERLANDS

*T.B.M.de Leede	c A.Sorovakatini b L.Sorovakatini	48
R.P.Lefebvre	c Mateyawa b Tawatatau	8
P.E.Cantrell	c Cakacaka b Maxwell	1
K-J.J.van Noortwijk	not out	24
R.F.van Oosterom	lbw b Batina	0
B.Zuiderent	not out	1
Zulfiqar Ahmed		
M.A.C.Nota		
G.L.Edwards		
K.A.Khan		
†R.H.Scholte		
Extras	b 3, lb 3, w 5, nb 7	18
Total	(4 wickets, 20.5 overs)	100

1-19(2), 2-24(3), 3-93(1), 4-93(5)

Netherlands Bowling

	O	M	R	W	
Lefebvre	10	3	16	4	(3w)
Khan	8	3	29	0	(5w)
Edwards	6	0	20	1	(1w,2nb)
Cantrell	10	3	10	4	(1w)
Nota	7.2	-	20	1	

Fiji Bowling

	O	M	R	W	
Tawatatau	8	0	23	1	(1w,2nb)
Batina	4.5	0	24	1	(3w,4nb)
Maxwell	5	0	18	1	
L.Sorovakatini	3	0	29	1	(1w,3nb)

Umpires: D.Beltran (Gibraltar) and H.Whitlock (Hong Kong)   Man of the Match: P.E.Cantrell

CANADA v EAST AND CENTRAL AFRICA   (First Round, Group C)

Played at Victoria Institute, Kuala Lumpur, March 29, 1997.

Canada won by 4 wickets   Toss: East and Central Africa

EAST AND CENTRAL AFRICA

M.B.Musoke	c and b Liburd	20
A.A.Dudhia	c and b Liburd	6
J.Lubya	c Bhansingh b Liburd	22
*Imran Brohi	b Seebaran	5
C.M.Gomm	c Glegg b Liburd	4
Y.S.Patel	st Glegg b Bhansingh	64
†J.Komakech	lbw b Seebaran	2
M.I.A.Jivraj	b Seebaran	0
T.L.Mbazzi	c Glegg b Isaacs	15
A.N.Paliwala	not out	13
I.I.Mohamed	run out	4
Extras	b 8, lb 7, w 9	24
Total	(all out, 50 overs)	179

1-34(1), 2-56(2), 3-61(3), 4-69(5), 5-71(4), 6-75(7), 7-75(8), 8-124(9), 9-170(6), 10-179(11)

CANADA

L.Bhansingh	c Komakech b Gomm	0
†A.Glegg	c Komakech b Gomm	3
D.Chumney	c Komakech b Gomm	18
M.Diwan	b Patel	15
N.Isaacs	c sub (F.Nsubuka) b Jivraj	51
D.Maxwell	c Lubya b Mbazzi	9
*I.Liburd	not out	47
D.Perera	not out	10
B.Seebaran		
D.Joseph		
D.Etwaroo		
Extras	b 6, lb 4, w 17	27
Total	(6 wickets, 46.3 overs)	180

1-1(1), 2-15(2), 3-33(3), 4-60(4), 5-102(6), 6-131(5)

Canada Bowling

	O	M	R	W	
Joseph	10	1	32	0	(3w,1nb)
Maxwell	3	0	17	0	(2w)
Liburd	10	0	38	4	(1w)
Seebaran	10	2	21	3	
Etwaroo	8	1	24	0	
Isaacs	7	1	27	1	(1w)
Bhansingh	2	0	5	1	(2w)

East and Central Africa Bowling

	O	M	R	W	
Gomm	8	2	22	3	(4w)
Jivraj	10	1	40	1	(4w)
Patel	6.3	0	23	1	(4w)
Lubya	5	0	22	0	(3w)
Mbazzi	9	0	37	1	(2w)
Paliwala	7	0	21	0	
Imran Brohi	1	0	5	0	

Umpires: Makbul Jaffer (Kenya) and Khoo Chai Huat (Malaysia)   Man of the Match: I.Liburd

FIJI v NAMIBIA   (First Round, Group C)

Played at Royal Selangor Club, Bukit Kiara, Kuala Lumpur, March 29, 1977.

Fiji won by 105 runs

Toss: Namibia

FIJI				NAMIBIA		
J.Rouse	b van Vuuren		0	D.Seager	lbw b Batina	3
*L.Sorovakatini	c Kotze b Barnard		37	M.Karg	c I.Cakacaka b Batina	2
J.Sorovakatini	c M.van Schoor			*D.Keulder	c T.Cakacaka	
	b van Vuuren		13		b Tawatatau	0
N.D.Maxwell	lbw b Keulder		28	B.G.Murgatroyd	b Tawatatau	1
T.Batina	lbw b van Vuuren		25	B.Kotze	lbw b Tawatatau	2
W.Tukana	c M.van Schoor			†M.van Schoor	c Batina b L.Sorovakatini	6
	b van Vuuren		24			
I.Cakacaka	not out		12	B.W.Ackerman	b Tukana	4
J.Mateyawa	not out		7	M.R.Barnard	b Tawatatau	0
A.Tawatatau				I.van Schoor	not out	21
A.Sorovakatini				D.Coetzee	c Batina b Mateyawa	6
†T.Cakacaka				R.van Vuuren	c I.Cakacaka b Maxwell	4
Extras	b 4, lb 8, w 18, nb 2		32	Extras	lb 6, w 16, nb 2	24
Total	(6 wickets, 50 overs)		178	Total	(all out, 33.5 overs)	73

1-10(1), 2-24(3), 3-81(4), 4-100(1), 5-141(5),
6-156(6)

1-2(2), 2-3(3), 3-7(1), 4-7(4), 5-21(6), 6-22(5),
7-22(8), 8-40(7), 9-65(10), 10-73(11)

Namibia Bowling	O	M	R	W		Fiji Bowling	O	M	R	W	
van Vuuren	10	1	39	4	(2w,1nb)	Tawatatau	10	6	9	4	(2w)
Ackerman	6	0	21	0	(6w,1nb)	Batina	10	5	12	2	(7w)
Coetzee	6	0	24	0	(1w)	L.Sorovakatini	4	0	20	1	(6w,2nb)
I.van Schoor	4	0	20	0	(3w)	Tukana	4	0	16	1	(1w)
Keulder	10	1	25	1	(2w)	Mayeyawa	3	0	6	1	
Barnard	10	1	17	1	(1w)	Maxwell	2.5	1	4	1	
Kotze	4	0	20	0	(1w)						

Umpires: I.Massey (Italy) and V.M.Rafik (East and Central Africa)   Man of the Match: A.Tawatatau

CANADA v NETHERLANDS   (First Round, Group C)

Scheduled for Perbadanan Kemajuan Negari Selangor, Kuala Lumpur, March 30, 1997.

Match abandoned without a ball being bowled.

Umpires: N.T.Plews (England) and A.A.Shaheen (Bangladesh)

Match Referee: J.R.Reid (New Zealand)

Just before the start of the match, around 500 people invaded the pitch thinking this was the Israel v Gibraltar match. They were protesting about the presence of Israel in the country. The venues of the two matches had been switched at short notice.

The match referee cancelled the match at 9.15am.

The organising committee and the two team managements agreed that the match would count as a 'no result' and the points would be shared.

ITALY v BERMUDA (First Round, Group D)

Played at Tenaga Nasional Sports Complex (Kilat Kelab), Kuala Lumpur, March 24, 1997.

Bermuda won by 7 wickets   Toss: Bermuda

ITALY			BERMUDA		
V.Zuppiroli	c Trott b Tucker	19	*A.B.Steede	c Kariyawasam b Rajapakse	9
A.Amati	lbw b Hurdle	2	R.L.Trott	lbw b Rajapakse	16
B.Giordano	c C.J.Smith b Tucker	23	C.J.Smith	not out	43
Akhlaq Qureshi	b Manders	18	C.M.Marshall	lbw b Sajjad Ahmed	47
Mohammad Razzaq	c Hurdle b Manders	12	G.S.Smith	not out	0
A.Pieri	run out (Manders)	11	J.J.Tucker		
†K.Kariyawasam	c Tucker b Manders	5	†D.A.Minors		
Sajjad Ahmed	not out	8	W.A.E.Manders		
M.G.L.Rajapakse	c C.J.Smith	0	R.W.Blades		
*A.Pezzi	not out	1	K.Hurdle		
R.Maggio			K.S.Fox		
Extras	b 4, lb 4, w 20, nb 1	29	Extras	b 2, lb 5, w 7	14
Total	(8 wickets, 50 overs)	128	Total	(3 wickets, 31.1 overs)	129

1-8(2), 2-61(1), 3-64(3), 4-95(5), 5-111(4), 6-113(6), 7-122(7), 8-125(9)

1-2(1), 2-33(2), 3-128(4)

Bermuda Bowling	O	M	R	W		Italy Bowling	O	M	R	W	
Blades	5	1	6	0	(1nb)	Akhlaq Qureshi	6	0	15	0	(4w)
Hurdle	8	0	16	1	(4w)	Rajapakse	8.1	0	40	2	(1w)
Tucker	10	1	31	2	(8w)	Giordano	5	1	14	0	(2w)
Fox	7	2	22	0	(2w)	Sajjad Ahmed	9	0	26	1	
Manders	10	3	18	3		Amati	1	0	9	0	
Marshall	5	0	17	0	(2w)	Maggio	2	0	18	0	
C.J.Smith	5	1	10	1	(1w)						

Umpires: A.F.M.Akhtaruddin (Bangladesh) and H.Reid (U.S.A.)   Man of the Match: C.M.Marshall

BERMUDA v HONG KONG (First Round, Group D)

Played at Victoria Institute, Kuala Lumpur, March 25, 1997.

Hong Kong won by 3 wickets   Toss: Hong Kong

BERMUDA			HONG KONG		
*A.B.Steede	c Fordham b Mohammed Zubair	65	M.R.Farcy	c Tucker b Perinchief	65
R.L.Trott	c Fordham b Brew	6	S.J.Brew	b Tucker	13
C.J.Smith	c Fordham b Mohammed Zubair	25	R.Sharma	c G.S.Smith b Blades	69
C.M.Marshall	c Mohammed Zubair b Raza	4	S.Foster	c Steede b Perinchief	5
G.S.Smith	c Sharma b Raza	10	*†J.P.Fordham	c Steede b Marshall	16
W.A.E.Manders	c Eames b Munir Hussain	65	Munir Hussain	c Marshall b Blades	21
†D.A.Minors	c Brew b Munir Hussain	1	Mohammed Zubair	b Blades	1
R.W.Blades	lbw b Mohammed Zubair	9	M.I.N.Eames	not out	16
J.J.Tucker	c Fordham b Munir Hussain	1	R.Sujanani	not out	5
B.D.Perinchief	not out	8	M.G.Lever		
K.Hurdle	not out	9	K.Raza		
Extras	lb 5, w 19	24	Extras	lb 4, w 12, nb 1	17
Total	(9 wickets, 50 overs)	227	Total	(7 wickets, 49.4 overs)	228

1-12(2), 2-62(3), 3-68(4), 4-91(5), 5-187(6), 6-192(7), 7-201(1), 8-204(9), 9-215(8)

1-51(2), 2-118(1), 3-142(4), 4-175(5), 5-205(3), 6-205(6), 7-211(7)

Hong Kong Bowling	O	M	R	W		Bermuda Bowling	O	M	R	W	
Brew	8	0	44	1	(4w)	Blades	10	1	42	3	(4w,1nb)
Farcy	3	0	10	0		Hurdle	3	0	15	0	(1w,1nb)
Munir Hussain	8	1	37	3	(2w)	Tucker	10	0	33	1	
Mohammed Zubair	8	0	31	3	(5w)	Marshall	7	0	46	1	(5w)
Lever	1	0	4	0	(2w)	Perinchief	10	1	35	2	(1w)
Sharma	10	0	38	0		Manders	6.4	0	39	0	(1w)
Raza	10	1	41	2	(3w)	C.J.Smith	3	0	14	0	
Sujanani	2	0	17	0							

Umpires: N.Gudker (Israel) and L.P.Hogan (Ireland)   Man of the Match: R.Sharma

PAPUA NEW GUINEA v SCOTLAND   (First Round, Group D)

Played at Kelab Aman, Kuala Lumpur, March 25, 1997.

Scotland won by 6 wickets

Toss: Papua New Guinea

PAPUA NEW GUINEA			SCOTLAND		
J.Maha	c Davies b Allingham	15	I.L.Philip	st Morea b Ipi	25
V.B.Kevau	c and b Sheridan	17	M.J.Smith	b Raka	3
L.Leka	c Davies b Allingham	0	D.R.Lockhart	c Raka b Pala	9
C.Amini	c Salmond b Blain	11	*G.Salmond	not out	37
N.Maha	c Allingham b Gourlay	8	J.G.Williamson	c Arua b N.Maha	14
*V.Pala	c Allingham b Sheridan	8	S.Gourlay	not out	11
†I.Morea	b Thomson	9	†A.G.Davies		
L.Ilaraki	b Thomson	7	N.J.de G.Allingham		
R.H.Ipi	c Davies b Thomson	6	J.A.R.Blain		
T.Raka	c Smith b Sheridan	2	K.Thomson		
F.Arua	not out	0	K.L.P.Sheridan		
Extras	b 3, lb 1, w 20, nb 13	37	Extras	lb 4, w 17, nb 1	22
Total	(all out, 36.1 overs)	120	Total	(4 wickets, 38.1 overs)	121

1-22(1), 2-22(3), 3-54(4), 4-71(5), 5-89(6), 6-90(2), 7-104(7), 8-111(8), 9-120(9), 10-120(10)

1-20(2), 2-52(3), 3-53(1), 4-97(5)

Scotland Bowling	O	M	R	W	
Thomson	8	0	37	3	(7w,1nb)
Allingham	5	0	13	3	(6w)
Williamson	5	0	17	0	(2w,6nb)
Blain	2	0	17	1	(4w,4nb)
Gourlay	8	1	20	1	(1w,2nb)
Sheridan	8.1	1	12	3	

Papua New Guinea Bowling	O	M	R	W	
Raka	9.1	1	18	1	(3w,1nb)
Arua	5	0	13	0	(8w)
Ipi	8	1	36	1	(3w)
Pala	8	1	17	1	(3w)
N.Maha	6	0	24	1	
Amini	2	0	9	0	

Umpires: A.A.Shaheen (Bangladesh) and E.D.Ohm (Netherlands)   Man of the Match: G.Salmond

SCOTLAND v HONG KONG   (First Round, Group D)

Played at Rubber Research Institute, Kuala Lumpur, March 26, 1997.

Scotland won by 87 runs

Toss: Hong Kong

SCOTLAND			HONG KONG		
I.L.Philip	c Fordham b Farcy	3	M.R.Farcy	b Blain	6
D.R.Lockhart	c Jones b Brew	7	K.Raza	b Blain	15
M.J.Smith	c Eames b Sujanani	67	S.J.Brew	b Williamson	6
*G.Salmond	c Fordham b Mohammed Zubair	34	R.Sharma	c Lockhart b Williamson	7
J.G.Williamson	c Sharma b Munir Hussain	27	S.Foster	b Blain	4
S.Gourlay	c Fordham b Brew	6	M.I.N.Eames	c Davies b Williamson	23
M.J.de G.Allingham	not out	35	*†J.P.Fordham	c Philip b Sheridan	32
†A.G.Davies	not out	18	R.Sujanani	b Kennedy	1
K.L.P.Sheridan			Munir Hussain	b Kennedy	2
J.A.R.Blain			D.Jones	c Blain b Kennedy	11
S.R.Kennedy			Mohammed Zubair	not out	2
Extras	b 4, lb 5, w 15	24	Extras	lb 12, w 11, nb 2	25
Total	(6 wickets, 50 overs)	221	Total	(all out, 40.4 overs)	134

1-9(1), 2-17(2), 3-99(4), 4-132(3), 5-152(6), 6-185(5)

1-6(1), 2-31(2), 3-31(3), 4-42(5), 5-46(4), 6-107(7), 7-111(8), 8-117(9), 9-126(6), 10-134(10)

Hong Kong Bowling	O	M	R	W	
Brew	10	1	46	2	(4w)
Farcy	3	0	9	1	(5w)
Mohammed Zubair	10	0	50	1	(3w)
Munir Hussain	8	0	36	1	
Sharma	3	0	12	0	
Raza	7	0	23	0	
Sujanani	6	0	20	1	
Jones	3	0	16	0	(3w)

Scotland Bowling	O	M	R	W	
Blain	7	1	23	3	(3w)
Allingham	4	0	24	0	(3w,1nb)
Williamson	8	2	26	3	(4w,1nb)
Gourlay	4	0	12	0	
Sheridan	10	1	22	1	
Kennedy	7.4	2	15	3	(1w,1nb)

Umpires: S.Bachitar (Singapore) and H.Reid (U.S.A.)   Man of the Match: J.G.Williamson

ITALY v PAPUA NEW GUINEA   (First Round, Group D)

Played at Perbadanan Kemajuan Negari Selangor, Kuala Lumpur, March 26, 1997.

Papua New Guinea won by 101 runs

Toss: Italy

PAPUA NEW GUINEA				ITALY		
V.B.Kevau	c Zuppiroli b Akhlaq Qureshi		0	V.Zuppiroli	lbw b Gaudi	5
K.Vuivagi	st Kariyawasam			A.Amati	b Arua	0
	b Sajjad Ahmed		29			
N.Maha	c Amati b Akhlaq Qureshi		2	B.Giordano	c Morea b Ilaraki	22
J.Ovia	run out		94	Akhlaq Qureshi	c Morea b Ilaraki	12
C.Amini	not out		45	S.V.de Mel	c Vuivagi b Ilaraki	12
T.Raka	not out		15	A.Pieri	b Gaudi	3
*V.Pala				*A.Pezzi	run out	9
K.Ilaraki				†K.Kariyawasam	c Ilaraki b Pala	13
†I.Morea				Sajjad Ahmed	c Amini b Arua	2
T.Gaudi				M.G.L.Rajapakse	not out	6
F.Arua				R.Maggio	b Pala	3
Extras	b 3, lb 12, w 18, nb 1		34	Extras	b 2, lb 8, w 18, nb 3	31
Total	(4 wickets, 50 overs)		219	Total	(all out, 48.4 overs)	118

1-0(1), 2-12(3), 3-74(2), 4-199(4)

1-4(2), 2-24(1), 3-50(4), 4-75(5), 5-75(3), 6-81(6), 7-99(7), 8-101(9), 9-108(8), 10-118(11)

Italy Bowling	O	M	R	W		Papua New Guinea Bowling	O	M	R	W	
Akhlaq Qureshi	10	1	29	2	(3w)	Raka	10	3	15	0	(5w)
Rajapakse	10	1	45	0	(4w,1nb)	Arua	10	2	21	2	(5w,1nb)
de Mel	10	1	33	0	(1w)	Gaudi	10	2	21	2	(3w,2nb)
Giordano	6	0	29	0	(5w)	Ilaraki	10	1	33	3	(2w)
Sajjad Ahmed	10	1	32	1		Amini	4.4	0	12	0	
Amati	2	0	17	0	(1w)	Pala	4	2	6	2	
Maggio	2	0	19	0	(1w)						

Umpires: G.F.Malik (U.A.E.) and J.K.Kruger (Namibia)   Man of the Match: J.Ovia

BERMUDA v PAPUA NEW GUINEA   (First Round, Group D)

Played at University of Malaya, Kuala Lumpur, March 28, 1997.

Bermuda won by 121 runs

Toss: Papua New Guinea

BERMUDA			PAPUA NEW GUINEA		
D.Smith	c Ilaraki b Raka	14	J.Maha	b Blades	9
G.S.Smith	b Arua	1	K.Vuivagi	lbw b Tucker	1
C.J.Smith	c Morea b Raka	2	J.Ovia	b Tucker	4
*A.B.Steede	c Ovia b Ilaraki	10	C.Amini	c D.Smith b Perinchief	7
C.M.Marshall	c J.Maha b Raka	4	N.Maha	c Minors b Blades	0
W.A.E.Manders	c Morea b Raka	7	†I.Morea	c Blades b Perinchief	38
J.J.Tucker	c N.Maha b Arua	104	K.Ilaraki	run out (Steede)	0
†D.A.Minors	c Morea b Ilaraki	17	*V.Pala	c G.S.Smith b Hollis	0
B.D.Perinchief	c Amini b Pala	12	T.Raka	c D.Smith b Perinchief	8
R.W.Blades	not out	2	T.Gaudi	b Perinchief	2
D.W.Hollis	not out	4	F.Arua	not out	0
Extras	lb 8, w 19	27	Extras	lb 1, w 12, nb 1	14
Total	(9 wickets, 50 overs)	204	Total	(all out, 28.2 overs)	83

1-10(2), 2-21(3), 3-27(1), 4-31(5), 5-42(6), 6-87(4), 7-139(8), 8-187(9), 9-199(7)

1-10(2), 2-10(1), 3-15(3), 4-19(5), 5-34(4), 6-36(7), 7-43(8), 8-56(9), 9-83(6), 10-83(10)

Papua New Guinea Bowling	O	M	R	W		Bermuda Bowling	O	M	R	W	
Raka	8	1	27	4	(4w)	Blades	6	2	14	2	(3w)
Arua	8	2	26	2	(7w)	Tucker	5	1	13	2	(3w)
Gaudi	4	1	24	0	(1w)	Marshall	3	0	10	0	(3w,1nb)
Pala	10	2	34	1	(1w)	Perinchief	8.2	1	33	4	(2w)
Ilaraki	10	1	42	2	(2w)	Hollis	6	1	12	1	(1w)
N.Maha	10	2	43	0	(4w)						

Umpires: N.T.Plews (England) and S.Bachitar (Singapore)   Man of the Match:

J.J.Tucker's 104 took 137 balls and included 13 fours and 2 sixes.

HONG KONG v ITALY   (First Round, Group D)

Played at Royal Selangor Club, Bukit Kiara, Kuala Lumpur, March 28, 1997.

Hong Kong won by 145 runs

HONG KONG			Toss: Italy		
			ITALY		
M.R.Farcy	c de Mel b Giordano	102	V.Zuppiroli	lbw b Farcy	0
K.Raza	c de Mel b Giordano	0	A.Amati	lbw b Raza	13
S.J.Brew	b Akhlaq Qureshi	39	*A.Pezzi	lbw b Farcy	0
R.Sharma	c Kariyawasam		Mohammad Razzaq	c Fordham	
	b Akhlaq Qureshi	1		b Mohammed Zubair	10
M.I.N.Eames	lbw b Giordano	17	Akhlaq Qureshi	b Jones	9
*†J.P.Fordham	c Zito b de Mel	36	S.V.de Mel	b Sharma	25
Munir Hussain	c Zuppiroli b de Mel	39	B.Giordano	c Eames b Sharma	32
Mohammed Zubair	c Kariyawasam		F.E.Zito	b Jones	7
	b Akhlaq Qureshi	0			
M.G.Lever	b de Mel	15	†K.Kariyawasam	lbw b Jones	0
A.N.French	c Mohammad Razzaq		Sajjad Ahmed	b Mohammed Zubair	8
	b Sajjad Ahmed	13			
D.Jones	not out	2	M.B.M.da Costa	not out	2
Extras	b 11, lb 1, w 6	18	Extras	b 6, lb 7, w 18	31
Total	(all out, 49.4 overs)	282	Total	(all out, 41 overs)	137

1-9(2), 2-123(3), 3-125(4), 4-163(5), 5-170(1), 6-241(7), 7-247(8), 8-253(6), 9-272(9), 10-282(10)

1-0(1), 2-0(3), 3-22(4), 4-45(5), 5-78(2), 6-93(6), 7-124(8), 8-124(78), 9-125(9), 10-137(10)

Italy Bowling	O	M	R	W	
Akhlaq Qureshi	10	1	67	3	(3w)
Giordano	10	1	35	3	
de Mel	10	0	40	3	(1w)
Amati	4	0	25	0	
Sajjad Ahmed	9.4	0	70	1	
da Costa	6	0	33	0	(2w)

Hong Kong Bowling	O	M	R	W	
Farcy	2	0	9	2	(3w)
Munir Hussain	4	2	9	0	(1w)
Mohammed Zubair	5	1	19	2	(6w)
Jones	6	1	14	3	(3w)
Lever	4	0	11	0	
Raza	10	2	35	1	
Sharma	10	2	27	2	(1w)

Umpires: T.Cooper (Fiji) and Khoo Chai Huat (Malaysia)   Man of the Match: M.R.Farcy

M.R.Farcy's 102 took 96 balls and included 12 fours.

HONG KONG v PAPUA NEW GUINEA   (First Round, Group D)

Played at Tenaga Nasional Sports Complex (Kilat Kelab), Kuala Lumpur, March 29, 1997.

Hong Kong won by 81 runs

HONG KONG			Toss: Hong Kong		
			PAPUA NEW GUINEA		
M.R.Farcy	lbw b Raka	21	V.B.Kevau	lbw b Farcy	0
K.Raza	b Arua	2	L.Leka	lbw b Brew	6
S.J.Brew	c and b Raka	1	K.Vuivagi	c Raza b Farcy	0
R.Sharma	b Gaudi	57	J.Ovia	st Fordham b Raza	62
M.I.N.Eames	b Amini	33	*C.Amini	run out	20
*†J.P.Fordham	b Ipi	71	W.Kila	b Mohammed Zubair	4
Munir Hussain	c Kila b Arua	7	†I.Morea	b Brew	2
M.G.Lever	not out	7	T.Raka	c and b Brew	0
A.N.French	run out	0	R.H.Ipi	b Mohammed Zubair	29
D.Jones	not out	1	T.Gaudi	run out	3
Mohammed Zubair			F.Arua	not out	0
Extras	b 3, lb 3, w 23, nb 3	32	Extras	b 5, lb 9, w 11	25
Total	(8 wickets, 50 overs)	232	Total	(all out, 42.1 overs)	151

1-8(2), 2-26(3), 3-43(1), 4-128(5), 5-169(4), 6-186(7), 7-231(6), 8-231(9)

1-5(1), 2-5(3), 3-7(2), 4-69(5), 5-84(6), 6-92(7), 7-92(8), 8-139(4), 9-149(9), 10-151(10)

Papua New Guinea Bowling	O	M	R	W	
Raka	10	0	45	2	(4w,1nb)
Arua	10	0	43	2	(7w)
Gaudi	10	1	42	1	(5w,1nb)
Ipi	6	0	30	1	(4w)
Ovia	4	0	20	0	(1w,2nb)
Amini	10	0	46	1	(2w)

Hong Kong Bowling	O	M	R	W	
Brew	7	2	22	3	(2w)
Farcy	6	1	15	2	(1w)
Munir Hussain	3	1	9	0	(1w)
Mohammed Zubair	8.1	1	31	2	(2w)
Raza	8	0	22	1	(1w)
Sharma	6	1	13	0	
Jones	2	0	13	0	
Lever	2	0	12	0	(1w)

Umpires: C.Horne (Canada) and J.Luther (Denmark)   Man of the Match: J.P.Fordham

ITALY v SCOTLAND (First Round, Group D)

Played at University of Malaya, Kuala Lumpur, March 29, 1997.

Scotland won by 131 runs   Toss: Scotland

SCOTLAND		
I.L.Philip	c Akhlaq Qureshi b de Mel	71
B.G.Lockie	c Zuppiroli b de Mel	58
M.J.Smith	c Akhlaq Qureshi b Rajapakse	10
*G.Salmond	c Zuppiroli b Parisi	43
J.G.Williamson	c and b Parisi	15
†D.R.Lockhart	c Zuppiroli b Giordano	18
S.R.Kennedy	st Pieri b de Mel	5
D.Cowan	b Akhlaq Qureshi	7
J.A.R.Blain	run out	9
A.M.Tennant	not out	3
I.R.Beven	lbw b Akhlaq Qureshi	1
Extras	(lb 8, w 23, nb 2)	33
Total	(all out, 48.1 overs)	273

1-127(2), 2-150(3), 3-186(1), 4-213(4), 5-223(5),
6-237(7), 7-257(6), 8-264(8), 9-270(9), 10-273(11)

ITALY		
V.Zuppiroli	c Lockhart b Beven	11
A.Amati	c Beven b Blain	9
*A.Pezzi	run out	0
S.V.de Mel	c Cowan b Beven	20
Akhlaq Qureshi	c Kennedy b Cowan	10
Mohammad Razzaq	c Kennedy b Beven	26
B.Giordano	c Kennedy b Tennant	25
F.E.Zito	lbw b Beven	0
T.Parisi	run out	0
†A.Pieri	b Cowan	17
M.G.L.Rajapakse	not out	0
Extras	lb 5, w 16, nb 3	24
Total	(all out, 37.2 overs)	142

1-14(1), 2-23(3), 3-24(2), 4-55(4), 5-56(5),
6-115(6), 7-115(8), 8-116(9), 9-135(7), 10-142(10)

Italy Bowling

	O	M	R	W	
Akhlaq Qureshi	9.1	1	30	2	(4w)
Rajapakse	10	0	60	1	(6w)
Parisi	10	0	81	2	(6w)
Giordano	9	0	51	1	(2w,2nb)
de Mel	10	1	43	3	(1w)

Scotland Bowling

	O	M	R	W	
Blain	9	0	40	1	(6w,2nb)
Beven	10	3	20	4	
Cowan	6.2	0	39	2	(6w,1nb)
Kennedy	6	2	14	0	(1w)
Tennant	6	0	24	1	(1w)

Umpires: D.Beltran (Gibraltar) and L.P.Hogan (Ireland)   Man of the Match: I.L.Philip

BERMUDA v SCOTLAND (First Round, Group D)

Played at Royal Selangor Club, Bukit Kiara, Kuala Lumpur, March 30, 1997.

Scotland won by 57 runs   Toss: Scotland

SCOTLAND		
I.L.Philip	st Minors b Manders	49
B.G.Lockie	st Minors b Hollis	33
M.J.Smith	c Steede b Manders	6
*G.Salmond	run out	44
J.G.Williamson	b Tucker	42
M.J.de G.Allingham	b Tucker	14
†A.G.Davies	b Tucker	3
S.R.Kennedy	c and b Blades	0
K.Thomson	not out	4
K.L.P.Sheridan	not out	6
I.R.Beven		
Extras	b 5, lb 10, w 12, nb 3	30
Total	(8 wickets, 50 overs)	231

1-98(2), 2-99(1), 3-112(3), 4-183(4), 5-203(5),
6-217(7), 7-218(9), 8-220(6)

BERMUDA		
D.Smith	b Kennedy	18
*A.B.Steede	b Allingham	1
R.L.Trott	c Davies b Kennedy	19
C.J.Smith	c Kennedy b Sheridan	11
C.M.Marshall	lbw b Sheridan	15
W.A.E.Manders	c Lockie b Beven	14
J.J.Tucker	c Allingham b Beven	10
†D.A.Minors	not out	18
B.D.Perinchief	c Davies b Williamson	19
R.W.Blades	c Smith b Allingham	13
D.W.Hollis	b Allingham	0
Extras	b 4, lb 9, w 16, nb 7	36
Total	(all out, 50 overs)	174

1-5(2), 2-52(1), 3-62(3), 4-88(4), 5-93(5), 6-115(6),
7-115(7), 8-154(9), 9-173(10), 10-174(11)

Bermuda Bowling

	O	M	R	W	
Blades	10	1	45	1	(2w)
Tucker	7	0	25	3	(2w)
Manders	10	1	49	2	(1w)
Perinchief	10	0	48	0	(1w)
Marshall	3	0	17	0	(2w,3nb)
Hollis	10	0	32	1	(3w)

Scotland Bowling

	O	M	R	W	
Thomson	9	1	34	0	(5w)
Allingham	4	0	34	3	(4w,5nb)
Williamson	7	1	20	1	(3w,2nb)
Kennedy	10	2	20	2	(2nb)
Sheridan	10	2	24	2	
Beven	10	1	29	2	(2w)

Umpires: J.K.Kruger (Namibia) and Makbul Jaffer (Kenya)   Man of the Match: I.L.Phlip

FIRST ROUND TABLES

	P	W	L	Nr	Points
GROUP A					
KENYA	5	5	-	-	10
IRELAND	5	4	1	-	8
U.S.A.	5	3	2	-	6
SINGAPORE	5	2	3	-	4
GIBRALTAR	5	1	4	-	2
ISRAEL	5	-	5	-	0

	P	W	L	Nr	Points
GROUP B					
BANGLADESH	5	5	-	-	10
DENMARK	5	4	1	-	8
UNITED ARAB EMIRATES	5	3	2	-	6
MALAYSIA	5	2	3	-	4
WEST AFRICA	5	1	4	-	2
ARGENTINA	5	-	5	-	0

	P	W	L	Nr	Points	Run Rate
GROUP C						
NETHERLANDS	4	3	-	1	7	2.94
CANADA	4	3	-	1	7	0.86
FIJI	4	2	2	-	4	
NAMIBIA	4	1	3	-	2	
EAST & CENTRAL AFRICA	4	-	4	-	0	

	P	W	L	Nr	Points
GROUP D					
SCOTLAND	4	4	-	-	8
HONG KONG	4	3	1	-	6
BERMUDA	4	2	2	-	4
PAPUA NEW GUINEA	4	1	3	-	2
ITALY	4	-	4	-	0

CANADA v KENYA   (Second Round, Group E)

Played at Tenaga Nasional Sports Complex (Kilat Kelab), Kuala Lumpur, April 1, 1997.

Kenya won on higher comparative scoring rate

Toss: Kenya

KENYA

A.Y.Karim	c Ramnarais b Rana	6
S.K.Gupta	c Rajadurai b Seeram	15
†K.Otieno	b Seeram	10
S.O.Tikolo	c Rajadurai b Seeram	93
*M.O.Odumbe	not out	148
T.Odoyo	c Bhansingh b Maxwell	7
H.S.Modi	c Diwan b Maxwell	0
A.Suji	not out	2
L.O.Tikolo		
M.A.Suji		
B.Patel		
Extras	lb 4, w 15, nb 3	22
Total	(6 wickets, 50 overs)	303

1-14(1), 2-33(3), 3-39(2), 4-240(4), 5-253(6),
6-258(7)

CANADA

*I.Liburd	st Otieno b Karim	28
L.Bhansingh	c Karim b M.A.Suji	10
M.Diwan	c Odumbe b Karim	21
M.Johnson	c Otieno b Odumbe	12
B.E.A.Rajadurai	retired hurt	7
N.Isaacs	c Otieno b A.Suji	17
D.Maxwell	c Otieno b A.Suji	2
S.Seeram	c Otieno b Patel	18
B.Seebaran	c S.O.Tikolo b A.Suji	8
†D.Ramnarais	not out	1
S.Rana	not out	1
Extras	lb 4, w 12, nb 2	18
Total	(8 wickets, 48 overs)	143

1-16(2), 2-64(3), 3-67(1), 4-81(4), 5-103(7),
6-122(6), 7-133(9), 8-142(8)

Canada Bowling

	O	M	R	W	
Rana	10	0	57	1	(4w)
Seeram	10	2	46	3	(1w,3nb)
Maxwell	6	0	52	2	(2w)
Liburd	5	0	42	0	(5w,1nb)
Seebaran	10	2	38	0	
Rajadurai	6	0	37	0	
Isaacs	3	0	27	0	

Kenya Bowling

	O	M	R	W	
M.A.Suji	7	0	25	1	(1w)
S.O.Tikolo	10	4	17	0	(3w)
Karim	10	1	25	2	
Odoyo	5	0	16	0	(2w,1nb)
Odumbe	8	0	16	1	(2w)
A.Suji	7	1	38	3	(4w,2nb)
Patel	1	0	2	1	

Umpires: L.P.Hogan (Ireland) and E.D.Ohm (Netherlands)   Man of the Match: M.O.Odumbe

B.Rajadurai retired hurt at 99/5. Play was abandoned due to rain after 48 overs of the Canada innings.

DENMARK v SCOTLAND   (Second Round, Group E)

Played at Rubber Research Institute, Kuala Lumpur, April 1, 1997.

Scotland won by 45 runs

Toss: Scotland

SCOTLAND

I.L.Philip	c and b Vestergaard	9
B.G.Lockie	b Sorensen	5
M.J.Smith	c J.S.Jensen b P.Jensen	26
*G.Salmond	run out	59
J.G.Williamson	b P.Jensen	0
S.Gourlay	lbw b P.Jensen	0
†A.G.Davies	b Sorensen	24
S.R.Kennedy	b Sorensen	3
K.Thomspn	c and b P.Jensen	4
K.L.P.Sheridan	not out	1
I.R.Beven	c Henriksen b Nielsen	10
Extras	b 4, lb 5, w 10, nb 7	26
Total	(all out, 48 overs)	167

1-11(1), 2-31(2), 3-63(3), 4-68(5), 5-68(6),
6-137(7), 7-149(8), 8-154(9), 9-156(4), 10-167(11)

DENMARK

†B.Singh	lbw b Beven	7
M.Lund	c Thomson b Beven	0
J.S.Jensen	c Williamson b Gourlay	21
C.R.Pedersen	c Davies b Thomson	2
S.A.Nielsen	c Davies b Sheridan	15
*S.Henriksen	b Williamson	3
M.H.Andersen	c Sheridan b Kennedy	6
S.Vestergaard	c Gourlay b Beven	20
P.Jensen	c Smith b Williamson	13
S.K.Kristenson	c Philip b Beven	0
S.R.M.Sorensen	not out	1
Extras	b 3, lb 7, w 15, nb 9	34
Total	(all out, 45.3 overs)	122

1-7(2), 2-13(1), 3-20(4), 4-48(3), 5-56(6), 6-73(7),
7-79(5), 8-110(8), 9-113(10), 10-122(9)

Denmark Bowling

	O	M	R	W	
Sorensen	9	0	29	3	(2w,1nb)
Vestergaard	2.3	1	4	1	(2w)
Nielsen	4.3	0	34	1	(1w,2nb)
Kristenson	10	1	33	0	
Andersen	10	3	16	0	(4w,4nb)
P.Jensen	10	4	25	4	(2nb)
Henriksen	2	0	17	0	(1w,2nb)

Scotland Bowling

	O	M	R	W	
Thomson	6	1	27	1	(7w)
Beven	10	2	23	4	(2w)
Gourlay	7	2	15	1	(5nb)
Williamson	5.3	1	22	2	(3w,4nb)
Kennedy	9	4	12	1	(2w,2nb)
Sheridan	8	2	13	1	

Umpires: A.F.M.Aktaruddin (Bangladesh) and H.Whitlock (Hong Kong)   Man of the Match: G.Salmond

S.Vestergaard was injured during his 3rd over (the 6th of the innings). The over was completed by S.A.Nielsen.

CANADA v SCOTLAND (Second Round, Group E)

Played at Royal Military College, Kuala Lumpur, April 2, 1997.

No result

Toss: Canada

CANADA			SCOTLAND
*I.Liburd	c Davies b Sheridan	39	I.L.Philip
D.Chumney	lbw b Beven	0	B.G.Lockie
M.Diwan	c Davies b Gourlay	5	M.J.Smith
N.Isaacs	not out	26	*G.Salmond
M.Johnson	c Thomson b Kennedy	1	J.G.Williamson
S.Seeram	not out	13	S.Gourlay
D.Maxwell			†A.G.Davies
B.Seebaran			S.R.Kennedy
†D.Ramnarais			K.Thomson
D.Joseph			K.L.P.Sheridan
S.Rana			I.R.Beven
Extras	lb 2, w 12, nb 1	15	
Total	(4 wickets, 29.4 overs)	99	

1-11(2), 2-31(3), 3-78(1), 4-79(5)

Scotland Bowling

	O	M	R	W	
Thomson	1.4	0	11	0	(1w)
Beven	6	1	13	1	(1w)
Williamson	1	0	12	0	(8w)
Gourlay	6	1	10	1	(2w,1nb)
Sheridan	9	0	32	1	
Kennedy	6	1	19	1	(1nb)

Umpires: A.A.Shaheen (Bangladesh) and E.D.Ohm (Netherlands)   Man of the Match: no award

Rain delayed the start of the match until 12.00pm and the match was reduced to 42 overs per side with 8 overs per bowler (2 bowlers may bowl 9 overs). Rain interrupted play at 1.52pm when Canada were 99/4 off 29 overs. Play resumed at 2.10pm with the match reduced to 39 overs per side. Rain interrupted play again at 2.14pm and the match was later abandoned.

DENMARK v KENYA (Second Round, Group E)

Played at Kelab Aman, Kuala Lumpur, April 2, 1997.

No result

Toss: Kenya

KENYA			DENMARK
A.Y.Karim	c Singh b Sorensen	6	†B.Singh
S.K.Gupta	c L.H.Andersen b Hansen	4	M.Lund
†K.Otieno	c M.H.Andersen b Sorensen	10	J.S.Jensen
S.O.Tikolo	c Nielsen b Hansen	2	L.H.Andersen
*M.O.Odumbe	not out	2	S.A.Nielsen
H.S.Modi			M.H.Andersen
M.A.Suji			*S.Henriksen
L.O.Tikolo			P.Jensen
A.Suji			T.M.Hansen
T.Odoyo			S.K.Kristenson
B.Patel			S.R.M.Sorensen
Extras	w 8, nb 1	9	
Total	(4 wickets, 9.4 overs)	33	

1-14(1), 2-29(2), 3-29(3), 4-33(4)

Denmark Bowling

	O	M	R	W	
Sorensen	5	1	12	2	(2w)
Hansen	4.4	0	21	2	(6w,1nb)

Umpires: I.Massey (Italy) and H.Whitlock (Hong Kong)   Man of the Match: no award

Play started at 1.00pm due to rain and a wet outfield with the match reduced to 42 overs per side. Rain stopped play at 1.47pm and the match was later abandoned.

CANADA v DENMARK (Second Round, Group E)

Played at Royal Selangor Club, Bukit Kiara, Kuala Lumpur, April 4, 1997.

Denmark won by 7 runs   Toss: Denmark

DENMARK			CANADA		
†B.Singh	lbw b Maxwell	29	*I.Liburd	c Singh b Hansen	9
M.Lund	c Ramnarais b Liburd	10	L.Bhansingh	c Nielsen b Hansen	17
J.S.Jensen	lbw b Liburd	0	M.Diwan	c P.Jensen b Hansen	2
L.H.Andersen	c Diwan b Liburd	0	D.Maxwell	c Singh b Sorensen	3
S.A.Nielsen	c Seebaran b Maxwell	10	N.Isaacs	not out	43
M.H.Andersen	run out	20	M.Johnson	c Singh b Sorensen	0
*S.Henriksen	b Maxwell	0	B.Seebaran	c Henriksen b Hansen	0
P.Jensen	c Liburd b Joseph	9	S.Seeram	c Lund b L.H.Andersen	25
T.M.Hansen	c Isaacs b Seebaran	8	†D.Ramnarais	c Nielsen b P.Jensen	1
S.K.Kristenson	lbw b Rana	3	D.Joseph	c Nielsen b Hansen	2
S.R.M.Sorensen	not out	0	S.Rana	run out	0
Extras	b 3, lb 5, w 24, nb 5	37	Extras	lb 3, w 11, nb 3	17
Total	(all out, 48.1 overs)	126	Total	(all out, 27.2 overs)	119

1-51(2), 2-51(3), 3-53(4), 4-71(5), 5-72(1), 6-72(7),
7-97(8), 8-116(6), 9-126(9), 10-126(10)

1-16(1), 2-31(3), 3-36(2), 4-38(4), 5-38(6), 6-39(7),
7-90(8), 8-97(9), 9-112(10), 10-119(11)

Canada Bowling	O	M	R	W	
Joseph	10	0	23	1	(3w,1nb)
Rana	9.1	1	21	1	(6w,2nb)
Seeram	8	0	18	0	(1w,3nb)
Liburd	5	1	14	3	(4w)
Seebaran	10	1	21	1	
Maxwell	6	0	21	3	(6w)

Denmark Bowling	O	M	R	W	
Sorensen	6	1	20	2	(2w)
Hansen	10	0	51	5	(5w,3nb)
M.H.Andersen	3.2	0	8	0	(2w)
Kristenson	2	0	16	0	(1w)
P.Jensen	5	1	18	1	(1w)
L.H.Andersen	1	0	3	1	

Umpires: J.K.Kruger (Namibia) and E.D.Ohm (Netherlands)   Man of the Match: T.M.Hansen

Rain interrupted play from 2.28pm until 3.31pm. Canada were 38/3 off 8 overs when play was suspended. There was no reduction in overs at the re-start.

KENYA v SCOTLAND (Second Round, Group E)

Played at Perbadanan Kemajuan Negari Selangor, Kuala Lumpur, April 4, 1997.

Kenya won on higher comparative scoring rate   Toss: Kenya

KENYA			SCOTLAND		
S.K.Gupta	b Williamson	19	I.L.Philip	c Otieno b M.A.Suji	0
L.Onyango	c Williamson b Beven	13	B.G.Lockie	not out	18
†K.Otieno	lbw b Allingham	7	M.J.Smith	c Odumbe b M.A.Suji	0
S.O.Tikolo	c Philip b Beven	32	*G.Salmond	c A.Suji b M.A.Suji	5
*M.O.Odumbe	c Philip b Kennedy	0	J.G.Williamson	not out	7
H.S.Modi	c and b Williamson	0	S.Gourlay		
A.Y.Karim	c Kennedy b Beven	14	†A.G.Davies		
L.O.Tikolo	c Sheridan b Gourlay	14	M.J.de G.Allingham		
T.Odoyo	c Sheridan b Gourlay	21	S.R.Kennedy		
A.Suji	c Philip b Gourlay	9	K.L.P.Sheridan		
M.A.Suji	not out	2	I.R.Beven		
Extras	lb 1, w 17, nb 4	22	Extras	b 1, w 5, nb 1	7
Total	(all out, 48.2 overs)	153	Total	(3 wickets, 23 overs)	37

1-28(2), 2-38(3), 3-60(1), 4-66(5), 5-67(6),
6-100(4), 7-106(7), 8-136(8), 9-146(10), 10-153(9)

1-1(1), 2-3(3), 3-19(4)

Scotland Bowling	O	M	R	W	
Gourlay	9.2	0	26	3	(3w,2nb)
Beven	10	1	34	3	(1w)
Allingham	7	0	28	1	(5w,1nb)
Kennedy	10	4	20	1	
Williamson	9	0	31	2	(8w,4nb)
Sheridan	3	0	13	0	

Kenya Bowling	O	M	R	W	
M.A.Suji	10	2	18	3	(4w,1nb)
S.O.Tikolo	7	1	10	0	(1w)
Karim	4	1	8	0	
Odoyo	2	2	0	0	

Umpires: L.P.Hogan (Ireland) and H.Whitlock (Hong Kong)   Man of the Match: no award

Rain stopped play at 3.15pm and the match was later abandoned. Under the Duckworth-Lewis method, Scotland needed to have scored 63 to win the match.

BANGLADESH v HONG KONG — (Second Round, Group F)

Played at Perbadanan Kemajuan Negari Selangor, Kuala Lumpur, April 1, 1997.

Bangladesh won by 7 wickets — Toss: Bangladesh

HONG KONG

M.R.Farcy	run out		38
S.J.Brew	b Khaled Mahmud		9
M.I.N.Eames	c and b Akram Khan		8
R.Sharma	c Enamul Hoque b Mohammed Rafique		23
*†J.P.Fordham	c and b Minhajul Abedin		6
M.G.Lever	run out		3
Munir Hussain	c Khaled Mashud b Mohammed Rafique		11
A.N.French	c Akram Khan b Minhajul Abedin		2
K.Raza	st Khaled Mashud b Mohammed Rafique		14
D.Jones	run out		12
Mohammed Zubair	not out		0
Extras	lb 3, w 16		19
Total	**(all out, 45.2 overs)**		**145**

1-44(2), 2-62(3), 3-76(1), 4-94(5), 5-100(6),
6-110(4), 7-118(7), 8-118(8), 9-145(10), 10-145(9)

BANGLADESH

Athar Ali Khan	st Fordham b Munir Hussain	29
Naimur Rahman	c sub (M.Swift) b Brew	8
Minhajul Abedin	lbw b Raza	13
Aminul Islam	not out	53
*Akram Khan	not out	25
Saiful Islam		
†Khaled Mashud		
Enamul Hoque		
Khaled Mahmud		
Mohammed Rafique		
Hasibul Hussain		
Extras	lb 4, w 16	20
Total	**(3 wickets, 38.2 overs)**	**148**

1-20(2), 2-52(1), 3-71(3)

Bangladesh Bowling

	O	M	R	W	
Saiful Islam	4	0	13	0	(6w)
Hasibul Hussain	5	1	21	0	(5w)
Khaled Mahmud	3	1	14	1	
Akram Khan	10	2	28	1	(2w)
Enamul Hoque	8	1	19	0	
Minhajul Abedin	8	0	27	2	(2w)
Mohammed Rafique	7.2	1	20	3	(1w)

Hong Kong Bowling

	O	M	R	W	
Brew	6	0	19	1	(3w)
Mohammed Zubair	6	0	22	0	(4w)
Munir Hussain	5	1	18	1	(7w)
Lever	5	0	20	0	(2w)
Sharma	3	0	14	0	
Raza	10	0	35	1	
Jones	3.2	0	16	0	

Umpires: J.Luther (Denmark) and W.Smith (Scotland)   Man of the Match: Aminul Islam

IRELAND v NETHERLANDS — (Second Round, Group F)

Played at Kelab Aman, Kuala Lumpur, April 1, 1997.

Ireland won on higher comparative scoring rate — Toss: Ireland

NETHERLANDS

*T.B.M.de Leede	b Gillespie	5
R.P.Lefebvre	c Eagleson b Gillespie	11
A.P.van Troost	c A.D.Patterson b Eagleson	15
B.Zuiderent	c A.D.Patterson b Doak	38
R.F.van Oosterom	c A.D.Patterson b Harrison	16
P.E.Cantrell	not out	53
Zulfiqar Ahmed	b McCrum	27
K.A.Khan	c Eagleson b Curry	15
M.A.C.Nota	b McCrum	4
†R.H.Scholte	not out	9
G.L.Edwards		
Extras	lb 11, w 6, nb 1	18
Total	**(8 wickets, 50 overs)**	**211**

1-17(1), 2-28(2), 3-62(3), 4-95(5), 5-109(4),
6-158(7), 7-192(8), 8-198(9)

IRELAND

J.D.Curry	c Nota b Lefebvre	30
D.A.Lewis	c Scholte b van Troost	19
*J.D.R.Benson	c Scholte b Khan	1
A.R.Dunlop	not out	26
N.G.Doak	not out	2
†A.D.Patterson		
R.L.Eagleson		
P.G.Gillespie		
G.D.Harrison		
M.W.Patterson		
P.McCrum		
Extras	lb 2, w 7, nb 4	13
Total	**(3 wickets, 23 overs)**	**91**

1-47(1), 2-48(3), 3-77(2)

Ireland Bowling

	O	M	R	W	
Gillespie	9	2	20	2	
M.W.Patterson	5	0	29	0	(2w,1nb)
Eagleson	4	1	19	1	
Harrison	10	1	28	1	
McCrum	7	0	39	2	(3w)
Doak	10	1	29	1	
Curry	5	0	36	1	

Netherlands Bowling

	O	M	R	W	
Lefebvre	6	2	12	1	(1w)
Khan	6	0	41	1	(4w,1nb)
Edwards	8	1	25	0	(1w)
van Troost	3	0	11	1	(1w,4nb)

Umpires: G.F.Mailk (U.A.E.) and J.K.Kruger (Namibia)   Man of the Match: no award

Rain interrupted play from 2.58pm until 4.00pm when Ireland were 73/2 off 17 overs. Rain halted play at 4.30pm and the match was abandoned at 5.20pm. Under the Duckworth-Lewis method Ireland need to have scored 87 to win.

BANGLADESH v IRELAND   (Second Round, Group F)

Played at Royal Selangor Club, Bukit Kiara, Kuala Lumpur, April 2, 1997.

No result   Toss: Ireland

IRELAND			BANGLADESH		
J.D.Curry	c Sanvar Hossain b Hasibul Hossain	15	Athar Ali Khan	not out	8
†A.D.Patterson	c Khaled Mashud b Hasibul Hossain	4	Naimur Rahman	not out	5
D.A.Lewis	c Minhajul Abedin b Enamul Hoque	14	Hasibul Hussain		
*J.D.R.Benson	b Enamul Hoque	17	Minhajul Abedin		
N.G.Doak	c Enamul Hoque b Mohammed Rafique	32	Saiful Islam		
A.R.Dunlop	c Khaled Mashud b Athar Ali Khan	2	†Khaled Mashud		
G.D.Harrison	st Khaled Mashud b Naimur Rahman	10	Sanvar Hossain		
P.G.Gillespie	b Hasibul Hossain	22	Enamul Hoque		
M.W.Patterson	run out	1	Mohammed Rafique		
R.L.Eagleson	b Mohammed Rafique	1	*Akram Khan		
P.McCrum	not out	0	Aminul Islam		
Extras	b 2, lb 2, w 5, nb 2	11	Extras	lb 5, w 6	11
Total	(all out, 49.1 overs)	129	Total	(no wicket, 6.4 overs)	24

1-15(2), 2-29(1), 3-53(3), 4-60(4), 5-63(6), 6-79(7),
7-116(5), 8-118(9), 9-129(8), 10-129(10)

Bangladesh Bowling	O	M	R	W	
Saiful Islam	7	3	15	0	(3w)
Hasibul Hussain	10	1	21	3	(1w,3nb)
Athar Ali Khan	10	2	18	1	
Akram Khan	2	0	7	0	
Enamul Hoque	10	3	20	2	
Naimur Rahman	5	0	20	1	
Mohammed Rafique	5.1	0	24	2	(1w)

Ireland Bowling	O	M	R	W	
Gillespie	3.4	0	11	0	
M.W.Patterson	3	1	8	0	(3w)

Umpires: J.K.Kruger (Namibia) and J.Luther (Denmark)   Man of the Match: no award
Rain stopped play at 2.15pm when Bangladesh were 23/0 from 6.1 overs. Play resumed at 5.17pm, Bangladesh being set a target of 63 runs in 20 overs. The match was abandoned due to a slippery outfield after 3 further balls.

HONG KONG v NETHERLANDS   (Second Round, Group F)

Played at Tenaga Nasional Sports Complex (Kilat Kelab), Kuala Lumpur, April 2, 1997.

No result   Toss: Hong Kong

HONG KONG			NETHERLANDS		
M.R.Farcy	c Lefebvre b Khan	28	B.Zuiderent	not out	7
S.J.Brew	c and b Lefebvre	1	R.P.Lefebvre	not out	7
*†J.P.Fordham	lbw b Cantrell	34	*T.B.M.de Leede		
R.Sharma	lbw b Khan	2	K-J.J.van Noortwijk		
M.I.N.Eames	run out	25	R.F.van Oosterom		
M.G.Lever	c Lefebvre b Edwards	3	P.E.Cantrell		
R.Sujanani	lbw b Lefebvre	23	Zulfiqar Ahmed		
D.Jones	c Cantrell b Khan	15	G.L.Edwards		
Munir Hussain	c van Oosterom b Edwards	11	K.A.Khan		
K.Raza	not out	5	†R.H.Scholte		
Mohammed Zubair	b Khan	6	S.van Dijk		
Extras	b 2, lb 6, w 7, nb 2	17	Extras	b 1, w 1	2
Total	(all out, 47.5 overs)	170	Total	(no wicket, 5.2 overs)	16

1-22(2), 2-34(1), 3-38(4), 4-91(3), 5-101(5),
6-101(6), 7-137(8), 8-152(9), 9-156(7), 10-170(11)

Netherlands Bowling	O	M	R	W	
Lefebvre	10	3	27	2	(2w)
Edwards	10	0	40	2	(1w,2nb)
Khan	8.5	0	28	4	(1w)
van Dijk	5	1	29	0	
Cantrell	10	1	19	1	
Zulfiqar Ahmed	4	0	19	0	(2w)

Hong Kong Bowling	O	M	R	W	
Brew	3	1	9	0	
Farcy	2.2	0	6	0	(1w)

Umpires: T.Cooper (Fiji) and Makbul Jaffer (Kenya)   Man of the Match: no award
Rain and lightning stopped play at 2.18pm and the match was abandoned at 4.30pm.

BANGLADESH v NETHERLANDS (Second Round, Group F)

Played at Rubber Research Institute, Kuala Lumpur, April 4, 1997.

Bangladesh won by 3 wickets   Toss: Bangladesh

NETHERLANDS			BANGLADESH		
B.Zuiderent	c Animul Islam		Athar Ali Khan	b Lefebvre	4
	b Hasibul Hussain	11			
R.P.Lefebvre	b Saiful Islam	1	Naimur Rahman	lbw b Lefebvre	0
*T.B.M.de Leede	st Khaled Mashud		Sanvar Hossain	c Scholte b Lefebvre	0
	b Athar Ali Khan	23			
P.E.Cantrell	run out	37	Aminul Islam	c van Noortwijk b Khan	4
R.F.van Oosterom	b Akram Khan	40	*Akram Khan	not out	68
K-J.J.van Noortwijk	c Khaled Mashud		Minhajul Abedin	run out	22
	b Mohammed Rafique	14			
Zulfiqar Ahmed	c Khaled Mashud		Enamul Hoque	c van Oosterom	
	b Mohammed Rafique	1		b Cantrell	3
†R.H.Scholte	run out	14	Saiful Islam	c Cantrell b Nota	18
M.A.C.Nota	run out	3	†Khaled Mashud	not out	0
K.A.Khan	b Akram Khan	9	Mohammed Rafique		
G.L.Edwards	not out	3	Hasibul Hussain		
Extras	lb 4, w 11	15	Extras	b 2, lb 8, w 10, nb 2	22
Total	(all out, 49.5 overs)	171	Total	(7 wickets, 31.4 overs)	141

1-8(2), 2-28(1), 3-60(3), 4-109(4), 5-135(5),
6-139(6), 7-139(7), 8-152(9), 9-162(8), 10-171(10)

1-7(2), 2-7(3), 3-13(4), 4-15(1), 5-77(6), 6-86(7),
7-136(8)

Bangladesh Bowling	O	M	R	W	
Saiful Islam	7	0	25	1	(9w)
Hasibul Hussain	7	2	10	1	
Athar Ali Khan	7	1	18	1	
Enamul Hoque	4	0	26	0	
Minhajul Abedin	10	0	34	0	(1w)
Mohammed Rafique	10	0	33	2	(1w)
Akram Khan	4.5	0	21	2	

Netherlands Bowling	O	M	R	W	
Lefebvre	7	4	8	3	(1w)
Khan	7	0	29	1	(6w,3nb)
Edwards	5	0	33	0	(2w,2nb)
Cantrell	7	0	22	1	(1w)
Bota	3.4	0	21	1	
Zulfiqar Ahmed	2	0	18	0	

Umpires: Makbul Jaffer (Kenya) and I.Massey (Italy)   Man of the Match: Akram Khan

Rain stopped play at 3.07pm. When play was resumed at 5.15pm, Bangladesh were required to score 141 runs in 33 overs to win.

HONG KONG v IRELAND (Second Round, Group F)

Played at Kelab Aman, Kuala Lumpur, April 4, 1997.

Ireland won by 51 runs   Toss: Hong Kong

IRELAND			HONG KONG		
J.D.Curry	b Jones	24	M.R.Farcy	c Curry b Gillespie	8
†A.D.Patterson	b Mohammed Zubair	12	K.Raza	c A.D.Patterson b Gillespie	1
D.A.Lewis	c Fordham b Jones	18	M.I.N.Eames	c Benson b Harrison	13
*J.D.R.Benson	c Eames b Sharma	33	S.J.Brew	c Harrison b McCrum	50
N.G.Doak	c Brew b Sharma	12	R.Sharma	c Curry b McCrum	21
A.R.Dunlop	b Mohammed Zubair	54	*†J.P.Fordham	c A.D.Patterson b Gillespie	4
P.G.Gillespie	c and b Sharma	19	Munir Hussain	c Dunlop b Eagleson	23
G.D.Harrison	not out	15	R.Sujanani	b McCrum	5
M.W.Patterson	not out	1	M.G.Lever	c Gillespie b Eagleson	9
P.McCrum			D.Jones	lbw b M.W.Patterson	5
R.L.Eagleson			Mohammed Zubair	not out	0
Extras	b 3, lb 9, w 23	35	Extras	b 1, lb 3, w 28, nb 1	33
Total	(7 wickets, 50 overs)	223	Total	(all out, 45.3 overs)	172

1-39(2), 2-58(1), 3-90(3), 4-116(4), 5-120(5),
6-158(7), 7-222(6)

1-16(2), 2-22(1), 3-55(3), 4-110(4), 5-118(5),
6-136(6), 7-146(8), 8-164(7), 9-166(9), 10-172(10)

Hong Kong Bowling	O	M	R	W	
Brew	8	2	35	0	(5w)
Farcy	3	0	26	0	(5w)
Mohammed Zubair	9	0	39	2	(5w)
Munir Hussain	8	1	32	0	(2w)
Jones	7	0	30	2	(2w)
Raza	2	0	8	0	
Sharma	10	1	29	3	(1w)
Sujanani	3	0	12	0	

Ireland Bowling	O	M	R	W	
Gillespie	7	0	42	3	(7w,2nb)
M.W.Patterson	4.3	0	14	1	(9w)
McCrum	10	1	30	3	(4w)
Eagleson	8	1	30	2	(5w)
Doak	8	2	19	0	(1w)
Harrison	5	2	21	1	
Curry	3	0	12	0	(1w)

Umpires: T.Cooper (Fiji) and J.Luther (Denmark)   Man of the Match: A.R.Dunlop

SECOND ROUND TABLES

GROUP E	P	W	L	Ab	Points
KENYA	3	2	-	1	5
SCOTLAND	3	1	1	1	3
DENMARK	3	1	1	1	3
CANADA	3	-	2	1	1

Scotland took second place, having beaten Denmark.

GROUP F	P	W	L	Ab	Points
BANGLADESH	3	2	-	1	5
IRELAND	3	2	-	1	5
HONG KONG	3	-	2	1	1
NETHERLANDS	3	-	2	1	1

CANADA v HONG KONG (Play-Off for Seventh Place)

Played at Perbadanan Kemajuan Negari Selangor, Kuala Lumpur, April 5, 1997.

Canada won by 4 wickets   Toss: Hong Kong

HONG KONG				CANADA		
Munir Hussain	b Joseph	0		D.Chumney	lbw b Munir Hussain	5
†R.D.Brewster	b Joseph	11		†A.Glegg	c Sharma b Sujanani	8
R.Sujanani	c Bhansingh b Joseph	7		M.Diwan	c Brew b Sharma	35
*S.J.Brew	b Bhansingh	46		D.Perera	b Sujanani	0
R.Sharma	st Glegg b Seebaran	10		N.Isaacs	c Brew b Raza	13
A.N.French	c Glegg b Seebaran	7		S.Seeram	lbw b Munir Hussain	18
J.P.R.Lamsam	c Diwan b Bhansingh	8		L.Bhansingh	not out	9
M.Swift	st Glegg b Diwan	11		*I.Liburd	not out	15
M.I.N.Eames	c and b Bhansingh	1		B.Seebaran		
K.Raza	not out	5		S.Rana		
Mohammed Zubair	c and b Diwan	0		D.Joseph		
Extras	b 2, lb 2, w 14, nb 1	19		Extras	b 1, w 22	23
Total	(all out, 42.4 overs)	125		Total	(6 wickets, 41.5 overs)	126

1-2(1), 2-16(3), 3-39(2), 4-56(5), 5-90(6), 6-97(4),
7-107(7), 8-111(9), 9-125(8), 10-125(11)

1-10(1), 2-28(2), 3-28(4), 4-64(5), 5-82(3), 6-93(6)

Canada Bowling	O	M	R	W		Hong Kong Bowling	O	M	R	W	
Joseph	7	0	25	3	(8w)	Munir Hussain	8.5	0	22	2	(5w)
Rana	6	0	18	0	(1w,1nb)	Raza	9	0	31	1	(3w)
Seebaran	10	1	25	2	(1w)	Mohammed Zubair	7	0	19	0	(6w)
Seeram	5	0	13	0		Sujanani	7	1	16	2	(2w)
Isaacs	6	0	16	0	(2w)	Sharma	6	1	21	1	
Bhansingh	5	0	13	3	(2w)	Brew	4	0	12	0	
Diwan	3.4	0	11	2		Lamsam	0.0	0	4	0	(2w)

Umpires: L.P.Hogan (Ireland) and Makbul Jaffer (Kenya)   Man of the Match: M.Diwan

Lamsam bowled 2 wides (the first of which was run for 3), was injured and the over was continued by Munir Hussain.

DENMARK v NETHERLANDS (Play-Off for Fifth Place)

Played at Rubber Research Institute, Kuala Lumpur, April 5, 1997.

Denmark won by 3 wickets   Toss: Denmark

NETHERLANDS				DENMARK		
B.Zuiderent	lbw b P.Jensen	25		S.A.Nielsen	lbw b Khan	26
R.P.Lefebvre	c P.Jensen b Sorensen	10		M.Lund	c Smits b Cantrell	11
K-J.J.van Noortwijk	b M.H.Andersen	17		J.S.Jensen	c and b van Dijk	24
*T.B.M.de Leede	st Singh b Kristenson	3		†B.Singh	c Smits b Khan	2
P.E.Cantrell	lbw b M.H.Andersen	1		M.H.Andersen	b van Dijk	4
R.F.van Oosterom	b Hansen	44		*S.Henriksen	lbw b de Leede	42
T.H.Groot	b Sorensen	35		L.H.Andersen	c Smits b van Dijk	0
K.A.Khan	not out	48		T.M.Hansen	not out	41
†J.Smits	run out	1		P.Jensen	not out	14
S.van Dijk	not out	5		S.K.Kristenson		
R.Singh				S.R.M.Sorensen		
Extras	b 1, lb 4, w 2, nb 2	9		Extras	b 3, lb 7, w 22, nb 4	36
Total	(8 wickets, 50 overs)	198		Total	(7 wickets, 49.4 overs)	200

1-18(2), 2-52(1), 3-56(3), 4-58(5), 5-69(4),
6-136(7), 7-172(6), 8-188(9)

1-52(2), 2-56(1), 3-78(4), 4-94(3), 5-96(5), 6-96(7),
7-176(6)

Denmark Bowling	O	M	R	W		Netherlands Bowling	O	M	R	W	
Sorensen	10	2	41	2	(1w)	Lefebvre	10	4	19	0	(3w)
Hansen	8	1	47	1		van Dijk	10	3	35	3	(6w,1nb)
P.Jensen	10	0	26	1	(1nb)	Cantrell	10	0	41	1	(3w)
M.H.Andersen	10	2	20	2	(1nb)	Khan	10	1	35	2	(4w,3nb)
Kristenson	8	1	39	1	(1w)	Singh	4	0	21	0	(2w)
L.H.Andersen	4	0	20	0		de Leede	4	0	19	1	
						Zuiderent	1.4	0	20	0	(1w)

Umpires: I.Kathiravel and H.Whitlock (Hong Kong)   Man of the Match: T.M.Hansen

IRELAND v KENYA　(Semi-Final)

Played at Tenaga Nasional Sports Complex (Kilat Kelab), Kuala Lumpur, April 6, 7, 1997.

Kenya won by 7 runs　　　　　　　　　　　　　　　　Toss: Ireland

KENYA				IRELAND		
A.Y.Karim	b Doak	23		J.D.Curry	c L.O.Tikolo b Odoyo	18
S.K.Gupta	c Heasley b M.W.Patterson	22		A.D.Patterson	b Karim	28
†K.Otieno	c Harrison b McCrum	51		*J.D.R.Benson	c Odumbe b Karim	35
S.O.Tikolo	b Doak	0		A.R.Dunlop	c Modi b Karim	1
*M.O.Odumbe	run out (Curry)	67		N.G.Doak	run out (M.A.Suji)	12
T.Odoyo	c A.D.Patterson b McCrum	0		D.Heasley	b M.A.Suji	51
A.Suji	not out	29		G.D.Harrison	c and b Karim	9
L.Onyango	b McCrum	1		M.W.Patterson	lbw b M.A.Suji	4
L.O.Tikolo	c Dunlop b McCrum	0		P.G.Gillespie	not out	24
M.A.Suji				P.McCrum	c Karim b S.O.Tikolo	3
H.S.Modi				†A.T.Rutherford	not out	3
Extras	b 4, lb 6, w 11, nb 1	22		Extras	b 1, lb 11, w 8	20
Total	(8 wickets, 50 overs)	215		Total	(9 wickets, 50 overs)	208

1-35(2), 2-83(1), 3-83(4), 4-158(3), 5-159(6), 6-201(5), 7-215(8), 8-215(9)

1-25(1), 2-62(2), 3-64(4), 4-88(5), 5-128(3), 6-146(7), 7-170(8), 8-178(6), 9-189(10)

Ireland Bowling	O	M	R	W		Kenya Bowling	O	M	R	W	
Gillespie	5	0	17	0	(2w)	M.A.Suji	9	1	33	2	(1w)
McCrum	9	0	51	4	(1w)	S.O.Tikolo	9	1	52	1	(3w)
M.W.Patterson	3	0	18	1	(4w,2nb)	Odoyo	10	3	41	1	(1w)
Heasley	8	0	39	0	(1w)	A.Suji	2	0	12	0	(2w)
Harrison	10	0	21	0		Karim	10	2	28	4	
Doak	10	0	32	2		Odumbe	10	0	30	0	
Curry	5	0	27	0	(3w)						

Umpires: D.B.Hair (Australia) and N.T.Plews (England)　　　Man of the Match: M.O.Odumbe
Third Umpire: S.Venkataraghavan (India)
Close of play score: 1st day: Kenya's innings completed
Due to a waterlogged field from a storm the previous night, the match did not start until 2.14pm. The match would still be 50 overs per side, continuing into the second day. Play was interrupted from 3.28pm until 3:59pm on the first day by rain.

BANGLADESH v SCOTLAND　(Semi-Final)

Played at Tenaga Nasional Sports Complex (Kilat Kelab), Kuala Lumpur, April 8, 9, 1997.

Bangladesh won by 72 runs　　　　　　　　　　　　　　Toss: Scotland

BANGLADESH				SCOTLAND		
Athar Ali Khan	c Davies b Beven	5		I.L.Philip	st Khaled Mashud b Naimur Rahman	37
Naimur Rahman	run out (Williamson)	26		B.G.Lockie	run out (Hasibul Hussain)	0
†Khaled Mashud	st Davies b Beven	70		D.R.Lockhart	c Athar Ali Khan b Enamul Hoque	19
Aminul Islam	b Blain	57		I.R.Beven	c Saiful Islam b Enamul Hoque	5
*Akram Khan	c Kennedy b Blain	4		*G.Salmond	st Khaled Mashud b Enamul Hoque	24
Saiful Islam	b Gourlay	15		J.G.Williamson	not out	39
Minhajul Abedin	not out	39		S.Gourlay	c and b Mohammed Rafique	4
Mohammed Rafique	c Lockie b Gourlay	16		†A.G.Davies	b Mohammed Rafique	12
Khaled Mahmud	not out	0		S.R.Kennedy	c Minhajul Abedin b Moh. Rafique	3
Hasibul Hussain				J.A.R.Blain	run out (Saiful Islam)	4
Enamul Hoque				K.L.P.Sheridan	c Aminul Islam b Moh. Rafique	2
Extras	b 3, lb 3, w 4, nb 1	11		Extras	b 1, lb 7, w 14	22
Total	(7 wickets, 50 overs)	243		Total	(all out, 44.5 overs)	171

1-12(1), 2-51(2), 3-166(4), 4-168(3), 5-172(5), 6-211(6), 7-233(8)

1-31(2), 2-62(1), 3-73(4), 4-80(3), 5-111(5), 6-123(7), 7-154(8), 8-162(9), 9-169(10), 10-171(11)

Scotland Bowling	O	M	R	W		Bangladesh Bowling	O	M	R	W	
Blain	10	0	49	2	(1w,3nb)	Saiful Islam	7	0	22	0	(4w)
Beven	10	2	29	2	(1w)	Hasibul Hussain	2	0	10	0	(5w)
Gourlay	7	0	62	2	(1nb)	Khaled Mahmud	6	1	18	0	(3w)
Kennedy	10	3	24	0		Enamul Hoque	10	0	31	3	
Williamson	8	0	43	0	(2w)	Naimur Rahman	9	1	30	1	(1w)
Sheridan	5	0	30	0		Mohammed Rafique	5.5	0	25	4	
						Minhajul Abedin	2	0	10	0	(1w)
						Akram Khan	3	0	17	0	

Umpires: N.T.Plews (England) and S.Venkataraghavan (India)　　　Man of the Match: Khaled Mashud
Third Umpire: D.B.Hair (Australia)
Close of play score: 1st day: Bangladesh innings competed
Due to a waterlogged field from a storm the previous night, play did not start until 2.43pm. It would continue until 6.15pm or the end of the first innings and continue on the second day.

IRELAND v SCOTLAND   (Play-Off for Third Place)

Played at Tenaga Nasional Sports Complex (Kilat Kelab), Kuala Lumpur, April 10,11, 1997.

Scotland won on higher comparative scoring rate
and qualify for the 1999 World Cup

Toss: Ireland

SCOTLAND			IRELAND		
I.L.Philip	c Doak b McCrum	11	J.D.Curry	c Salmond b Thomson	7
D.R.Lockhart	c Benson b Doak	21	†A.D.Patterson	c Davies b Thomson	6
M.J.Smith	run out (Doak)	49	D.A.Lewis	c Thomson b Allingham	11
*G.Salmond	st A.D.Patterson b Curry	7	*J.D.R.Benson	c Smith b Sheridan	26
J.G.Williamson	c and b M.W.Patterson	27	N.G.Doak	c Thomson b Sheridan	7
M.J.de G.Allingham	run out (Gillespie)	22	A.R.Dunlop	c Salmond b Sheridan	10
†A.G.Davies	b Heasley	17	D.Heasley	c Lockhart b Sheridan	18
I.R.Beven	c A.D.Patterson		P.G.Gillespie	st Davies b Beven	9
	b M.W.Patterson	3			
S.R.Kennedy	not out	4	G.D.Harrison	c Lockhart b Williamson	16
K.Thomson			M.W.Patterson	c Kennedy b Williamson	6
K.L.P.Sheridan			P.McCrum	not out	2
Extras	lb 4, w 22	26	Extras	b 1, lb 1, w 15, nb 6	23
Total	(8 wickets, 45 overs)	187	Total	(all out, 39 overs)	141

1-19(1), 2-75(2), 3-94(4), 4-132(3), 5-136(5),
6-172(7), 7-177(8), 8-187(6)

1-9(1), 2-20(2), 3-46(3), 4-72(5), 5-80(4), 6-88(6),
7-111(7), 8-115(8), 9-137(10), 10-141(9)

Ireland Bowling	O	M	R	W	
Gillespie	5	1	10	0	(1w)
McCrum	7	1	14	1	(3w)
Heasley	8	0	44	1	(3w)
M.W.Patterson	8	0	42	2	(12w,1nb)
Harrison	8	0	34	0	(1w)
Doak	6	0	28	1	
Curry	3	0	11	1	(1w)

Scotland Bowling	O	M	R	W	
Beven	9	0	35	1	(2w)
Thomson	6	1	27	2	(6w,4nb)
Kennedy	9	3	14	0	
Allingham	3	0	13	1	(4w)
Sheridan	9	1	34	4	
Williamson	3	0	16	2	(2w,4nb)

Umpires: D.B.Hair (Australia) and S.Venkataraghavan (India)   Man of the Match: M.J.Smith
Third Umpire: N.T.Plews (England)
Close of play score: 1st day: Scotland 56/1 (Lockhart 19*, Smith 13*) off 19 overs

On the first day rain interrupted play at 10.47 am and play was abandoned for the day at 1.00pm. Play did not begin until
11.58pm on the second day due to a waterlogged ground, the match being reduced to 45 overs per side. Under the
Duckworth-Lewis method the Ireland target was 192 in 45 overs.

KENYA v BANGLADESH   (Final – For the Carlsberg I.C.C. Trophy)

Played at Tenaga Nasional Sports Complex (Kilat Kelab, Kuala Lumpur, April 12, 13, 1997.

Bangladesh won on higher comparative scoring rate   Toss: Bangaldesh

KENYA			BANGLADESH		
A.Y.Karim	b Saiful Islam	0	Naimur Rahman	b M.A.Suji	0
S.K.Gupta	c and b Khaled Mahmud	16	Mohammed Rafique	c Odumbe b A.Suji	26
†K.Otieno	lbw b Saiful Islam	2	Minhajul Abedin	c Patel b Odoyo	26
S.O.Tikolo	c Saiful Islam		Aminul Islam	b Karim	37
	b Khaled Mahmud	147			
*M.O.Odumbe	st Khaled Mashud		*Akram Khan	c Odoyo b Odumbe	22
	b Mohommed Rafique	43			
T.Odoyo	b Mohommed Rafique	1	Enamul Hoque	c Gupta b Karim	5
H.S.Modi	not out	12	Saiful Islam	c Odumbe b Karim	14
A.Suji	st Khaled Mashud		†Khaled Mashud	not out	15
	b Mohommed Rafique	1			
L.O.Tikolo			Khaled Mahmud	st Otieno b Odumbe	5
M.A.Suji			Hasibul Hussain	not out	4
B.Patel			Athar Ali Khan		
Extras	b 1, lb 9, w 9	19	Extras	b 3, lb 4, w 5	12
Total	(7 wickets, 50 overs)	241	Total	(8 wickets, 25 overs)	166

1-0(1), 2-15(3), 3-58(2), 4-196(5), 5-212(6),
6-230(4), 7-241(8)

1-0(1), 2-50(2), 3-63(3), 4-116(4), 5-118(5),
6-123(6), 7-139(7), 8-151(9)

Bangladesh Bowling	O	M	R	W		Kenya Bowling	O	M	R	W	
Saiful Islam	9	0	39	2	(3w)	M.A.Suji	4	0	28	1	(1w)
Hasibul Hussain	6	0	15	0	(4w)	S.O.Tikolo	4	0	29	0	(2w)
Athar Ali Khan	5	0	22	0		Odoyo	5	0	27	1	
Khaled Mahmud	7	1	31	2	(1w)	A.Suji	5	0	26	1	(2w)
Enamul Hoque	10	0	41	0		Karim	4	0	31	3	
Naimur Rahman	4	0	21	0		Odumbe	3	0	18	2	
Mohammed Rafique	6	1	40	3	(1w)						
Akram Khan	3	0	22	0							

Umpires: D.B.Hair (Australia) and S.Venkataraghavan (India)   Man of the Match: S.O.Tikolo
Third Umpire: N.T.Plews (England)
Close of play score: 1st day: Kenya innings completed

Play did not start on the first day until 1.45pm due to rain. Play would continue until the end of the first innings, with the second innings on the reserve day. On the second day, rain delayed the start until 3.30pm. Under the Duckworth-Lewis method, the Bangladesh targert was reduced to 166 in 25 overs.

Bangladesh still required 11 off the final over, but 1 six from the first ball by M.A.Suji eased the pressure and helped them to win.

Man of the Series:	M.O.Odumbe (Kenya)
Batsman of the Series:	S.O.Tikolo (Kenya)
Bowler of the Series:	management did not nominate a bowler of the series
Fielder of the Series:	Aminul Islam (Bangladesh)
Wicket-keeper of the Series:	Khaled Mashud (Bangladesh)

ISRAEL v WEST AFRICA   (Minor Placings Play-Off Match)

Played at Royal Military College, Kuala Lumpur, April 1, 1997.

West Africa won by 190 runs   Toss: Israel

WEST AFRICA		
K.Sagoe	lbw b Ashton	10
O.E.Ukpong	not out	78
†A.Kpundeh	c Perlman b Kehimkar	24
*O.O.Agodo	c Ashton b Hall	42
S.Kpundeh	c Smith b Kehimkar	0
U.Ntinu	c Smith b Hall	12
G.I.Wiltshire	b Moss	24
J.Omoigui	not out	31
O.Idowu		
P.D.Vanderpuje-Orgle		
S.Fadahunsi		
Extras	b 1, lb 5, w 20	26
Total	(6 wickets, 50 overs)	247

1-38(1), 2-94(3), 3-119(5), 4-163(6), 5-164(4),
6-198(7)

ISRAEL		
L.Hall	b Fadahunsi	7
Y.Nagavkar	run out (Vanderpuje-Orgle)	0
S.B.Perlman	c Agodo b Vanderpuje-Orgle	11
A.Talkar	c S.Kpundeh b Vanderpuje-Orgle	16
*H.Awasker	b Vanderpuje-Orgle	0
R.Ashton	b Fadahunsi	0
A.Vard	b Vanderpuje-Orgle	8
A.Moss	c Omoigui b Fadahunsi	0
B.Kehimkar	lbw b S.Kpundeh	1
†P.Smith	st A.Kpundeh b Vanderpuje-Orgle	4
V.E.Worrell	not out	2
Extras	b 4, w 4	8
Total	(all out, 21.1 overs)	57

1-6(2), 2-11(1), 3-28(3), 4-28(5), 5-29(6), 6-45(4),
7-49(7), 8-49(8), 9-53(10), 10-57(9)

Israel Bowling

	O	M	R	W	
Moss	10	1	41	1	(3w)
Kehimkar	10	1	28	2	(1w)
Worrell	7	0	43	0	(5w)
Ashton	7	0	32	1	(6w)
Awasker	10	1	51	0	(4w)
Hall	4	0	32	2	(1w)
Nagavkar	2	0	14	0	

West Africa Bowling

	O	M	R	W	
Fadahunsi	10	2	22	3	
Vanderpuje-Orgle	10	3	31	5	(4w)
Ntinu	1	1	0	0	
S.Kpundeh	0.1	0	0	1	

Umpires: D.Ker (Argentina) and H.Reid (U.S.A.)   Man of the Match: O.E.Ukpong

O.E.Ukpong retired hurt on 51 with the score at 118/2 and returned at the fall of the sixth wicket.

NAMIBIA v PAPUA NEW GUINEA   (Minor Placings Play-Off Match)

Played at University of Malaya, Kuala Lumpur, April 1, 1997.

Papua New Guinea won by 5 runs   Toss: Papua New Guinea

PAPUA NEW GUINEA		
L.Leka	b Coetzee	35
K.Vuivagi	c Barnard b Ackerman	2
J.Ovia	b Coetzee	0
†J.Maha	b Coetzee	4
N.Maha	lbw b Ackerman	0
*V.Pala	c B.Kotze b Keulder	39
W.Kila	st M.van Schoor b Barnard	19
K.Ilaraki	b Barnard	7
R.H.Ipi	lbw b Barnard	0
T.Raka	not out	6
F.Arua	run out	9
Extras	lb 2, w 10, nb 1	13
Total	(all out, 27.3 overs)	134

1-31(2), 2-32(3), 3-43(4), 4-50(5), 5-50(1), 6-84(7),
7-104(8), 8-104(9), 9-118(6), 10-134(10)

NAMIBIA		
D.Seager	c J.Maha b Arua	4
I.J.Stevenson	run out	32
*D.Keulder	b Ilaraki	13
B.G.Murgatroyd	run out	5
D.Kotze	c Ipi b Pala	19
†M.van Schoor	c J.Maha b Pala	6
B.W.Ackerman	c Ilaraki b N.Maha	1
M.R.Barnard	b Pala	14
I.van Schoor	b Pala	5
B.Kotze	not out	8
D.Coetzee	b Pala	0
Extras	b 3, lb 9, w 9, nb 1	22
Total	(all out, 47.5 overs)	129

1-5(1), 2-48(3), 3-55(4), 4-87(2), 5-101(6),
6-102(5), 7-103(7), 8-110(9), 9-129(8), 10-129(11)

Namibia Bowling

	O	M	R	W	
Ackerman	6	0	26	2	(5w,1nb)
B.Kotze	2	0	17	0	(3w)
Coetzee	7	0	24	3	
I.van Schoor	5	0	33	0	(2w,1nb)
Barnard	5.3	0	18	3	
Keulder	2	0	14	1	

Papua New Guinea Bowling

	O	M	R	W	
Raka	7	1	22	0	(3w)
Arua	7	1	15	1	(3w)
Ipi	7	1	11	0	(1w,1nb)
Ilaraki	10	1	33	1	(1w)
N.Maha	10	2	20	1	
Pala	6.5	2	16	5	

Umpires: D.Beltran (Gibraltar) and N.Gudker (Israel)   Man of the Match: V.Pala

EAST AND CENTRAL AFRICA v ITALY   (Minor Placings Play-Off Match)
Played at University of Malaya, Kuala Lumpur, April 2, 1997.

No result   Toss: East and Central Africa

EAST AND CENTRAL AFRICA			ITALY
A.Ebrahim	st Kariyawasam b Giordano	12	*A.Pezzi
M.B.Musoke	st Kariyawasam b de Mel	1	†K.Kariyawasam
H.Bags	c Akhlaq Qureshi b Giordano	34	Ahklaq Qureshi
*Imran Brohi	c and b da Costa	32	Mohammad Razzaq
Y.S.Patel	b Akhlaq Qureshi	95	S.de Mel
C.M.Gomm	c Maggio b da Costa	5	B.Giordano
T.L.Mbazzi	lbw b Zuppiroli	6	V.Zuppiroli
J.Komakech	b Zuppiroli	0	A.Amati
†A.N.Paliwala	not out	15	A.Pieri
F.Nsubuka	c Kariyawasam		M.B.M.da Costa
	b Akhlaq Qureshi	4	
I.I.Mohamed	b Akhlaq Qureshi	0	R.Maggio
Extras	b 1, lb 8, w 19	28	
		—	
Total	(all out, 49.5 overs)	232	

1-3(2), 2-48(3), 3-64(1), 4-97(4), 5-119(6), 6-159(7),
7-161(8), 8-224(5), 9-232(10), 10-232(11)

Italy Bowling

	O	M	R	W	
Akhlaq Qureshi	9.5	2	30	3	(1w)
de Mel	10	2	30	1	
Giordano	10	0	61	2	(1w)
da Costa	10	0	35	2	
Mohammad Razzaq	2	0	19	0	(4w)
Amati	4	0	18	0	(4w)
Zuppiroli	4	0	30	2	(9w)

Umpires: S.Bachitar (Singapore) and A.O.D.George (West Africa)   Man of the Match: no award

Play started 75 minutes late at 10:45am with 50 overs per side still scheduled. Heavy rain during the lunch interval caused the match to be abandoned.

GIBRALTAR v WEST AFRICA   (Minor Placings Play-Off Match)
Played at Victoria Institute, Kuala Lumpur, April 2, 1997.

No result   Toss: Gibraltar

WEST AFRICA			GIBRALTAR		
K.Sagoe	c Shephard b De'Ath	1	D.Robeson	b Fadahunsi	0
O.E.Ukpong	lbw b Churaman	7	R.Phillips	not out	4
†A.Kpundeh	b De'Ath	23	R.Buzaglo	not out	3
G.I.Wiltshire	c Cary b De'Ath	6	N.Churaman		
S.Kpundeh	c Shephard b Mills	7	D.De'Ath		
U.Ntinu	c Cary b De'Ath	2	G.Mills		
*O.O.Agodo	st Shephard b Phillips	36	T.Garcia		
J.Omoigui	c and b Garcia	12	S.Cary		
S.Fadahunsi	c Garcia b Cary	3	†S.Shephard		
O.Idowu	not out	18	T.Buzaglo		
P.D.Vanderpuje-Orgle	c anb Churaman	4	*C.Rocca		
Extras	b 1, lb 3, w 9	13	Extras	nb 3	3
		—			—
Total	(all out, 49.2 overs)	132	Total	(1 wicket, 2 overs)	10

1-3(1), 2-22(2), 3-34(4), 4-49(3), 5-49(5), 6-51(6),   1-0(1)
7-84(8), 8-97(9), 9-119(7), 10-132(11)

Gibraltar Bowling						West Africa Bowling					
	O	M	R	W			O	M	R	W	
Churaman	9.2	2	23	2	(3w)	Fadahunsi	1	0	4	1	(1nb)
De'Ath	10	1	25	4	(1w)	Vanderpuje-Orgle	1	0	6	0	
Mills	7	1	26	1	(2w)						
Garcia	10	2	24	1							
Cary	10	4	20	1							
Phillips	3	0	10	1							

Umpires: G.F.Malik (U.A.E) and W.Maha (Papua New Guinea)   Man of the Match: no award

Rain caused the match to be abandoned. West Africa advance on overall tournament net run-rate.

MALAYSIA v SINGAPORE (Minor Placings Play-Off Match)
Played at Rubber Research Institute, April 2, 1997.

Singapore won on higher comparative scoring rate   Toss: Singapore

MALAYSIA			SINGAPORE		
S.V.Segeran	c and b Muruthi	41	M.H.Sithawalla	st K.Ramadas	15
				b D.Ramadas	
Saat Jalil	lbw b Wilson	0	A.J.Ranggi	c K.Ramadas b Navaratnam	1
V.R.Rajah	c Mohamed b Martens	1	D.J.Chelvathurai	lbw b Menon	9
M.A.Williams	c Stone b Martens	6	*R.T.Y.Mohamed	not out	11
*R.Menon	lbw b Martens	3	G.S.Wilson	not out	7
S.N.Jeevandran	c Muruthi b David	11	R.S.R.Martens		
S.Navaratnam	b David	13	†J.H.Stone		
†K.Ramadas	run out	0	C.J.F.Gunningham		
R.M.Selvaratnam	c Wilson b David	9	S.Muruthi		
D.Ramadas	lbw b Mohamed	19	R.Chandran		
M.A.Muniandy	not out	13	R.David		
Extras	lb 2, w 11, nb 1	14	Extras	lb 2, w 9	11
Total	(all out, 48.2 overs)	130	Total	(3 wickets, 18.1 overs)	54

1-3(2), 2-10(3), 3-23(4), 4-38(5), 5-66(6), 6-76(1),
7-78(8), 8-97(9), 9-98(7), 10-130(10)

1-2(2), 2-34(3), 3-38(1)

Singapore Bowling	O	M	R	W		Malaysia Bowling	O	M	R	W	
Wilson	10	2	30	1	(1w)	Muniandy	4	0	12	0	(4w)
Martens	9	0	42	3	(6w,2nb)	Navaratnam	4	1	15	1	(2w)
Mohamed	9.2	2	17	1	(1w)	Selvaratnam	3	0	7	0	(2w)
Muruthi	10	2	20	1		Menon	3.1	0	8	1	(1w)
David	10	4	19	3	(3w,2nb)	D.Ramadas	3	1	4	1	
						Jeevandran	1	0	6	0	

Umpires: R.Butler (Bermuda) and N.Gudker (Israel)   Man of the Match: no award

Rain stopped play at 2.41pm with Singapore on 31/1 after 14 overs. Play was resumed at 5.51pm with Singapore set a target of 54 in 20 overs under the Duckworth-Lewis method.

ARGENTINA v ISRAEL (Minor Placings Play-Off Match)
Played at Victoria Institute, Kuala Lumpur, 6 April 1997.

Argentina won by 9 wickets   Toss: Israel

ISRAEL			ARGENTINA		
L.Hall	run out	7	M.J.Paterlini	not out	29
Y.Nagavkar	lbw b Irigoyan	26	B.C.Roberts	c Talkar b Hall	30
A.Talkar	c Perez Rivero b Tunon	1	*G.P.Kirschbaum	not out	1
D.Silver	c Arizaga b Irigoyan	2	G.F.Arizaga		
*H.Awasker	c Roberts b Arizaga	0	B.I.Irigoyan		
R.Ashton	c Roberts b Arizaga	3	†M.O.Juarez		
B.Kehimkar	c Juarez b Arizaga	5	D.M.Lord		
M.Jawalekar	lbw b Irigoyan	3	M.D.Morris		
M.Wadavakar	c Roberts b Pereyra	2	H.P.Pereyra		
†P.Smith	lbw b Irigoyan	0	A.Perez Rivero		
V.E.Worrell	not out	0	C.J.Tunon		
Extras	w 14, nb 1	15	Extras	w 5	5
Total	(all out, 21.5 overs)	64	Total	(1 wicket, 27.3 overs)	65

1-12(1), 2-17(3), 3-37(4), 4-42(2), 5-43(5), 6-52(7),
7-55(6), 8-62(8), 9-62(10), 10-64(9)

1-61(2)

Argentina Bowling	O	M	R	W		Israel Bowling	O	M	R	W	
Lord	3	0	17	0	(1w,1nb)	Worrell	4	0	13	0	
Tunon	5	2	15	1	(4w)	Kehimkar	6	2	8	0	(2w)
Irigoyan	8	2	13	4	(2w)	Awasker	10	2	19	0	(1w)
Arizaga	5	1	17	3	(7w)	Ashton	2	0	10	0	
Pereyra	0.5	0	2	1		Wadavakar	2	0	11	0	(2w)
						Hall	3.3	1	4	1	

Umpires: R.Butler (Bermuda) and H.Reid (U.S.A.)   Man of the Match: B.Irigoyan

ARGENTINA v GIBRALTAR (Play-Off for Nineteenth Place)
Played at Royal Selangor Club, Bukit Kiara, Kuala Lumpur, April 1, 1997.

Gibraltar won by 4 wickets Toss: Gibraltar

ARGENTINA		
M.J.Paterlini	b Cary	11
B.C.Roberts	c Cary b Mills	2
*G.P.Kirschbaum	c Mills b De'Ath	17
M.D.Morris	b De'Ath	18
B.I.Irigoyan	c Shephard b Churaman	39
†M.O.Juarez	c Shephard b Garcia	6
A.Perez Rivero	c Garcia b Churaman	13
H.P.Pereyra	lbw b Garcia	1
G.F.Arizaga	run out	5
C.J.Tunon	c Rocca b Mills	19
D.M.Lord	not out	1
Extras	b 6, lb 3, w 7, nb 2	18
Total	(all out, 46.3 overs)	150

1-8(2), 2-34(1), 3-56(3), 4-58(4), 5-85(6), 6-122(5),
7-124(7), 8-124(8), 9-136(9), 10-150(10)

GIBRALTAR		
R.Buzaglo	c Juarez b Irigoyan	4
N.Churaman	lbw b Irigoyan	2
*C.Rocca	run out	22
T.Buzaglo	lbw b Lord	48
D.Johnson	lbw b Perez Rivero	21
†S.Shephard	c and b Lord	2
R.Phillips	not out	15
T.Garcia	not out	4
G.De'Ath		
S.Cary		
G.Mills		
Extras	b 1, lb 3, w 27, nb 2	33
Total	(6 wickets, 41.1 overs)	151

1-10(1), 2-25(2), 3-67(3), 4-105(4), 5-112(6),
6-146(5)

Gibraltar Bowling

	O	M	R	W	
Mills	6.3	0	24	2	(2w,2nb)
Churaman	10	2	26	2	(2w,1nb)
Cary	8	0	30	1	(1w,1nb)
De'Ath	10	2	21	2	
Garcia	10	1	26	2	(2w)
Johnson	2	0	14	0	

Argentina Bowling

	O	M	R	W	
Irigoyan	10	0	40	2	(9w,1nb)
Tunon	4	0	17	0	(5w)
Perez Rivero	7	1	28	1	(1nb)
Arizaga	7	0	25	0	(5w)
Pereyra	8.1	1	21	0	
Lord	5	1	16	2	(8w)

Umpires: C.Hoare (Canada) and Khoo Chai Huat (Malaysia)   Man of the Match: T.Buzaglo

EAST AND CENTRAL AFRICA v WEST AFRICA (Play-Off for Seventeenth Place)
Played at Royal Military College, Kuala Lumpur, April 4, 1997.

East and Central Africa won by 45 runs   Toss: East and Central Africa

EAST AND CENTRAL AFRICA		
A.Ebrahim	c Omoigui b Ukpong	42
M.B.Musoke	b Fadahunsi	4
H.Bags	c Ntinu b Vanderpuje-Orgle	9
*Imran Brohi	b Ntinu	15
C.M.Gomm	c A.Kpundeh b Idowu	7
Y.S.Patel	b Ntinu	1
T.L.Mbazzi	c Nutsugah b Idowu	7
†J.Komakech	c Ukpong b Fadahunsi	26
A.N.Paliwala	not out	11
F.Nsubuka	lbw b Fadahunsi	0
I.I.Mohamed	run out	3
Extras	b 9, lb 5, w 18, nb 1	33
Total	(all out, 49.4 overs)	158

1-14(2), 2-46(3), 3-77(4), 4-80(5), 5-83(6), 6-97(7),
7-136(1), 8-150(8), 9-151(10), 10-158(11)

WEST AFRICA		
K.Sagoe	c Mbazzi b Mohamed	17
†A.Kpundeh	b Gomm	11
O.Ukpong	run out	20
J.Omoigui	lbw b Imran Brohi	32
U.Ntinu	c Imran Brohi b Mohamed	0
*O.O.Agodo	run out	7
E.Nutsugah	lbw b Imran Brohi	0
S.Kpundeh	c Komakech b Imran Brohi	5
O.Idowu	not out	1
S.Fadahunsi	c Komakech b Mbazzi	0
P.D.Vanderpuje-Orgle	b Mbazzi	0
Extras	b 3, lb 5, w 11, nb 1	20
Total	(all out, 42.2 overs)	113

1-18(2), 2-60(1), 3-62(3), 4-62(5), 5-95(6), 6-95(7),
7-107(8), 8-112(4), 9-113(10), 10-113(11)

West Africa Bowling

	O	M	R	W	
Fadahunsi	8.4	1	23	3	(1w)
Vanderpuje-Orgle	10	0	40	1	(2w)
Ntinu	10	2	22	2	(6w,1nb)
Idowu	10	0	25	2	(3w)
Ukpong	7	1	21	1	(1w)
S.Kpundeh	4	1	13	0	(1w)

East and Central Africa Bowling

	O	M	R	W	
Gomm	4	0	16	1	(4w)
Patel	4	0	17	0	(4w,1nb)
Mbazzi	7.2	0	26	2	(2w)
Nsubuka	10	4	15	0	
Mohamed	10	1	15	2	
Paliwala	3	0	10	0	
Imran Brohi	4	1	6	3	

Umpires: D.Beltran (Gibraltar) and A.S.Peter (Malaysia)   Man of the Match: Imran Brohi

A.Ebrahim retired hurt on 26 with the score at 56/3 and returned at the fall of the fifth wicket.

MALAYSIA v NAMIBIA   (Play-Off for Fifteenth Place)

Played at Tenaga Nasional Sports Complex (Kilat Kelab), Kuala Lumpur, April 4, 1997.

Namibia won by 7 wickets   Toss: Namibia

MALAYSIA			NAMIBIA		
S.V.Segeran	c Keulder b Thirion	27	M.R.Barnard	c K.Ramadas b Selvaratnam	19
V.R.Rajah	c Keulder b Barnard	19	I.J.Stevenson	lbw b D.Ramadas	29
*D.Ramadas	b Keulder	1	*D.Keulder	c K.Ramadas b Selvaratnam	45
M.A.Williams	b Keulder	0	B.G.Murgatroyd	not out	29
S.Navaratnam	c I.van Schoor b Van Vuuren	41	D.Kotze	not out	12
Tan Kim Hing	c and b Kotze	9	J.Thirion		
†K.Ramadas	c Keulder b Kotze	1	M.Karg		
R.M.Selvaratnam	c Murgatroyd b van Vuuren	9	†M.van Schoor		
S.N.Jeevandran	b van Vuuren	11	I.van Schoor		
M.A.Muniandy	b van Vuuren	0	D.Coetzee		
V.Ramadass	not out	0	R.van Vuuren		
Extras	b 3, lb 5, w 16	24	Extras	b 1, lb 1, w 11	13
Total	(all out, 48.3 overs)	142	Total	(3 wickets, 35.3 overs)	147

1-56(2), 2-61(3), 3-61(4), 4-65(1), 5-108(6),   1-25(1), 2-70(2), 3-111(3)
6-111(7), 7-120(5), 8-130(8), 9-131(10), 10-142(9)

Namibia Bowling	O	M	R	W		Malaysia Bowling	O	M	R	W	
van Vuuren	8.3	0	27	4	(8w)	Muniandy	6	1	13	0	(1w)
Coetzee	3	0	17	0	(4w)	Jeevandran	6	0	19	0	
Barnard	10	2	17	1	(1w)	Navaratnam	3	0	18	0	(3w)
I.van Schoor	7	1	19	0	(1w)	Tan Kim Hing	3	0	11	0	
Keulder	9	4	19	2	(2w)	Selvaratnam	8	1	25	2	(1w)
Thirion	6	0	19	1		Ramadass	6	1	26	0	(4w,1nb)
Kotze	5	2	16	2		D.Ramadas	2	0	13	1	
						Williams	1	0	11	0	
						Segeran	0.3	0	9	0	(1w)

Umpires: R.Mahomed (East and Central Africa) and W.Smith (Scotland)   Man of the Match: D.Keulder

PAPUA NEW GUINEA v SINGAPORE   (Play-Off for Thirteenth Place)

Played at Royal Selangor Club, Bukit Kiara, Kuala Lumpur, April 5, 1997.

Papua New Guinea won by 70 runs   Toss: Papua New Guinea

PAPUA NEW GUINEA			SINGAPORE		
†I.Morea	b Wilson	0	M.H.Sithawalla	c Ovia b Raka	11
C.Amini	lbw b Martens	6	A.J.Ranggi	b Raka	14
V.B.Kevau	lbw b Mohamed	32	D.J.Chelvathurai	b N.Maha	2
J.Ovia	lbw b Wilson	8	R.Chandran	c Arua b Pala	10
J.Maha	c Muruthi b Mohamed	18	*R.T.Y.Mohamed	c Pala b N.Maha	0
N.Maha	b Chelvathurai	45	G.S.Wilson	c Pala b N.Maha	8
R.H.Ipi	c Stone b Wilson	24	C.J.F.Gunningham	c Arua b Pala	1
*V.Pala	b Muruthi	0	R.David	c Kevau b N.Maha	0
T.Raka	run out	12	†J.H.Stone	b Amini	11
T.Gaudi	not out	3	S.Muruthi	run out	7
F.Arua	lbw b Chelvathurai	1	R.S.R.Martens	not out	3
Extras	b 3, lb 5, w 9	17	Extras	b 2, lb 4, w 23	29
Total	(all out, 45.1 overs)	166	Total	(all out, 41.4 overs)	96

1-0(1), 2-12(2), 3-36(4), 4-71(5), 5-94(6), 6-141(7),   1-29(1), 2-36(3), 3-36(2), 4-41(5), 5-56(4), 6-59(7),
7-142(8), 8-162(9), 9-164(6), 10-166(11)   7-60(8), 8-67(6), 9-87(10), 10-96(9)

Singapore Bowling	O	M	R	W		Papua New Guinea Bowling	O	M	R	W	
Wilson	10	1	53	3	(4w)	Raka	10	2	19	2	(5w)
Martens	6	1	11	1	(1w)	Arua	10	0	23	0	(5w)
Mohamed	10	3	18	2	(2w)	Gaudi	10	2	23	4	(8w)
David	7	1	29	0	(2w)	Pala	8	2	14	2	(3w)
Muruthi	9	0	35	1		Amini	3.4	0	11	1	(1w)
Chelvathurai	3.1	1	12	2							

Umpires: G.F.Mailk (U.A.E.) and C.Hoare (Canada)   Man of the Match: T.Gaudi

UNITED ARAB EMIRATES v UNITED STATES OF AMERICA
(Philip Snow Plate Semi-Final)

Played at Victoria Institute, Kuala Lumpur, April 1, 1997.

United Arab Emirates won by 34 runs · Toss: United Arab Emirates

U.A.E.		
Azhar Saeed	c Kallicharran b Dennis	12
Adnan Mushtaq	c Denny b Dennis	0
M.V.Perera	c Denny b Benjamin	5
†Ali Akbar Rana	c Denny b Kallicharran	32
Salim Raza	st Denny b Kallicharran	30
*Saeed-al-Saffar	run out	5
M.Hyder	not out	29
Mohammed Tauqeer	b Benjamin	24
Asim Saeed	c Lachman b Bacchus	11
Ahmed Nadeem	not out	15
Mohammad Atif		
Extras	lb 5, w 21	26
Total	(8 wickets, 50 overs)	189

1-7(2), 2-25(1), 3-25(3), 4-81(5), 5-99(6), 6-99(4),
7-145(8), 8-162(9)

U.S.A.		
M.C.Adams	c Ali Akbar Rana b Salim Raza	13
P.Singh	c Ali Akbar Rana b Asim Saeed	9
†R.Denny	run out	12
A.D.Texeira	b Asim Saeed	0
*S.F.A.F.Bacchus	c and b Azhar Saeed	51
R.Lachman	c Ali Akbar Rana b Azhar Saeed	20
Z.Amin	c Saeed-al-Saffar b Ahmed Nadeem	16
D.I.Kallicharran	c Ahmed Nadeem b Azhar Saeed	3
K.Dennis	not out	15
E.Grant	run out	4
R.Benjamin	lbw b Ahmed Nadeem	0
Extras	b 1, w 8, nb 3	12
Total	(all out, 40.2 overs)	155

1-32(2), 2-32(1), 3-39(4), 4-54(3), 5-105(6), 6-128(5),
7-136(8), 8-137(7), 9-153(10), 10-155(11)

U.S.A. Bowling

	O	M	R	W	
Dennis	9	3	37	2	(7w)
Grant	8	2	23	0	(4w)
Benjamin	10	1	41	2	(4w)
Amin	10	1	43	0	
Kallicharran	10	1	32	2	(6w)
Bacchus	3	0	8	1	

U.A.E. Bowling

	O	M	R	W	
Ahmed Nadeem	9.2	2	26	2	(5w)
Asim Saeed	8	1	25	2	(2w,3nb)
Salim Raza	9	1	39	1	
Saeed-al-Saffar	3	1	15	0	(1w)
Azhar Saeed	9	0	30	3	
Perera	1	0	11	0	
Mohammad Atif	1	0	8	0	

Umpires: T.Cooper (Fiji) and V.M.Rafik (East and Central Africa)   Man of the Match: S.F.A.F.Bacchus

BERMUDA v FIJI   (Philip Snow Plate Semi-Final)

Played at Perbadanan Kemajuan Negari Selangor, Kuala Lumpur, April 2, 1997.

No result · Toss: Bermuda

BERMUDA		
*A.B.Steede	lbw b Maxwell	21
R.L.Trott	c T.Cakacaka b Batina	1
G.S.Smith	b Bartina	8
C.J.Smith	b Batina	6
J.J.Tucker	c I.Cakacaka b Maxwell	17
†D.A.Minors	c Tukana b Mateyawa	18
W.A.E.Manders	c Maxwell b Mateyawa	28
C.S.T.Hill	c and b Maxwell	22
D.W.Hollis	lbw b Maxwell	0
K.Hurdle	c Seuvou b Mateyawa	0
K.S.Fox	not out	0
Extras	(b 3, lb 7, w 10, nb 5)	25
Total	(all out, 46 overs)	146

1-5(2), 2-20(3), 3-32(4), 4-62(1), 5-68(5), 6-107(6),
7-145(8), 8-145(9), 9-146(10), 10-146(7)

FIJI		
*L.Sorovakatini	c and b Hill	7
†T.Cakacaka	st Minors b Hill	0
J.Sorovakatini	c Manders b Hurdle	17
N.D.Maxwell	not out	5
T.Batina	not out	2
W.Tukana		
I.Cakacaka		
A.Sorovakatini		
J.Mateyawa		
J.Seuvou		
A.Tawatatau		
Extras	w 14, nb 1	15
Total	(3 wickets, 12.3 overs)	46

1-7(2), 2-32(3), 3-32(1)

Fiji Bowling

	O	M	R	W	
Tawatatau	10	5	12	0	(2w)
Batina	7	0	23	3	(3w)
Seuvou	7	1	35	0	(2w)
Maxwell	9	3	17	4	(2w,2nb)
Mateyawa	9	0	35	3	(2nb)
L.Sorovakatini	4	0	14	0	(1w,1nb)

Bermuda Bowling

	O	M	R	W	
Hurdle	5	2	16	1	(7w,1nb)
Hill	6	0	27	2	(7w)
Tucker	1.3	0	3	0	

Umpires: D.Beltran (Gibraltar) and C.Sen (Malaysia)   Man of the Match: no award

Rain stopped play at 2.41pm and the match was later abandoned.

Bermuda advanced to the Philip Snow Trophy Final on net run rate.

FIJI v UNITED STATES OF AMERICA   (Play-Off for Eleventh Place)

Played at Royal Military College, Kuala Lumpur, April 5, 1997.

Fiji won by 5 wickets   Toss: United States of America

U.S.A.			FIJI		
M.C.Adams	c Batina b Mateyawa	27	J.Bulabalavu	lbw b Amin	37
Sohail Alvi	b Mateyawa	24	E.Tadu	c Sohail Alvi b Kallicharran	36
†A.D.Texeira	c Sorovakatini b Tukana	9	J.Sorovakatini	run out	0
*S.F.A.F.Bacchus	c Tukana b Maxwell	1	N.D.Maxwell	c Texeira b Abdul Nazir	33
R.Lachman	b Tawatatau	30	*T.Batina	lbw b Kallicharran	6
D.I.Kallicharran	lbw b Tukana	2	W.Tukana	not out	34
Aijaz Ali	c Bulabalavu b Tukana	44	I.Cakacaka	not out	29
Z.Amin	c Tadu b Tukana	11	J.Mateyawa		
K.Dennis	c Bulabalavu b I.Cakacaka	13	A.Tawatatau		
Nazir Islam	c Bulabalavu b Tukana	0	J.Seuvou		
Abdul Nazir	not out	0	†T.Cakacaka		
Extras	lb 11, w 18, nb 3	32	Extras	b 4, lb 5, w 10, nb 3	22
Total	(all out, 48.3 overs)	193	Total	(5 wickets, 47 overs)	197

1-63(1), 2-66(2), 3-67(4), 4-76(3), 5-81(6),
6-144(5), 7-172(7), 8-189(8), 9-191(10), 10-193(9)

1-80(2), 2-81(3), 3-83(1), 4-100(5), 5-151(4)

Fiji Bowling	O	M	R	W		U.S.A. Bowling	O	M	R	W	
Tawatatau	10	3	27	1	(2w,1nb)	Dennis	8	0	33	0	(1w,3nb)
Batina	7	0	32	0	(6w)	Abdul Nazir	10	0	54	1	(5w,1nb)
Seuvou	3	0	14	0	(1w)	Nazir Islam	2	0	11	0	
Maxwell	7	1	24	1	(2w,2nb)	Kallicharran	10	1	33	2	(2w,1nb)
Mateyawa	10	1	34	2	(2w)	Amin	10	1	27	1	(1w)
Tukana	7	0	31	5	(7w)	Bacchus	7	1	30	0	(1w)
I.Cakacaka	4.3	0	20	1							

Umpires: A.A.Shaheen (Bangladesh) and Ismail Khan   Man of the Match: W.Tukana

Rain stopped play at 3.09pm after 20 overs. Play resumed at 3.35pm.

BERMUDA v UNITED ARAB EMIRATES   (Philip Snow Plate Final – Ninth Place)

Played at Kelab Aman, Kuala Lumpur, April 5, 1997.

Bermuda won by 57 runs   Toss: Bermuda

BERMUDA			U.A.E.		
*A.B.Steede	c Ali Akbar Khan b Asim Saeed	14	Azhar Saeed	c Manders b Hill	2
R.L.Trott	c Mohammed Tauqeer b Arshad Laeeq	37	Arif Yousuf	run out	14
G.S.Smith	c Mohammed Tauqeer b Saeed-al-Saffar	41	Salim Raza	lbw b Hill	37
C.J.Smith	c Saeed-al-Saffar b Hyder	39	†Ali Akbar Rana	b Hollis	29
J.J.Tucker	b Arshad Laeeq	42	Arshad Laeeq	c Manders b Hollis	17
†D.A.Minors	c Ali Akbar Rana b Hyder	0	M.Hyder	run out	2
W.A.E.Manders	lbw b Arshad Laeeq	14	Ahmed Nadeem	c Tucker b Hollis	14
C.S.T.Hill	b Arshad Laeeq	0	*Saeed-al-Saffar	c Trott b Fox	1
D.W.Hollis	not out	3	Mohammed Tauqeer	not out	15
K.Hurdle	not out	3	Asim Saeed	c Trott b Fox	0
K.S.Fox			Mohammad Atif	run out	2
Extras	lb 10, w 9, nb 2	21	Extras	lb 2, w 19, nb 2	23
Total	(8 wickets, 50 overs)	214	Total	(all out, 40.2)	157

1-39(1), 2-86(2), 3-116(3), 4-177(4), 5-177(6),
6-202(7), 7-202(8), 8-209(5)

1-10(1), 2-52(2), 3-64(3), 4-104(5), 5-116(6),
6-120(4), 7-121(8), 8-143(9), 9-151(10), 1-157(11)

U.A.E. Bowling	O	M	R	W		Bermuda Bowling	O	M	R	W	
Ahmed Nadeem	8	0	39	0	(5w)	Hurdle	5.2	0	26	0	(5w,1nb)
Asim Saeed	6	0	25	1	(2w,1nb)	Hill	9	0	39	2	(7w,1nb)
Salim Raza	9	1	36	0		Tucker	6	1	22	0	(5w)
Arshad Laeeq	7	0	28	4	(2w)	Hollis	10	3	20	3	
Saeed-al-Saffar	7	1	23	1		Fox	10	0	48	2	(3w)
Mohammad Atif	1	0	11	0							
Azhar Saeed	6	0	22	0	(1nb)						
Hyder	6	0	20	2							

Umpires: D.Ker (Argentina) and Khoo Chai Huat (Malaysia)   Man of the Match: G.S.Smith

FINAL RANKINGS

1st	Bangladesh	**Winner of the Carlsberg ICC Trophy** Participate in the 1999 World Cup
2nd	Kenya	Participate in the 1999 World Cup
3rd	Scotland	Participate in the 1999 World Cup
4th	Ireland	
5th	Denmark	
6th	Netherlands	
7th	Canada	
8th	Hong Kong	
9th	Bermuda	**Winner of the Philip Snow Plate**
10th	United Arab Emirates	
11th	Fiji	
12th	United States of America	
13th	Papua New Guinea	
14th	Singapore	
15th	Namibia	
16th	Malaysia	
17th	East and Central Africa	
18th	West Africa	
19th	Gibraltar	
20th	Argentina	
21st	Israel Italy	(shared)

A helicopter helps to dry the ground after rain

HIGHLIGHTS OF THE

1997

ICC TROPHY

HIGHEST TEAM TOTALS

312-5	United States of America	v Gibraltar	RRI
303-6	Kenya	v Canada	Tenaga NSC
282	Hong Kong	v Italy	Royal Selangor
278-2	Ireland	v Scotland	Victoria Institute
273	Scotland	v Italy	Univ of Malaya
264-8	Canada	v Namibia	Kelab Aman

LOWEST TEAM TOTALS
(Completed Innings)

26	East & Central Africa	v Netherlands	RMC
32	United States of America	v Kenya	Univ of Malaya
44	Gibraltar	v Kenya	RMC
57	Israel	v West Africa	RMC
64	Israel	v Argentina	Victoria Institute
72	West Africa	v U.A.E.	Royal Selangor
73	Namibia	v Fiji	Royal Selangor

HIGHEST INDIVIDUAL INNINGS

148*	M.O.Odumbe	Kenya	v Canada	Tenaga NSC
147	S.O.Tikolo	Kenya	v Bangladesh	Tenaga NSC
127*	D.A.Lewis	Ireland	v Gibraltar	Victoria Institute
125	M.Diwan	Canada	v Namibia	Kelab Aman
104	J.Tucker	Bermuda	v P.N.G.	Univ of Malaya
102	M.R.Farcy	Hong Kong	v Italy	Royal Selangor
100*	S.F.A.F.Bacchus	U.S.A.	v Gibraltar	RRI

NOTABLE WICKET PARTNERSHIPS

1st	127	I.L.Philip & B.G.Lockie	Scotland	v Italy	Univ of Malaya
	113*	J.D.Curry & A.D.Patterson	Ireland	v Singapore	Kelab Aman
2nd	162	D.A.Lewis & J.D.R.Benson	Ireland	v Gibraltar	Victoria Institute
	134	Azhar Saeed & Arshad Laeeq	U.A.E.	v Argentina	Victoria Institute
	123	I.Liburd & M.Diwan	Canada	v Namibia	Kelab Aman
	114	M.R.Farcy & S.J.Brew	Hong Kong	v Italy	Royal Selangor
3rd	120	M.Diwan & B.E.A.Rajadurai	Canada	v Namibia	Kelab Aman
4th	199	S.O.Tikolo & M.O.Odumbe	Kenya	v Canada	Tenaga NSC
	138	S.O.Tikolo & M.O.Odumbe	Kenya	v Bangladesh	Tenaga NSC
	125	J.Ovia & C.Amini	P.N.G.	v Italy	PKNS
	124	K.M.Deshpande & R.T.Y.Mohamed			
			Singapore	v Gibraltar	Tenaga NSC
	112*	S.O.Tikolo & M.O.Odumbe	Kenya	v Israel	Kelab Aman
7th	111	B.Singh & M.H.Andersen	Denmark	v Argentina	PKNS

BEST INDIVIDUAL BOWLING

7-9	K.A.Khan	Netherlands	v E & C Africa	RMC
5-7	M.A.Suji	Kenya	v U.S.A.	Univ of Malaya
5-14	N.Churaman	Gibraltar	v Israel	RRI
5-16	V.Pala	P.N.G.	v Namibia	Univ of Malaya
5-19	M.H.Andersen	Denmark	v Malaysia	RRI
5-29	S.Rana	Canada	v Fiji	Univ of Malaya
5-31	P.D.Vanderpuje-Orgle	West Africa	v Israel	RMC
5-31	W.Tukana	Fiji	v U.S.A.	RMC
5-51	T.M.Hansen	Denmark	v Canada	Royal Selangor

MOST WICKET-KEEPING DISMISSALS IN A MATCH

5 (4c,1s)	K.Otieno	Kenya	v Canada	Tenaga NSC
5 (4c,1s)	Ali Akbar Rana	U.A.E.	v Denmark	Univ of Malaya

BATSMEN SCORING 250 RUNS IN THE TOURNAMENT

		M	I	NO	Runs	HS	Ave	100	50
M.O.Odumbe	Kenya	10	10	5	493	148*	98.60	1	3
S.O.Tikolo	Kenya	10	10	1	399	147	44.33	1	2
J.D.Curry	Ireland	10	10	2	291	65*	36.37	-	3
M.R.Farcy	Hong Kong	7	7	0	268	102	38.28	1	1
D.A.Lewis	Ireland	9	8	2	256	127*	42.66	1	-
G.Salmond	Scotland	9	8	1	253	59	36.14	-	1

BOWLERS TAKING 15 WICKETS IN THE TOURNAMENT

		O	M	R	W	Ave	BB	4w
A.Y.Karim	Kenya	61.1	12	157	19	8.26	4-7	2
K.A.Khan	Netherlands	57.1	7	195	19	10.26	7-9	3
I.Beven	Scotland	65	10	183	19	9.63	4-20	2
Mohammed Rafique	Bangladesh	57.4	6	203	19	10.68	4-25	1
S.R.M.Sorensen	Denmark	65.5	10	183	18	10.16	3-19	-
M.A.Suji	Kenya	69.4	15	159	17	9.35	5-7	1
N.Churaman	Gibraltar	65.2	12	227	17	13.35	5-14	1
N.G.Doak	Ireland	74.5	11	234	16	14.62	4-9	1
R.P.Lefebvre	Netherlands	58.5	17	105	15	7.00	4-16	1
Arshad Laeeq	U.A.E.	56.3	11	172	15	11.46	4-14	2
B.I.Irigoyan	Argentina	57	4	203	15	13.53	4-13	2

ICC TROPHY
RECORDS

Throughout the record section East & Central Africa records include East Africa in the 1979-86 competitions.

COMPLETE TEAM RECORDS 1979-1997

		M	*W*	*L*	*NR*
Argentina	1979-97	31	4	26	1
Bangladesh	1979-97	43	26	14	3
Bermuda	1979-97	45	30	12	3
Canada	1979-97	42	22	14	6
Denmark	1979-97	36	23	12	1
East & Central Africa	1982-97	37	9	23	5
Fiji	1979-97	39	12	22	5
Gibraltar	1982-97	35	6	24	5
Hong Kong	1982-97	37	15	19	3
Ireland	1994-97	17	9	7	1
Israel	1979-97	40	3	35	2
Italy	1997	5	-	4	1
Kenya	1982-97	39	24	12	3
Malaysia	1979-97	38	8	26	4
Namibia	1994-97	14	7	7	-
Netherlands	1979-97	47	29	12	6
Papua New Guinea	1979-97	41	22	16	3
Scotland	1997	9	6	2	1
Singapore	1979-97	31	8	17	6
Sri Lanka	1979	6	4	1	1
United Arab Emirates	1994-97	16	13	3	-
United States of America	1979-97	39	22	12	5
Wales †	1979	4	2	1	1
West Africa	1982-97	22	5	11	6
Zimbabwe	1982-90	25	23	-	2

† In 1979 Wales (other than Glamorgan), though not an ICC Associate member, filled a vacancy without gaining official points when Gibraltar were a late withdrawal.

HIGHEST TEAM TOTALS

455-9	Papua New Guinea	v Gibraltar	Cannock	1986
425-4	Netherlands	v Israel	Old Silhillians	1986
407-8	Bermuda	v Hong Kong	Griff & Coton	1986
402-4	Netherlands	v Israel	ACC, Amsterdam	1990
396-4	United States of America	v Israel	Solihull Mun.	1986
381-8	Papua New Guinea	v Fiji	Old Hill	1986
377-6	Papua New Guinea	v Israel	Worcester	1986
357-7	Zimbabwe	v Argentina	Fordhouses	1986
356-2	Canada	v Fiji	Kings Heath	1986
356-5	Canada	v P.N.G.	Walsall	1986
355-8	Hong Kong	v West Africa	Sir Ali Muslim	1994

LOWEST TEAM TOTALS
(Completed Innings)

26	East & Central Africa	v Netherlands	RMC	1997
32	United States of America	v Kenya	Univ of Malaya	1997
44	Gibraltar	v Kenya	RMC	1997
45	Israel	v Denmark	Impala	1994
46	Gibraltar	v Canada	Swindon	1986
51	Namibia	v Canada	Nairobi CG	1994
52	Papua New Guinea	v Netherlands	Wolverhampton	1986
55	Gibraltar	v P.N.G.	Market Harborough	1982
57	Israel	v West Africa	RMC	1997

HIGHEST INDIVIDUAL INNINGS

172	S.D.Myles	Hong Kong	v Gibraltar	Bridgnorth	1986
169*	R.Gomes	Netherlands	v Israel	ACC, Amsterdam	1990
164*	P.Prashad	Canada	v P.N.G.	Walsall	1986
162	S.R.Atkinson	Netherlands	v Israel	Old Silhillians	1986
162	B.Harry	P.N.G.	v Israel	Worcester	1986
158*	M.O.Odumbe	Kenya	v Bermuda	Aga Khan	1994
155*	R.E.Lifmann	Netherlands	v Malaysia	Redditch	1982
154*	R.J.Elferink	Netherlands	v Fiji	Hinckley	1982
154	N.E.Clarke	Netherlands	v Israel	ACC, Amsterdam	1990

HIGHEST WICKET PARTNERSHIPS

1st	257	R.F.Schoonheim & R.E.Lifmann	Netherlands	v Malaysia	Redditch	1986
2nd	248	R.Gomes & N.E.Clarke	Netherlands	v Israel	Amsterdam	1990
3rd	194	S.D.Myles & N.P.Stearns	Hong Kong	v Gibraltar	Bridgnorth	1986
4th	199	S.O.Tikolo & M.O.Odumbe	Kenya	v Canada	Tenaga NSC	1997
5th	135*	K.S.Khan & K.Lorick	U.S.A.	v Israel	Solihull Mun.	1986
6th	174	G.C.Wallace & P.W.E.Rawson	Zimbabwe	v Argentina	Fordhouses	1986
7th	107	A.Leka & Raki Ila	P.N.G.	v Bermuda	Nuneaton	1986
8th	86*	V.Pala & G.Ravu	P.N.G.	v Canada	Kenilworth	1982
9th	62	M.Yazid Imran & Lim Ju Jing	Malaysia	v Bangladesh	Moseley Ash.	1986
10th	49*	A.Tawatatau & S.K.G.Amin	Fiji	v E&C Africa	ACC, Amst.	1990

BEST INDIVIDUAL BOWLING

7-9	K.A.Khan	Netherlands	v E & C Africa	RMC	1997
7-19	O.H.Mortensen	Denmark	v Israel	Impala	1994
7-21	B.Singh	Canada	v Namibia	Nairobi CG	1994
7-23	S.Ashraful Huq	Bangladesh	v Fiji	Water Orton	1979
6-11	B.Gohel	Hong Kong	v Fiji	Knowle & Dorridge	1986
6-14	R.J.Elferink	Netherlands	v Fiji	Gloucester Spa	1986
6-22	R.J.Elferink	Netherlands	v Israel	Old Silhillians	1986
6-26	A.Kumar	East Africa	v Argentina	Stourbridge	1986
6-38	A.Edwards	Bermuda	v Fiji	Wellington	1986
6-41	P-J.Bakker	Netherlands	v Kenya	HCC, The Hague	1990

MOST WICKET-KEEPING DISMISSALS IN A MATCH

6 (6c)	M.Saddique	Denmark	v Israel	Impala	1994
5 (3c,2s)	R.F.Schoonheim	Netherlands	v Israel	Banbury	1979
5 (4c,1s)	Nasir Ahmed	Bangladesh	v Kenya	VRA, Amsterdam	1990
5 (2c,3s)	Nasir Ahmed	Bangladesh	v Fiji	VOC, Rotterdam	1990
5 (5c)	N.Alu	P.N.G.	v U.S.A.	VRA, Amsterdam	1990
5 (5c)	R.Denny	U.S.A.	v E & C Africa	Nairobi CG	1994
5 (5c)	M.van Schoor	Namibia	v Kenya	Simba Union	1994
5 (4c,1s)	K.Otieno	Kenya	v Canada	Tenaga NSC	1997
5 (4c,1s)	Ali Akbar Rana	U.A.E.	v Denmark	Univ of Malaya	1997

MOST CATCHES BY A FIELDER IN A MATCH

4	M.P.Jarvis	Zimbabwe	v Bangladesh	HCC, The Hague	1990
4	Enamul Hoque	Bangladesh	v Kenya	Simba Union	1994

BATSMEN SCORING 650 RUNS IN A CAREER

		Years	M	I	NO	Runs	HS	Ave	100	50
M.O.Odumbe	Kenya	1990-97	25	24	7	1173	158*	69.00	3	6
N.E.Clarke	Netherlands	1990-94	18	18	4	1040	154	74.28	5	3
R.Gomes	Netherlands	1986-90	18	17	4	772	169*	59.38	3	2
Minhajul Abedin	Bangladesh	1986-97	30	28	4	761	68	31.70	-	4
P.Prashad	Canada	1986-94	18	18	5	747	164*	57.46	3	2
S.W.Lubbers	Netherlands	1979-94	35	30	7	733	81	31.86	-	5
S.O.Tikolo	Kenya	1994-97	19	19	4	719	147	47.93	1	5
W.A.Reid	Bermuda	1979-86	22	22	3	697	128	36.68	1	2
R.P.Lefebvre	Netherlands	1986-97	34	29	6	688	109*	29.91	1	1

BATSMEN SCORING 400 RUNS IN A TOURNAMENT

		Year	M	I	NO	Runs	HS	Ave	100	50
P.Prashad	Canada	1986	8	8	2	533	164*	88.83	3	-
N.E.Clarke	Netherlands	1990	9	9	1	523	154	65.37	2	2
N.E.Clarke	Netherlands	1994	9	9	3	517	121*	86.16	3	1
S.R.Atkinson	Netherlands	1986	10	10	3	508	162	72.57	2	2
R.Gomes	Netherlands	1986	10	9	3	499	127*	83.16	2	2
M.O.Odumbe	Kenya	1997	10	10	5	493	148*	98.60	1	3
S.D.Myles	Hong Kong	1986	8	8	1	408	172	58.28	1	2

BOWLERS TAKING 35 WICKETS IN A CAREER

		Years	O	M	R	W	Ave	BB	4w
O.H.Mortensen	Denmark	1979-94	207.4	52	656	63	10.41	7-19	7
R.P.Lefebvre	Netherlands	1986-97	262.1	60	606	51	11.88	4-16	1
A.Y.Karim	Kenya	1986-97	261.1	41	798	48	16.62	5-20	3
A.Edwards	Bermuda	1986-94	218.2	28	764	44	17.36	6-38	2
N.A.Gibbons	Bermuda	1979-94	251.3	26	960	42	22.85	4-18	2
Minhajul Abedin	Bangladesh	1986-97	161.2	19	579	37	15.64	4-40	1
Enamul Hoque	Bangladesh	1994-97	216.2	34	649	35	18.54	3-18	-

BOWLERS TAKING 20 WICKETS IN A TOURNAMENT

		Year	O	M	R	W	Ave	BB	4w
O.H.Mortensen	Denmark	1986	78.5	11	207	22	9.40	4-15	2
P-J.Bakker	Netherlands	1986	90	15	286	21	13.61	5-18	2

MOST WICKET-KEEPING DISMISSALS IN A CAREER

		Year	Total	Ct	St
A.C.Douglas	Bermuda	1982-90	38	36	2
Nasir Ahmed	Bangladesh	1982-94	35	25	10
R.Denny	U.S.A.	1994-97	26	18	8
R.F.Schoonheim	Netherlands	1979-86	25	22	3
R.H.Scholte	Netherlands	1990-97	24	21	3
M.Harris Abu Bakar	Malaysia	1979-90	24	23	1

Note that D.L.Houghton (Zimbabwe, 1982-90) made 24 dismissals - 7 of these were as an outfielder.

MOST CATCHES BY A FIELDER IN A CAREER

		Year	Total
S.W.Lubbers	Netherlands	1979-97	20
R.P.Lefebvre	Netherlands	1986-97	20
M.O.Odumbe	Kenya	1990-97	18
Enamul Hoque	Bangladesh	1994-97	16
A.Y.Karim	Kenya	1986-97	16
Minhajul Abedin	Bangladesh	1986-97	15

ALL-ROUNDERS SCORING 350 RUNS AND TAKING 25 WICKETS IN A CAREER

			Batting		Bowling	
		Year	Runs	Ave	Wkts	Ave
Minhajul Abedin	Bangladesh	1986-97	761	31.70	37	15.64
N.A.Gibbons	Bermuda	1979-94	631	30.04	42	22.85
S.Henriksen	Denmark	1986-97	459	22.95	27	16.14
G.De'Ath	Gibraltar	1986-97	429	18.65	29	32.75
S.J.Brew	Hong Kong	1994-97	420	30.00	25	17.00
R.J.Elferink	Netherlands	1979-86	387	48.37	28	10.42
R.P.Lefebvre	Netherlands	1986-97	688	29.91	51	11.88
S.W.Lubbers	Netherlands	1979-94	733	31.86	34	22.79
V.Pala	P.N.G.	1979-97	471	27.70	33	19.93

28 OR MORE APPEARANCES IN A CAREER

		Year	Total
H.Awasker	Israel	1982-97	35
S.W.Lubbers	Netherlands	1979-94	35
N.A.Gibbons	Bermuda	1979-94	34
R.P.Lefebvre	Netherlands	1986-97	34
Minhajul Abedin	Bangladesh	1986-97	30
A.Y.Karim	Kenya	1986-97	30
W.A.E.Manders	Bermuda	1986-97	29
J.Mateyawa	Fiji	1982-97	29
T.Buzaglo	Gibraltar	1982-97	29
S.B.Perlman	Israel	1979-97	29
A.Tawatatau	Fiji	1986-97	28
G.De'Ath	Gibraltar	1986-94	28
W.Maha	P.N.G.	1982-94	28

Only career figures for players in the 1997 competition are listed for each country.
† Indicates players who have played first-class cricket.

ARGENTINA

ARIZAGA, Gaston Felipe b 8.5.1974 Buenos Aires. rhb rm. Club: Belgrano Athletic Club.
CIABURRI, Sergio Javier b 20.7.1964 Buenos Aires. rhb rm. Club: Lomas Athletic Club.
FORRESTER, Donald b 11.08.1969 Buenos Aires. rhb ob. Club: Belgrano Athletic Club.
IRIGOYAN, Bernardo Iritxity 3.9.1969 Buenos Aires. rhb rm. Club: Lomas Athletic Club.
JUAREZ, Martin Oscar b 29.9.1964 Lomas De Zamora. rhb wkt. Club: Lomas Athletic Club.
KIRSCHBAUM, Guillermo Patricio b 28.3.1968 Buenos Aires. rhb. Club: Belgrano Athletic
    Club.
LORD, Diego Martin b 26.9.1977 Lomas De Zamora. rhb rm. Club: Lomas Athletic Club.
MORRIS, Miguel David b 15.5.1964 Buenos Aires. rhb. Club: Hurlingham.
PATERLINI, Matias Joaquin b 31.12.1977 Buenos Aires. rhb. Club: St. Alban's Former Pupils.
PEREYRA, Hernan Pablo b 16.3.1970 Lomas De Zamora. rhb sla. Club: St. Alban's Former
    Pupils.
PEREZ RIVERO, Andres Roberto 15.4.1975 Buenos Aires. rhb rm. Belgrano Athletic Club.
RIVEROS, Maximiliano Jose b 7.8.1975 Argentina. rhb rm. Club: Belgrano Athletic Club.
ROBERTS, Brian Cammy b 21.9.1963 Buenos Aires. rhb. Club: Hurlingham.
ROWE, Andres Miguel b 1.8.1975 Buenos Aires. rhb rm. St. Alban's Former Pupils.
TUNON, Christian Jose b 18.6.1971 Lanu's, Buenos Aires. rhb rm. St. Alban's Former Pupils.
VAN STEEDEN, Malcolm Kevin b 10.9.1978 Buenos Aires. rhb wkt. Club: Hurlingham.

Batting	Year	M	I	NO	Runs	HS	Ave	100	50	Ct/St
G.F.Arizaga	1997	5	4	1	20	8*	6.66	-	-	2
S.J.Ciaburri	1990-1997	3	3	1	4	4*	4.00	-	-	1
D.Forrester	1990-1997	15	15	0	325	79	21.66	-	1	10
B.I.Irigoyan	1990-1997	17	16	2	200	43	14.28	-	-	2
M.O.Juarez	1997	6	5	0	23	9	4.60	-	-	6/1
G.P.Kirschbaum	1990-1997	21	21	1	367	57	18.35	-	2	7
D.M.Lord	1997	5	4	3	1	1*	1.00	-	-	2
M.D.Morris	1986 1997	23	22	1	321	61	15.28	-	1	7
M.J.Paterlini	1997	7	7	2	152	77*	30.40	-	1	1
H.P.Pereyra	1990-1997	21	18	4	76	16	5.42	-	-	6
A.R.Perez Rivero	1994-1997	8	7	0	37	13	5.28	-	-	5
M.J.Riveros	1997	2	1	0	4	4	4.00	-	-	1
B.C.Roberts	1986-1997	19	19	1	164	30	9.11	-	-	5
A.M.Rowe	1997	1	-	-	-	-	-	-	-	-
C.J.Tuñón	1994-1997	10	9	0	46	19	5.11	-	-	1
M.K.van Steeden	1997	3	3	0	6	4	2.00	-	-	1

Bowling	Year	O	M	R	W	Ave	BB	4w
G.F.Arizaga	1997	25.3	1	128	6	21.33	3-17	-
S.J.Ciaburri	1990-1997	6	0	71	0	-	-	-
D.Forrester	1990-1997	85.3	1	458	12	38.16	3-66	-
B.I.Irigoyan	1990-1997	79	4	307	16	19.18	4-13	2
D.M. Lord	1997	24	1	112	5	22.40	2-16	-
H.P.Pereyra	1990-1997	177.2	14	630	28	22.50	4-28	1
A.R.Perez Rivero	1994-1997	40	2	185	8	23.12	4-47	1
M.J.Riveros	1997	5	0	34	0	-	-	-
A.M.Rowe	1997	2	0	17	0	-	-	-
C.J.Tuñón	1994-1997	52	2	225	10	22.50	5-37	1

Highest Totals
For: 226-6   v U.S.A.   Sir Ali Muslim   1994
Against: 357-7   by Zimbabwe   Fordhouses   1986

Highest Individual Innings
For: 79   D.Forrester   v Fiji   Impala   1994
Against: 125   P.W.E.Rawson   for Zimbabwe   Fordhouses   1986

Best Bowling Analysis

For:	5-37	C.J.Tuñón	v E & C Africa	Premier	1994
Against:	6-26	Anil Kumar	for East Africa	Stourbridge	1986

Most in a Career

Runs:	367	(Ave 18.35)	G.P.Kirschbaum	1990-97
Wickets:	28	(Ave 22.50)	H.P.Pereyra	1990-97
Matches:	23		M.D.Morris	1986-97

Most in a Tournament

Runs:	230	(Ave 32.86)	D.Forrester	1994
Wickets:	15	(Ave 13.53)	B.I.Irigoyan	1997

Record Wicket Partnerships

1st	87	G.P.Kirschbaum & B.I.Irigoyen	v U.S.A.	Sir Ali Muslim	1994
2nd	48	L.Alonso & A.G.Morris	v Zimbabwe	Fordhouses	1986
3rd	54	G.P.Kirschbaum & D.Forrester	v Fiji	Impala	1994
4th	77	M.D.Morris & G.P.Kirschbaum	v Fiji	Klein Zwitserland	1990
5th	55	M.J.Paterlini and H.P.Pereyra	v U.A.E.	Victoria Institute	1997
6th	42	M.E.Ryan & A.G.Morris	v E & C Africa	HCC, The Hague	1990
7th	28	P.R.Stocks & M.Morris	v East Africa	Stourbridge	1986
8th	32	D.A.Culley & P.R.Stocks	v Malaysia	Studley	1986
9th	36	L.A.Jooris & C.J.Tuñón	v P.N.G.	Sir Ali Muslim	1994
10th	26	G.P.Kirschbaum & A.H.Gooding	v Israel	HCC, The Hague	1990

BANGLADESH

AKRAM Hussain KHAN, Mohammed b 1.2.1967 Chittagong. rhb rm.
AMINUL ISLAM b 2.2.1968 Dhaka. rhb ob.
ATHAR ALI KHAN b 10.2.1962 Dhaka rhb rm.
ENAMUL HOQUE "Moni" b 27.2.1966 Comilla (shown in previous books as E.H.Moni). rhb sla.
HASIBUL HUSSAIN b 3.6.1977 Dhaka.
JAHANGIR ALAM b 5.3.1973 Narayangonj.
KHALED MAHMUD "Sujan" b 26.7.1971 Dhaka.
KHALED MASHUD "Pilot" b 8.2.1976 Rajshahi. wkt.
MINHAJUL ABEDIN "Nannu" b 25.9.1965 Chittagong. rhb ob.
MOHAMMED RAFIQUE b 15.5.1970 Dhaka. sla.
NAIMUR RAHMAN "Durjoy" b 19.9.1974 Dhaka.
SAIFUL ISLAM KHAN b 1.4.1969 Mymensingh.
SANVAR HOSSAIN b 5.8.1973 Mymensingh.

Batting	Year	M	I	NO	Runs	HS	Ave	100	50	Ct/St
Akram Khan	1990-1997	24	20	7	476	68*	36.61	-	3	8
Aminul Islam	1990-1997	22	20	2	448	74	24.88	-	3	7
Athar Ali Khan	1994-1997	17	16	3	260	41	20.00	-	-	4
Enamul Hoque	1990-1997	24	17	3	209	37	14.92	-	-	16
Hasibul Hussain	1997	10	3	2	13	7*	13.00	-	-	2
Jahangir Alam	1994-1997	8	8	1	291	117*	41.57	1	1	1/4
Khaled Mahmud	1997	4	3	1	38	33	19.00	-	-	1
Khaled Mashud	1997	10	5	4	92	70	92.00	-	1	12/11
Minhajul Abedin	1986-1997	30	28	4	761	68	31.70	-	4	15
Mohammed Rafique	1997	9	5	1	76	26	19.00	-	-	3
Naimur Rahman	1997	10	10	2	173	53	21.62	-	1	1
Saiful Islam	1994-1997	10	5	0	78	19	15.60	-	-	2
Sanvar Hossain	1997	6	5	1	30	13*	7.50	-	-	2

Bowling	Year	O	M	R	W	Ave	BB	4w
Akram Khan	1990-1997	55.2	7	187	10	18.70	2-10	-
Athar Ali Khan	1994-1997	81	10	274	6	45.66	1-16	-
Enamul Hoque	1990-1997	216.2	34	649	35	18.54	3-18	-

Hasibul Hussain	1997	64.2	10	159	11	14.45	3-21	-
Khaled Mahmud	1997	26	7	90	4	22.50	2-31	-
Minhajul Abedin	1986-1997	161.2	19	579	37	15.64	4-40	1
Mohammed Rafique	1997	57.4	6	203	19	10.68	4-25	1
Naimur Rahman	1997	40	4	126	8	15.75	3-21	-
Saiful Islam	1994??-1997	71	7	195	9	21.66	2-12	-

Highest Totals
For:	282-8		v Kenya	Simba Union	1994
Against:	315-7		by Zimbabwe	Moseley	1986

Highest Individual Innings
For:	117*	M.J.Alam	v U.A.E.	Ngara	1994
Against:	147	S.O.Tikolo	for Kenya	Tenaga NSC	1997

Best Bowling Analysis
For:	7-23	S.Ashraful Huq	v Fiji	Water Orton	1979
Against:	5-14	La's Aukopi	for P.N.G.	Bournville	1982

Most in a Career
Runs:	761	(Ave 31.70)	Minhajul Abedin	1986-97
Wickets:	37	(Ave 15.64)	Minhajul Abedin	1986-97
Matches:	30		Minhajul Abedin	1986-97

Most in a Tournament
Runs:	283	(Ave 47.17)	M.J.Alam	1994
Wickets:	19	(Ave 10.68)	Mohammed Rafique	1997

Record Wicket Partnerships
1st	170	Y.R.Rahman & S.N.Shirazi	v P.N.G.	Bournville	1982
2nd	50	Mohammed Rafique & Minhajul Abedin	v Kenya	Tenaga NSC	1997
3rd	121	N.Abedin & F.Ahmed	v Canada	Rood en Wit	1990
4th	106	F.Ahmed & Minhajul Abedin	v Hong Kong	Aga Khan	1994
5th	62	Akram Khan & Minhajul Abedin	v Netherlands	RRI	1997
6th	118	M.J.Alam & Salim Shahed	v U.A.E.	Ngara	1994
7th	60	Enamul Hoque & M.Akram Khan	v U.S.A.	Jaffery	1994
	60	Akram Khan & Khaled Mahmud	v Malaysia	Tenaga NSC	1997
8th	42*	M.Akram Khan & M.A.Hossain	v Fiji	VOC, Rotterdam	1990
9th	53	Enamul Hoque & Mizanur Rahman	v Netherlands	Premier	1994
10th	23	D.R.Chowdhury & K.Z.Islam	v Fiji	Water Orton	1979

BERMUDA

BLADES, Roger W. b 25.5.1963 Barbados. rhb. Club: Police Recreation Club.

FOX, Kameron Shaun b 16.11.1977 St. Davids. rhb, sla. Club: St. David's County Cricket Club.

HILL, Corey Shea Tchombe b 28.3.1969 Bailey's Bay. rm. Club: Bailey's Bay

HOLLIS, Delano Wayne b 17.9.1969 Bermuda. rhb, ob. Clubs: Freuchie (Scotland), Cleveland County Cricket Club.

HURDLE, Kevin b 30.12.1976 Bermuda. rhb, rf. Club: Flatt's Victoria Recreation Club.

MANDERS, Willard Arnold E. b 26.4.1959 Bermuda. rhb ob. Club: Western Stars Sports Club.

MARSHALL, Charles MacDonald b 10.5.1961 Baileys Bay. lhb lm. Club: Bailey's Bay.

MINORS, Dean Anthony 6.1.1970 Hamilton. lhb wkt. Club: St. George's.

PERINCHIEF, Bruce Dwayne b 27.11.1960 Paget. rhb lbg. Club: National Sports Club.

SMITH, Clay James b 15.1.1971 Bermuda. rhb ob. Club: St. George's.

SMITH, Dexter b 22.5.1961 Bermuda. lhb. Club: St. George's.

SMITH, Glenn Shane b 22.1.1973 Bailey's Bay. lhb. Club: Bailey's Bay.

STEEDE, Albert B. b 17.5.1968 Bermuda. rhb. Club: Western Stars Sports Club.

TROTT, Roger Lee b 25.6.1963 Paget. rhb wkt. Club: Bailey's Bay.

TUCKER, Janeiro J. b 15.3.1975 Bermuda. rhb rmf. Club: Southampton Rangers Sports Club.

Batting	Year	M	I	NO	Runs	HS	Ave	100	50	Ct/St
R.W.Blades	1997	4	3	1	24	13	12.00	-	-	2
K.S.Fox	1997	3	1	1	0	0*	-	-	-	-
C.S.T.Hill	1997	2	2	0	22	22	11.00	-	-	1
D.W.Hollis	1997	4	4	2	7	4*	3.50	-	-	-
K.Hurdle	1997	4	3	2	12	9*	12.00	-	-	1
W.A.E.Manders	1986-1997	29	23	2	566	75	26.95	-	3	11
C.M.Marshall	1986-1997	20	16	4	335	62*	27.91	-	1	6
D.A.Minors	1994-1997	15	9	2	142	46*	20.28	-	-	15/3
B.D.Perinchief	1994-1997	11	5	3	42	19	21.00	-	-	1
C.J.Smith	1994-1997	15	15	3	517	108*	43.08	1	3	2
D.Smith	1994-1997	11	11	2	424	110	47.11	1	2	4
G.S.Smith	1997	5	5	1	60	41	15.00	-	-	2
A.B.Steede	1994-1997	15	15	0	344	76	22.93	-	2	6
R.L.Trott	1997	5	5	0	79	37	15.80	-	-	3
J.J.Tucker	1997	6	5	0	174	104	34.80	1	-	3

Bowling	Year	O	M	R	W	Ave	BB	4w
R.Blades	1997	31	5	107	6	17.83	3-42	-
K.S.Fox	1997	17	2	70	2	35.00	2-48	-
C.S.T.Hill	1997	15	0	66	4	16.50	2-27	-
D.W.Hollis	1997	26	4	64	5	12.80	3-20	-
K.Hurdle	1997	21.2	2	72	2	36.00	1-16	-
W.A.E.Manders	1986-1997	123.4	15	423	14	30.21	3-18	-
C.M.Marshall	1986-1997	40.2	0	193	4	48.25	2-34	-
B.D.Perinchief	1994-1997	94.5	8	380	13	29.23	4-33	1
C.J.Smith	1994-1997	28	1	121	1	121.00	1-10	-
J.J.Tucker	1997	39.3	3	127	8	15.87	3-25	-

Highest Totals

For:	407-8		v Hong Kong	Griff & Coton	1982
Against:	330-9		by U.A.E.	Nairobi CG	1994

Highest Individual Innings

For:	128	W.A.Reid	v Malaysia	Wednesbury	1982
Against:	158*	M.O.Odumbe	for Kenya	Aga Khan	1994

Best Bowling Analysis

For:	6-38	A.Edwards	v Fiji	Wellington	1986
Against:	4-17	N.D.Maxwell	for Fiji	PKNS	1997

Most in a Career

Runs:	697	(Ave 36.68)	W.A.Reid	1979-86
Wickets:	44	(Ave 17.36)	A.Edwards	1986-94
Matches:	34		N.A.Gibbons	1979-94

Most in a Tournament

Runs:	391	(Ave 55.86)	C.J.Smith	1994
Wickets:	18	(Ave 18.61)	A.Edwards	1994

Record Wicket Partnerships

1st	211	G.A.Brown & W.A.Reid	v Malaysia	Wednesbury	1982
2nd	137	A.B.Steede & C.J.Smith	v Kenya	Aga Khan	1994
3rd	106	R.Hill & W.A.E.Manders	v P.N.G.	Nuneaton	1986
4th	125*	G.A.Brown & C.F.Blades	v West Africa	Olton	1982
5th	100*	C.F.Blades & J.J.Tucker	v P.N.G.	Mitchell & Butler	1986
6th	62	W.A.E.Manders & T.Smith	v Kenya	ACC, Amsterdam	1990
7th	59	N.A.Gibbons & R.Leverock	v Singapore	Klein Zwitserland	1990
8th	59	A.C.Douglas & E.G.James	v East Africa	Stratford-u-Avon	1982
9th	48*	D.A.Minors & T.Burgess	v Hong Kong	Jaffery	1994
10th	30*	K.Phillip & B.D.Perinchief	v Kenya	Aga Khan	1994

BHANSINGH, Latchman b 26.11.1966 Guyana. lhb sla. Club: Viking. †
CHUMNEY, Desmond b 8.1.1968 St.Kitts. ob. Club: Victoria Park.
DIWAN, Muneeb b 20.3.1972 St.Stephen. rhb ob. Clubs: Nova Scotia, Essex CCC. †
ETWAROO, Derick b 6.1.1964 Guyana. ob. Club: Viking.
GLEGG, Alex b 9.8.1971 Zimbabwe. wkt. Club: Vancouver.
ISAACS, Nigel b 26.12.1971 Colombo, Sri Lanka. lhb ob. Club: Grace Church.
JOHNSON, Martin b 18.3.1964 Dominica. Club: Malton.
JOSEPH, Davis b 31.7.1963 Grenada. rmf. Club: Victoria Park.
LIBURD, Ingleton b 27.4.1961 Trinidad. lhb rm. Club: Malton.
MAXWELL, Don b 23.2.1971 Barbados. Club: York.
PERERA, Derek b 13.10.1977 Canada. Club: Toronto.
RAJADURAI, Brian Eric Anton b 24.8.1965 Colombo, Sri Lanka. rhb lb. Club: Grace Church. †
RAMNARAIS, Danny b 20.6.1964 Guyana. wkt. Club: Cavaliers.
RANA, Sukhjinder b 17.2.69 Punjab, India. lm.
SEEBARAN, Barry b 12.9.1972 Vancouver, British Columbia. sla. Club: Vancouver.
SEERAM, Shiv b 25.9.1963 Guyana. rm. Club: Cavaliers. †

Batting	Year	M	I	NO	Runs	HS	Ave	100	50	Ct/St
L.Bhansingh	1997	5	5	2	76	40*	25.33	-	-	4
D.Chumney	1997	4	4	0	23	18	5.75	-	-	2
M.Diwan	1997	7	7	0	204	125	29.14	1	-	5
D.Etwaroo	1986-1997	17	10	2	54	18	6.75	-	-	6
A.Glegg	1997	2	2	0	11	8	5.50	-	-	3/3
N.Isaacs	1994-1997	11	10	3	264	51	37.71	-	1	1
M.Johnson	1997	5	5	0	47	34	9.40	-	-	2
D.Joseph	1990-1997	17	8	2	24	10	4.00	-	-	4
I.Liburd	1990-1997	20	20	3	631	87	37.11	-	3	4
D.Maxwell	1994-1997	11	8	0	98	40	12.25	-	-	6
D.Perera	1997	2	2	1	10	10*	10.00	-	-	-
B.E.A.Rajadurai	1997	3	3	1	77	62	38.50	-	1	2
D.Ramnarais	1994-1997	12	4	2	9	5	4.50	-	-	8/4
S.Rana	1997	6	2	1	1	1*	1.00	-	-	-
B.Seebaran	1990-1997	15	7	3	10	8	2.50	-	-	2
S.Seeram	1997	6	6	1	76	25	15.20	-	-	-

Bowling	Year	O	M	R	W	Ave	BB	4w
L.Bhansingh	1997	10	0	34	4	8.50	3-13	-
M.Diwan	1997	3.4	0	11	2	5.50	2-11	-
D.Etwaroo	1986-1997	153.3	32	437	17	25.70	4-64	1
N.Isaacs	1994-1997	24.1	1	109	2	54.50	1-2	-
D.Joseph	1990-1997	136.2	13	463	23	20.13	5-19	1
I.Liburd	1990-1997	48	2	213	9	23.66	4-38	1
D.Maxwell	1994-1997	50.3	1	252	10	25.20	3-21	-
B.E.A.Rajadurai	1997	18.2	1	78	3	26.00	2-7	-
S.Rana	1997	39.2	3	148	7	21.14	5-29	1
B.Seebaran	1990-1997	128	20	314	19	16.52	4-34	1
S.Seeram	1997	33	3	127	7	18.14	4-50	1

Highest Totals
For:	356-2	v Fiji	Kings Heath	1986
	356-5	v P.N.G.	Walsall	1986
Against:	324-8	by Sri Lanka	Worcester	1979

Highest Individual Innings
For:	164*	P.Prashad	v P.N.G.	Walsall	1986
Against:	148*	M.O.Odumbe	for Kenya	Tenaga NSC	1997

Best Bowling Analysis
For:	7-21	B.Singh	v Namibia	Nairobi CG	1994
Against:	5-38	E.Dulfer	for Netherlands	Koninklijke	1990

Most in a Career

Runs:	747	(Ave 57.46)	P.Prashad		1986-94
Wickets:	26	(Ave 15.88)	T.Gardner		1990-94
Matches:	23		O.Singh		1982-94

Most in a Tournament

Runs:	533	(Ave 88.83)	P.Prashad		1986
Wickets:	14	(Ave 15.50)	D.A.Abraham		1986

Record Wicket Partnerships

1st	233	O.Dipchand & P.Prashad	v Fiji	Kings Heath	1986
2nd	126	P.Prashad & I.F.Kirmani	v Israel	Shrewsbury	1986
3rd	120	M.Diwan & I.Liburd	v Namibia	Kelab Aman	1997
4th	136	P.Prashad & D.Singh	v P.N.G.	Walsall	1986
5th	65	P.Prashad & C.Neblett	v P.N.G.	Walsall	1986
6th	111	Tariq Javed & B.M.Mauricette	v Bermuda	Burton-on-Trent	1979
7th	75	D.Singh & T.Gardner	v Netherlands	Koninklijke	1990
8th	41	D.Singh & D.A.Abraham	v Netherlands	Cheltenham	1986
9th	50	D.Singh & D.A.Abraham	v U.S.A.	Sutton Coldfield	1982
10th	16	D.Singh & A.Hakim	v P.N.G.	Kenilworth	1982

DENMARK

ANDERSEN, Lars Hedegaard b 14.8.1975 Grena. rfm. Club: Nykobing Mors.

ANDERSEN, Morton Hedegaard b 19.2.1972 Grena. rfm. Club: Nykobing Mors.

HANSEN, Thomas Munkholt b 25.3.1976 Glostrup. rhb lfm. Club: Svanholm.

HENRIKSEN, Soren b 1.12.1964 Rodoure, Copenhagen. rfm. Clubs: Svanholm, Lancashire CCC. †

JENSEN, Johnny Soby b 2.4.1968 Silkeborg. rm. Club: Herning.

JENSEN, Peer b 30.4.1965 Esbjerg. lhb sla. Club: Glostrup.

KRISTENSEN, Soren Klitgaard b 29.3.1971 Aalborg. rhb sla. Club: Aalborg Chang.

LUND, Mickey b 21.8.1972 Frederiksberg. Club: Svanholm.

NIELSEN, Steen Anker b 11.7.1968 Denmark. rhb wkt. Club: Glostrup.

PEDERSEN, Carsten Refstrup b 18.5.1977 Herning. Club: Herning.

RASMUSSEN, Anders b 25.2.1975 Glostrup. rhb ob. Club: Glostrup.

SINGH, Baljit b 23.2.1977 Frederiksberg. rhb wkt. Club: Kjobenhavn Boldklub.

SORENSEN, Soren Roar Markvad b 13.11.1968 Koge. rhb rfm. Club: Glostrup.

VESTERAARD, Soren b 1.3.1972 Copenhagen. rhb rf. Clubs: Svanholm. Glamorgan CCC, Warwickshire CCC.

Batting	Year	M	I	NO	Runs	HS	Ave	100	50	Ct/St
L.H.Andersen	1997	4	3	0	15	15	5.00	-	-	1
M.H.Andersen	1997	9	7	1	122	52*	20.33	-	1	2
T.M.Hansen	1997	5	4	2	55	41*	27.50	-	-	-
S.Henriksen	1986-1997	25	22	2	459	56	22.95	-	2	14
J.S.Jensen	1986-1997	20	19	1	427	57	23.72	-	2	6
P.Jensen	1990-1997	13	12	1	178	48	16.18	-	-	6/2
S.K.Kristensen	1997	9	6	2	16	5*	4.00	-	-	-
M.Lund	1997	9	8	0	95	43	11.87	-	-	2
S.A.Nielsen	1997	9	7	0	101	26	14.42	-	-	7/2
C.R.Pedersen	1997	5	5	1	40	34*	10.00	-	-	1
A.Rasmussen	1997	2	1	0	14	14	14.00	-	-	-
B.Singh	1997	9	8	0	111	57	13.87	-	1	7/1
S.R.M.Sorensen	1990-1997	12	6	4	13	7	6.50	-	-	4
S.Vestergaard	1994-1997	14	12	3	189	25	21.00	-	-	5

Bowling	Year	O	M	R	W	Ave	BB	4w
L.H.Andersen	1997	7	0	29	1	29.00	1-3	-
M.H.Andersen	1997	58.2	11	121	9	13.44	5-19	1
T.M.Hansen	1997	31	2	143	10	14.30	5-51	1
S.Henriksen	1986-1997	121.1	15	436	27	16.14	5-56	3
J.S.Jensen	1986-1997	9.5	3	33	3	11.00	2-18	-

P.Jensen	1990-1997	49	13	134	8	16.75	4-25	1
S.K.Kristensen	1997	58.1	9	187	10	18.70	3-16	-
S.A.Nielsen	1997	7.1	1	44	1	44.00	1-34	-
C.R.Pedersen	1997	3	1	4	1	4.00	1-4	-
A.Rasmussen	1997	12	0	50	0	-	-	-
S.R.M.Sorensen	1990-1997	100.2	16	290	28	10.35	4-43	1
S.Vestergaard	1994-1997	86.1	13	284	16	17.75	3-15	-

Highest Totals

For:	274-7		v Argentina	Kenilworth	1986
Against:	318-8		by Sri Lanka	Mitchell & Butler	1979

Highest Individual Innings

For: 86 J.Morild v Netherlands Mitchell & Butler 1986
Against: 127* R.Gomes for Netherlands Mitchell & Butler 1986

Best Bowling Analysis

For: 7-19 O.H.Mortensen v Israel Impala 1994
Against: 4-16 M.P.Stead for Canada Knowle & Dorridge 1979

Most in a Career

Runs: 459 (Ave 22.95) S.Henriksen 1986-97
Wickets: 63 (Ave 10.41) O.H.Mortensen 1979-94
Matches: 26 O.H.Mortensen 1979-94

Most in a Tournament

Runs: 238 (Ave 34.00) S.Henriksen 1986
Wickets: 22 (Ave 9.41) O.H.Mortensen 1986

Record Wicket Partnerships

1st	121	P.Jensen & J.S.Jensen	v U.S.A.	ACC, Amsterdam	1990
2nd	84	A.Butt & M.Christiansen	v Malaysia	Sir Ali Muslim	1994
3rd	92*	J.S.Jensen & C.R.Pedersen	v West Africa	RMC	1997
4th	123	A.Butt & J.Gregersen	v Bermuda	Ruaraka	1994
5th	99	S.Henriksen & J.Morild	v Netherlands	Mitchell & Butler	1986
6th	47	J.Morild & O.H.Mortensen	v Netherlands	Mitchell & Butler	1986
7th	111	B.Singh & M.H.Andersen	v Argentina	PKNS	1997
8th	47	L.Slebsager & O.H.Mortensen	v Namibia	Premier	1994
9th	49*	M.Saddique & M.Seider	v Malaysia	Sir Ali Muslim	1994
10th	26*	M.Seider & T.Skov Nielsen	v Kenya	Kenilworth	1986

EAST & CENTRAL AFRICA

Records include matches played by East Africa in 1979-1986

BAGS, Haroon b 28.12.1963 Lusaka, Zambia (shown in previous books as H.Bagas). rhb lbg. Club: Metropolitan SC.

DUDHIA, Arshad Abdulla b 25.11.1970 Lusaka, Zambia. rhb rm. Club: Colts CC.

EBRAHIM, Arif b 8.1.1966 Lusaka, Zambia. rhb ob. Club: Municipal SC.

GOMM, Chad Matthew b 22.1.1977 Lincoln, England. rhb rm wkt. Club: Colts CC.

IMRAN Ahmed BROHI b 1.10.1963 Hyderabad, Pakistan. rhb.

JIVRAJ, Murtaza Ibrahim Ali b 28.3.1973 Dar-Es-Salaam, Tanzania. rhb rfm. Club: Eaglets SC.

KOMAKECH, James b 4.8.1975 Mulago, Uganda. rhb ob wkt. Club: Wanderers CC.

LUBYA, John b 15.9.1971 Lugazi, Uganda. rhb rm. Club: Wanderers CC.

MBAZZI, Tendo Lubwiawa b 17.10.1974 Mulago, Uganda. rhb rm.

MOHAMED, Imran Ismail b 2.11.1971 Kazmad, India. rhb rm. Club: Metropolitan SC.

MUSOKE, Mayambala Benjamin b 23.10.1976 Rubaga, Kampala, Uganda. rhb. Club: Tornado CC.

NSUBUKA, Frank b 28.8.1980 Nsambia, Uganda. rhb rm. Club: Wanderers CC.

PALIWALA, Arif Noordin b 5.8.1975 Dar-Es-Saraam, Tanzania. rhb lg wkt. Club: Anadil Burhxni SC.

PATEL, Yekesh Shantilal b 27.12.1970 Dar-Es-Salaam, Tanzania. rhb rm. Club: D.B.S.C.

SARIGAT, Faizel Mohamed b 5.3.1963 Chipata, Zambia. rhb rm. Club: Metropolitan SC.

Batting	Year	M	I	NO	Runs	HS	Ave	100	50	Ct/St
H.Bags	1990-1997	16	16	1	175	34	11.66	-	-	3
A.A.Dudhia	1997	3	3	0	23	14	7.66	-	-	3
A.Ebrahim	1997	4	4	0	56	42	14.00	-	-	-
C.M.Gomm	1997	6	6	0	45	29	7.50	-	-	-
Imran Brohi	1994-1997	13	12	0	291	141	24.25	1	-	4
M.I.A.Jivraj	1997	3	3	0	8	6	2.66	-	-	-
J.Komakech	1997	6	6	0	52	26	8.66	-	-	8
J.Lubya	1997	4	4	0	24	22	6.00	-	-	1
T.L.Mbazzi	1997	6	6	1	33	15	6.60	-	-	4
I.I.Mohamed	1997	3	3	0	7	4	2.33	-	-	-
M.B.Musoke	1997	5	5	0	57	30	11.40	-	-	-
F.Nsubuka	1997	4	4	1	6	4	2.00	-	-	2
A.N.Paliwala	1997	5	5	4	46	15*	46.00	-	-	-
Y.S.Patel	1994-1997	14	13	2	268	95	24.36	-	2	2
F.M.Sarigat	1990-1997	13	13	0	156	57	12.00	-	1	1

Bowling	Year	O	M	R	W	Ave	BB	4w
H.Bags	1990-1997	52.1	1	253	7	36.14	3-47	-
C.M.Gomm	1997	30	3	110	10	11.00	3-22	-
Imran Brohi	1994-1997	29	1	103	6	17.16	3-6	-
M.I.A.Jivraj	1997	27	2	82	4	20.50	2-12	-
J.Lubya	1997	18	2	62	3	20.66	2-26	-
T.L.Mbazzi	1997	30.1	2	95	5	19.00	2-26	-
I.I.Mohamed	1997	10	1	15	2	7.50	2-15	-
F.Nsubuka	1997	14	4	27	0	-	-	-
A.Paliwala	1997	14.3	1	44	1	44.00	1-13	-
Y.S.Patel	1994-1997	63	4	253	15	16.86	3-28	-

Highest Totals

For:	266-8		v Singapore	Nairobi CG	1994
Against:	274-7		by Denmark	Old Edwardians	1986

Highest Individual Innings

For:	141	Imran Brohi	v Singapore	Nairobi CG	1994
Against:	87*	D.L.Houghton	for Zimbabwe	Nantwich	1986
	87	T.Buzaglo	for Gibraltar	Gymkhana	1994

Best Bowling Analysis

For:	6-26	A.Kumar	v Argentina	Stourbridge	1986
Against:	5-27	R.Benjamin	for U.S.A.	Quick (N)	1990

Most in a Career

Runs:	328	(Ave 25.23)	B.R.Bouri	1982-90
Wickets:	22	(Ave 14.72)	S.M.Lakha	1982-90
Matches:	17		S.Walusimbi	1982-90

Most in a Tournament

Runs:	221	(Ave 36.83)	Imran Brohi	1994
Wickets:	11	(Ave 26.90)	D.M.Patel	1982
	11	(Ave 7.63)	B.R.Desai	1986
	11	(Ave 12.00)	S.M.Lakha	1994

Record Wicket Partnerships

1st	84	K.W.Arnold & D.C.Patel	v Fiji	Stafford	1982
2nd	158	D.Patel & M.Dhirani	v Gibraltar	Gymkhana	1994
3rd	75	F.Sarigat & I.Brohi	v Singapore	Nairobi CG	1994
4th	125	F.G.Patel & B.K.Bouri	v Bangladesh	Coventry & N.W.	1986
5th	61	B.R.Bouri & S.Walusimbi	v Malaysia	Hermes	1990
6th	113	Imran Brohi & H.Bags	v Singapore	Nairobi CG	1994
7th	67	A.Kumar & V.M.Tarmohamed	v Argentina	Stourbridge	1986
8th	63	Y.S.Patel & A.N.Paliwala	v Italy	Univ of Malaya	1997
9th	54	H.Bags & Y.Warakabulo	v U.S.A.	Quick (N)	1990
10th	18	Y.Warakabulo & Janak Patel	v U.S.A.	Quick (N)	1990

BATINA, Taione b 28.1.1964 Fiji. rhb rfm.
BULABALAVU, Jioji b 20.2.1972 Lakeba. rhb.
CAKACAKA, Iniasi b 17.7.1968 Korotolu. rhb ob wkt.
CAKACAKA, Taione b 15.7.1967 Lakeba. rhb wkt.
MATEYAWA, Joeli b 12.4.1962 Lakeba. rhb rmf.
MAXWELL, Neil Donald b 12.6.1967 Lautoka. rhb rf. Clubs: Victoria, New South Wales. †
ROUSE, Jason b 31.7.1970 Fiji. rhb.
SEUVOU, Jone b 17.6.1966 Lakeba. lfm.
SOROVAKATINI, Asaeli b 2.3.1966 Lakeba. lhb.
SOROVAKATINI, Josefa b 19.3.1964 Lakeba. rhb.
SOROVAKATINI, Lesivou b 28.12.1962 Lakeba. rhb rfm.
TADU, Eroni b 15.2.1962 Lakeba. rhb.
TAWATATAU, Atunaisa b 6.11.1965 Lakeba. lf.
TUKANA, Waisake b 15.8.1974 Lakeba. lhb rmf.

Batting	Year	M	I	NO	Runs	HS	Ave	100	50	Ct/St
T.Batina	1986-1997	26	24	1	238	47	10.34	-	-	4
J.Bulabalavu	1997	2	2	0	38	37	19.00	-	-	3
I.Cakacaka	1997	5	4	2	62	29*	31.00	-	-	5
T.Cakacaka	1994-1997	11	9	0	107	46	11.88	-	-	11/1
J.Mateyawa	1982-1997	29	23	6	212	50	12.47	-	1	6
N.D.Maxwell	1990-1997	13	13	2	346	84	31.45	-	1	4
J.Rouse	1994-1997	11	11	1	208	87	20.80	-	2	-
J.Seuvou	1986-1997	12	10	2	62	12	7.75	-	-	1
A.Sorovakatini	1990-1997	17	13	3	127	31	12.70	-	-	7
J.Sorovakatini	1986-1997	20	20	2	444	63	24.66	-	2	10
L.Sorovakatini	1990-1997	16	15	1	263	84	18.78	-	1	3
E.Tadu	1997	3	3	0	40	36	13.33	-	-	2
A.Tawatatau	1986-1997	28	19	8	139	31*	12.63	-	-	8
W.Tukana	1997	6	5	2	92	34*	30.66	-	-	3

Bowling	Year	O	M	R	W	Ave	BB	4w
T.Batina	1986-1997	205.5	32	702	30	23.40	3-7	-
I.Cakacaka	1997	4.3	0	20	1	20.00	1-20	-
J.Mateyawa	1982-1997	207	21	796	33	24.12	4-28	1
N.D.Maxwell	1990-1997	83.5	19	205	20	10.25	4-17	2
J.Seuvou	1986-1997	77.3	8	316	6	52.66	2-17	-
L.Sorovakatini	1990-1997	51.3	3	234	11	21.27	3-37	-
A.Tawatatau	1986-1997	265	53	792	31	25.54	4-9	1
W.Tukana	1997	23	0	80	8	10.00	5-31	1

Highest Totals
For: 288-8 v Argentina Klein Zwitserland 1990
Against: 381-8 by P.N.G. Old Hill 1986

Highest Individual Innings
For: 87 J.Rouse v P.N.G. Ngara 1994
Against: 154* R.Elferink for Netherlands Hinckley 1982

Best Bowling Analysis
For: 5-31 W.Tukana v U.S.A. RMC 1997
Against: 7-23 S.Ashraful Huq for Bangladesh Water Orton 1979

Most in a Career
Runs: 626 (Ave 25.04) C.A.C.Browne 1979-94
Wickets: 33 (Ave 24.12) J.Mateyawa 1982-97
Matches: 27 C.A.C.Browne 1979-94

Most in a Tournament

Runs:	259	(Ave 43.17)	J.T.Sorovakatini	1990
Wickets:	11	(Ave 20.81)	A.Waqaninamata	1990
	11	(Ave 7.27)	N.D.Maxwell	1997

Record Wicket Partnerships

1st	104	V.S.J.Campbell & L.Sorovakatini	v Bermuda	Hermes	1990
2nd	119	C.A.C.Browne & J.T.Sorovakatini	v Hong Kong	VOC, Rotterdam	1990
3rd	67	J.T.Sorovakatini & T.Batina	v Gibraltar	Banbury	1986
4th	61	C.A.C.Browne & J.T.Sorovakatini	v P.N.G.	Old Hill	1986
5th	115	L.Sorovakatini & T.Cakacaka	v West Africa	Jaffery	1994
6th	46*	W.Tukana & I.Cakacaka	v U.S.A.	RMC	1997
7th	35	I.Vuli & R.G.Jepsen	v Denmark	Wellington	1979
8th	40	I.Vuli & T.Korocowiri	v Singapore	Solihull	1982
9th	34	I.V.Tambualevu & F.L.C.Valentine			
			v Canada	Solihull	1979
10th	49*	A.Tawatatau & S.K.G.Amin	v E & C Africa	ACC, Amsterdam	1990

GIBRALTAR

BUZAGLO, Richard b 30.12.1965 Gibraltar. rhb.
BUZAGLO, Timothy b 21.6.1961 Gibraltar. rhb.
CARY, Stephen b 20.6.1968 Cornwall, England.
CHURAMAN, Nigel b 28.3.1969 Gibraltar. lhb rm.
CLINTON, Clive b 10.12.1945 Gibraltar. rhb ob.
DE'ATH, Gary b 14.8.1957 Grantham, Lincolnshire, England. lhb ob.
GARCIA, Terrance b 31.7.1977 Gibraltar. rhb lb.
HEWITT, Adrian b 28.7.1959 Gibraltar. rhb rm.
JOHNSON, Daniel b 12.7.1979 Gibraltar. rhb ob.
MILLS, Geoffrey b 7.3.1969 Gibraltar. rhb rm.
PHILLIPS, Rudolph b 27.1.1948 Barbados. rhb ob.
ROBESON, David b 17.6.1976 Gibraltar. rhb.
ROCCA, Christian b 8.3.1965 Gibraltar. rhb.
SHEPHARD, Stephen b 13.4.1976 Gibraltar. rhb wkt.

Batting	Year	M	I	NO	Runs	HS	Ave	100	50	Ct/St
R.Buzaglo	1986-1997	27	27	2	392	49	15.68	-	-	12/1
T.Buzaglo	1982-1997	29	27	1	590	98	22.69	-	3	10
S.Cary	1997	7	2	2	7	7*	-	-	-	6
N.Churaman	1997	7	6	0	44	14	7.33	-	-	3
C.Clinton	1994-1997	8	8	1	42	16*	6.00	-	-	1
G.De'Ath	1986-1997	28	25	2	429	63	18.65	-	1	5
T.Garcia	1994-1997	13	11	5	25	5*	4.16	-	-	4
A.Hewitt	1994-1997	9	9	2	57	14*	8.14	-	-	3
D.Johnson	1997	6	6	0	72	28	12.00	-	-	1
G.Mills	1997	4	1	0	0	0	0.00	-	-	1
R.Phillips	1994-1997	7	7	2	56	15*	11.20	-	-	1
D.Robeson	1997	4	4	0	7	5	1.75	-	-	1
C.Rocca	1986-1997	18	16	2	285	58	20.35	-	1	4
S.Shephard	1994-1997	8	7	0	43	21	6.14	-	-	5/2

Bowling	Year	O	M	R	W	Ave	BB	4w
S.Cary	1997	53	6	229	5	45.80	1-17	-
N.Churaman	1997	65.2	12	227	17	13.35	5-14	1
C.Clinton	1994-1997	6.4	0	30	1	30.00	1-20	-
G.De'Ath	1986-1997	231.5	29	950	29	32.75	5-88	2
T.Garcia	1994-1997	83.3	6	390	8	48.75	2-26	-
A.Hewitt	1994-1997	55	5	268	7	38.28	2-38	-
D.Johnson	1997	30	0	164	4	41.00	2-52	-
G.Mills	1997	29.3	4	87	4	21.75	2-24	-
R.Phillips	1994-1997	3	0	10	1	10.00	1-10	-
D.Robeson	1997	0.4	0	6	0	-	-	-

Highest Totals
For:	263-7		v Israel	Warwick	1986
Against:	455-9		by P.N.G.	Cannock	1986

Highest Individual Innings
For:	98	T.Buzaglo	v Singapore	Ruaraka	1994
Against:	172	S.D.Myles	for Hong Kong	Bridgnorth	1986

Best Bowling Analysis
For:	5-14	N.Churaman	v Israel	RRI	1997
Against:	5-9	D.A.Abraham	for Canada	Swinton	1986

Most in a Career
Runs:	590	(Ave 22.69)	T.Buzaglo	1982-97
Wickets:	29	(Ave 32.75)	G.De'Ath	1986-97
Matches:	29		T.Buzaglo	1982-97

Most in a Tournament
Runs:	257	(Ave 36.71)	T.Buzaglo	1994
Wickets:	17	(Ave 13.35)	N.Churaman	1997

Record Wicket Partnerships
1st	61	W.T.Scott & C.Robinson	v Israel	Warwick	1986
2nd	83	R.Buzaglo & T.Buzaglo	v E & C Africa	HBS	1990
3rd	55	R.Buzaglo & G.De'Ath	v Ireland	Sir Ali Muslim	1994
4th	63	G.De'Ath & S.Chinnappa	v Singapore	Hermes	1990
5th	78	S.Shephard & C.Rocca	v Singapore	Tenaga NSC	1997
6th	73*	A.Raikes & H.Finch	v Israel	VOC, Rotterdam	1990
7th	58	C.Rocca & T.Buzaglo	v Israel	Warwick	1986
8th	29	W.T.Scott & T.J.Finlayson	v Kenya	Solihull	1982
	29	C.Rocca & S.J.Boylan	v Fiji	Banbury	1986
9th	23	S.Chinnappa & S.J.Boylan	v Denmark	Koninklijke	1990
10th	21	M.Smith & P.White	v U.S.A.	Aston Manor	1986

HONG KONG

BREW, Stewart John b 5.1.1965 Brisbane, Australia. rhb rm. Club: Hong Kong CC Optimists.

BREWSTER Raymond David b 26.3.1951 Brisbane, Australia. rhb wkt. Club: Kowloon CC Infidels.

EAMES, Mark Ian Neil b 19.8.1961 Coventry, England. lhb. Club: Kowloon CC Infidels.

FARCY, Mohamed Riaz b 15.1.1967 Hong Kong. rhb rm. Club: Little Sai Wan. †

FORDHAM, John Patrick b 9.7.1959 Leeds, England. rhb wkt. Club: Kowloon CC Templars.

FOSTER, Steven b 10.3.1967 London, England. rhb rm. Club: Hong Kong CC Scorpions.

FRENCH, Alexander Nial b 1.12.1980 Hong Kong. rhb ob. Club: Hong Kong CC Scorpions.

JONES, David b 11.9.1964 Hong Kong. rhb rm. Club: Kowloon CC Infidels.

LAMSAM, John Patrick Roy b 15.5.1980 Hong Kong. rhb rm. Club: Kowloon CC Dragons.

LEVER, Martin Geoffrey b 19.3.1969 Heswell, England. rhb rm. Club: Vagabonds.

MOHAMMAD ZUBAIR b 22.1.1975 Pakistan. rhb rm. Club: Pakistan Association.

MUNIR HUSSAIN b 17.11.1967 Pakistan. rhb rm. Club: Pakistan Association.

RAZA, Kamran b 30.10.1977 Hong Kong. rhb rm. Club: Little Sai Wan.

SHARMA, Rahul b 14.9.1960 New Dehli, India. rhb rm lb. Club: Kowloon CC Templars. †

SUJANANI, Ravi b 11.6.1970 Hong Kong (shown in previous books as S.Ravi). rhb rm. Club: Kowloon CC Dragons.

SWIFT, Michael b 5.5.1963 Calgary, Canada. lhb. Club: Hong Kong CC Scorpions.

Batting	Year	M	I	NO	Runs	HS	Ave	100	50	Ct/St
S.J.Brew	1994-1997	15	14	0	420	124	30.00	1	2	9
R.D.Brewster	1986-1997	10	10	1	184	55	20.44	-	1	5/3
M.I.N.Eames	1994-1997	15	14	1	212	33	16.30	-	-	7
M.R.Farcy	1994-1997	14	14	0	387	102	27.64	1	1	-
J.P.Fordham	1994-1997	14	14	1	453	79	34.84	-	4	14/2
S.Foster	1997	2	2	0	9	5	4.50	-	-	-
A.N.French	1997	4	4	0	22	13	5.50	-	-	-

	Year									
D.Jones	1990-1997	12	11	2	157	71	17.44	-	1	5
J.P.R.Lamsam	1997	1	1	0	8	8	8.00	-	-	-
M.G.Lever	1997	6	5	1	37	15	9.25	-	-	-
Mohammed Zubair	1997	8	7	3	9	6	2.25	-	-	1
Munir Hussain	1997	8	8	0	114	39	14.25	-	-	-
K.Raza	1997	8	7	2	42	15	8.40	-	-	1
R.Sharma	1997	8	8	0	190	69	23.75	-	2	4
R.Sujanani	1994-1997	6	6	2	45	23	11.25	-	-	-
M.Swift	1997	1	1	0	11	11	11.00	-	-	-

Bowling	Year	O	M	R	W	Ave	BB	4w
S.J.Brew	1994-1997	100	13	425	25	17.00	4-16	2
M.R.Farcy	1994-1997	68.2	7	245	12	20.41	2-9	-
D.Jones	1994-1997	50.2	5	165	8	20.62	3-14	-
J.P.R.Lamsam	1997	0.0	0	4	0	-	-	-
M.G.Lever	1997	12	0	47	0	-	-	-
Mohammed Zubair	1997	53.1	2	211	10	21.10	3-31	-
Munir Hussain	1997	44.5	6	163	7	23.28	3-37	-
K.Raza	1997	56	3	195	6	32.50	2-41	-
R.Sharma	1997	48	5	154	6	25.66	3-29	-
R.Sujanani	1994-1997	21	1	79	3	26.33	2-16	-

Highest Totals

For:	355-8		v West Africa	Sir Ali Muslim	1994
Against:	407-8		by Bermuda	Griff & Coton	1986

Highest Individual Innings

For:	172	S.D.Myles	v Gibraltar	Bridgnorth	1986
Against:	125*	N.A.Gibbons	for Bermuda	Griff & Coton	1986

Best Bowling Analysis

For:	6-11	B.Gohel	v Fiji	Knowle & Dorridge	1986
Against:	5-24	A.Njuguna	for Kenya	Gymkhana	1994

Most in a Career

Runs:	453	(Ave 34.84)	J.P.Fordham	1994-97
Wickets:	25	(Ave 17.00)	S.J.Brew	1994-97
Matches:	20		N.P.Stearns	1982-90

Most in a Tournament

Runs:	408	(Ave 58.28)	S.D.Myles	1986
Wickets:	18	(Ave 13.22)	S.J.Brew	1994

Record Wicket Partnerships

1st	89	B.C.Catton & R.D.Brewster	v P.N.G.	Olton	1986
2nd	161	S.J.Brew & S.R.Atkinson	v West Africa	Sir Ali Muslim	1994
3rd	194	S.D.Myles & N.P.Stearns	v Gibraltar	Bridgnorth	1986
4th	85	R.Sharma & M.I.N.Eames	v P.N.G.	Tenaga NSC	1997
5th	88*	A.A.Lorimer & P.W.Anderson	v Zimbabwe	Wellesbourne	1982
6th	73	J.O.D.Orders & J.P.Garden	v Denmark	Gymkhana	1994
7th	52	C.Collins & Y.J.Vachha	v U.S.A.	Leamington	1986
8th	34*	R.Farooq & G.Davies	v Malaysia	DVS Schiedam	1990
9th	54*	Y.J.Vachha & B.Gohel	v P.N.G.	Olton	1986
10th	34*	G.Lalchandani & R.C.Gill	v Kenya	Streetley	1982

IRELAND

BENSON, Justin David Ramsay b 1.3.1967 Dublin. rhb rm. Clubs: Malahide, Leicestershire CCC. †

CURRY, John Desmond b 20.12.1966 Strabane, Co Tyrone. lhb ob. Club: Limavady. †

DOAK, Neil George b 21.6.1972 Lisburn, Co Antrim. rhb ob. Club: Lisburn. †

DUNLOP, Angus Richard b 17.3.1967 Dublin. rhb ob. Club: Dublin YMCA. †

EAGLESON, Ryan Logan b 17.12.1974 Carrickfergus, Co Antrim. rhb rfm. Club: Carrickfergus. †

GILLESPIE, Peter Gerard b 11.5.1974 Strabane, Co Tyrone. rhb rf. Club: Strabane. †

GRAHAM, Samuel (known as Uel) b 9.1.1967 Lisburn, Co Antrim. rhb rm. Club: Lisburn. †

HARRISON, Garfield David b 8.5.1961 Lurgan, Co Armagh. lhb ob. Club: Waringstown. †
HEASLEY, Derek b 15.1.1972 Lisburn, Co Antrim. rhb rm. Club: Lisburn.
LEWIS, David Alan b 1.6.1964 Cork. rhb rm. Club: Dublin YMCA. †
MCCRUM, Paul Michael b 11.8.1962 Waringstown, Co Armagh. rhb rfm. Club: Muckamore. †
MOLINS, Gregory Lee b 19.3.1976 Dublin. rhb sla. Club: Carlisle. †
PATTERSON, Andrew David b 4.9.1975 Belfast. rhb wkt. Club: Cliftonville. †
PATTERSON, Mark William b 2.2.1974 Belfast. rhb rfm. Club: Cliftonville. †
RUTHERFORD, Allan Thomas b 2.6.1967 Strabane, Co Tyrone. rhb wkt. Club: Bready. †

Batting	Year	M	I	NO	Runs	HS	Ave	100	50	Ct/St
J.D.R.Benson	1994-1997	17	15	1	459	74*	32.78	-	2	8
J.D.Curry	1994-1997	12	11	2	309	65*	34.33	-	3	3
N.G.Doak	1994-1997	11	8	2	119	35	19.83	-	-	2
A.R.Dunlop	1994-1997	16	13	3	232	54	23.20	-	1	5
R.L.Eagleson	1997	7	3	0	6	4	2.00	-	-	4
P.G.Gillespie	1997	9	6	1	93	24*	18.60	-	-	3
S.Graham	1994-1997	6	5	2	91	28	30.33	-	-	1
G.D.Harrison	1994-1997	16	12	2	204	36	20.40	-	-	3
D.Heasley	1997	3	2	0	69	51	34.50	-	1	2
D.A.Lewis	1994-1997	16	14	2	405	127*	33.75	1	1	5
P.McCrum	1994-1997	11	5	3	14	7*	7.00	-	-	4
G.L.Molins	1997	3	2	2	5	5*	-	-	-	1
A.D.Patterson	1997	7	5	1	94	44*	23.50	-	-	11/2
M.W.Patterson	1997	10	6	2	52	27*	13.00	-	-	2
A.T.Rutherford	1997	4	2	2	28	25*	-	-	-	2

Bowling	Year	O	M	R	W	Ave	BB	4w
J.D.Curry	1994-1997	48.5	3	213	7	30.42	3-28	-
N.G.Doak	1994-1997	82.5	12	272	16	17.00	4-9	1
R.L.Eagleson	1997	21.2	3	86	4	21.50	2-30	-
P.G.Gillespie	1997	51.4	7	168	7	24.00	3-42	-
S.Graham	1994-1997	7	2	20	1	20.00	1-20	-
G.D.Harrison	1994-1997	134	27	386	13	29.69	3-19	-
D.Heasley	1997	20	0	102	2	51.00	1-19	-
P.McCrum	1994-1997	75	10	274	15	18.26	4-51	1
G.L.Molins	1997	27	5	94	2	47.00	1-33	-
M.W.Patterson	1997	51.3	5	206	14	14.71	4-22	1

Highest Totals
For: 278-2   v Gibraltar   Victoria Institute   1997
Against: 295-4   by U.A.E.   Ruaraka   1994

Highest Individual Innings
For: 127*   D.A.Lewis   v Gibraltar   Victoria Institute   1997
Against: 122   S.M.Hussain   for U.A.E.   Ruaraka   1994

Best Bowling Analysis
For: 5-29   C.J.Hoey   v P.N.G.   Ngara   1994
Against: 4-28   A.Y.Karim   for Kenya   Tenaga NSC   1997

Most in a Career
Runs: 459   (Ave 32.78)   J.D.R.Benson   1994-97
Wickets: 16   (Ave 17.00)   N.G.Doak   1994-97
Matches: 17   J.D.R.Benson   1994-97

Most in a Tournament
Runs: 291   (Ave 36.37)   J.D.Curry   1997
Wickets: 16   (Ave 14.62)   N.G.Doak   1997

Record Wicket Partnerships
1st   113*   J.D.Curry & A.D.Patterson   v Singapore   Kelab Aman   1997
2nd   162   D.A.Lewis & J.D.R.Benson   v Gibraltar   Victoria Institute 1997
3rd   50   J.D.R.Benson & D.A.Lewis   v P.N.G.   Ngara   1994
4th   69   D.A.Lewis & G.D.Harrison   v Gibraltar   Sir Ali Muslim   1994
5th   66   M.F.Cohen & C.McCrum   v Canada   Premier   1994

6th	60	A.R.Dunlop & C.McCrum	v U.A.E.	Ruaraka	1994
7th	64	A.R.Dunlop & G.D.Harrison	v Hong Kong	Kelab Aman	1997
8th	47	G.D.Harrison & M.W.Patterson	v U.S.A.	Tenaga NSC	1997
9th	38	A.T.Rutherford & A.D.Patterson	v Kenya	RRI	1997
10th	19*	P.G.Gillespie & A.T.Rutherford	v Kenya	Tenaga NSC	1997

ISRAEL

ASHTON, Raymond b 1.5.1976 India.
AWASKER, Hillel b 10.10.1959 India.
HALL, Louis b 7.8.1955 Barbados.
JAWALEKAR, Moses b 7.12.1961 Bombay, India.
KEHIMKAR, Bension b 11.8.1960 Mumbai, India.
MOSS, Alan b 2.12.1964 South Africa.
NAGAVKAR, Yefeth b 19.12.1975 India.
PERLMAN, Stanley B. b 22.12.1950 Cape Town, South Africa.
SILVER, David b 17.4.1957 Melbourne, Australia.
SMITH, Paul b 21.1.1965 Cape Town, South Africa. wkt.
TALKAR, Avshalom b 13.8.1973 Israel.
TALKER, Moses b 1.7.1967 India.
VARD, Adrian b 9.2.1970 Dublin, Eire.
WADAVAKAR, Menashe b 27.9.1968 India.
WORRELL, Valice Edgar b 9.7.1950 Barbados.

Batting	Year	M	I	NO	Runs	HS	Ave	100	50	Ct/St
R.Ashton	1994-1997	13	13	3	117	23*	11.70	-	-	4
H.Awasker	1982-1997	35	34	2	323	66	10.09	-	1	10
L.Hall	1997	6	6	0	37	14	6.16	-	-	-
M.Jawalekar	1997	3	3	0	12	8	4.00	-	-	-
B.Kehimkar	1990-1997	9	9	1	46	12	5.75	-	-	-
A.Moss	1982-1997	25	24	3	271	42	12.90	-	-	4
Y.Nagavkar	1997	7	7	0	62	26	8.85	-	-	1
S.B.Perlman	1979-1997	29	28	2	639	75*	24.57	-	3	14
D.Silver	1997	6	6	0	113	40	18.83	-	-	1
P.Smith	1997	7	7	3	29	11	7.25	-	-	6
A.Talkar	1994-1997	8	8	0	48	16	6.00	-	-	4
M.Talker	1997	2	2	0	7	7	3.50	-	-	-
A.Vard	1997	3	3	0	13	8	4.33	-	-	2
M.Wadavakar	1997	3	3	0	5	2	1.66	-	-	1
V.E.Worrell	1986-1997	18	15	3	40	12	3.33	-	-	3

Bowling	Year	O	M	R	W	Ave	BB	4w
R.Ashton	1994-1997	64.5	2	307	12	25.58	4-54	1
H.Awasker	1982-1997	228.5	21	358	19	18.84	3-44	-
L.Hall	1997	21.3	2	90	4	22.50	2-32	-
B.Kehimkar	1990-1997	45	6	139	5	27.80	2-28	-
A.Moss	1982-1997	168.5	14	810	20	40.50	5-27	1
Y.Nagavkar	1997	9.2	0	58	0	-	-	-
D.Silver	1997	3	0	18	0	-	-	-
M.Wadavakar	1997	7	0	37	0	-	-	-
V.E.Worrell	1986-1997	115.5	6	575	8	71.87	3-86	-

Highest Totals
For:	269-9		v Gibraltar	VOC, Rotterdam	1990
Against:	425-4		by Netherlands	Old Silhillians	1986

Highest Individual Innings
For:	108	D.Moss	v Fiji	Birmingham Mun	1986
Against:	169*	R.Gomes	for Netherlands	ACC, Amsterdam	1990

Best Bowling Analysis

For:	5-27	A.P.Moss	v Argentina	HCC, The Hague	1990
Against:	7-19	O.H.Mortensen	for Denmark	Impala	1994

Most in a Career

Runs:	639	(Ave 24.57)	S.B.Perlman	1979-97
Wickets:	20	(Ave 40.50)	A.Moss	1982-97
Matches:	35		H.Awasker	1982-97

Most in a Tournament

Runs:	222	(Ave 31.71)	D.Moss	1986
Wickets:	11	(Ave 20.09)	A.P.Moss	1990

Record Wicket Partnerships

1st	47	S.Erulkar & J.Kessel	v Hong Kong	VRA, Amsterdam	1990
2nd	109	S.Erulkar & H.Awaskar	v Gibraltar	VOC, Rotterdam	1990
3rd	33	S.B.Perlman & A.P.Moss	v Hong Kong	Burnt Green	1986
4th	109	Z.Moshe & S.B.Perlman	v Gibraltar	Warwick	1986
5th	85	Z.Moshe & S.M.Nemblette	v Gibraltar	Warwick	1986
6th	92	N.Ward & M.Hamburger	v Namibia	Impala	1994
7th	50	S.B.Perlman & A.P.Moss	v P.N.G.	Cheltenham	1982
8th	33	S.B.Perlman & Z.Moshe	v P.N.G.	Hermes	1990
9th	35	D.Moss & N.Davidson	v Fiji	Birmingham Mun.	1986
10th	31	D.Moss & M.Jacob	v Canada	Ruaraka	1994

ITALY

AKHLAQ Ahmed QURESHI b 7.2.1962 Lahore, Pakistan. rhb. Club: Como. †
AMATI, Andrea b 7.6.1964 Rome. rhb rm. Club: Capannelle.
DA COSTA, Massimo Brian Michael b 21.4.1947 Bangalore, India. lhb sla. Club: Capannelle.
DE MEL, Samantha V. b 12.12.1965 Colombo, Sri Lanka. rhb, sla. Club: Bergamo. †
GIORDANO, Benito b 20.12.1971 Warrington, England. rhb rm. Club: Trentino.
KARIYAWASAM, I. Kamal b 7.7.1958 Ambalangoda, Sri Lanka. rhb wkt. Club: Bergamo.
MAGGIO, Riccardo b 24.1.1970 Rome. rhb ob. Club: Lazio.
MOHAMMAD RAZZAQ b 15.12.1959 Gujrat, Pakistan. Club: Como.
PARISI, Thomas b 12.8.1976 Bologna. rhb rm. Club: Pianoro.
PEZZI, Andrea b 13.4.1965 Cesena. rhb rm. Club: Cesena.
PIERI, Alessandro b 23.7.1963 Cesena. rhb wkt. Club: Cesena.
RAJAPAKSE, Mohottilage Gamini Lekau b 13.6.1957 Dehiwala, Sri Lanka. rhb rm. Club: Grosseto.
SAJJAD AHMED b 15.1.1963 Rawalpindi, Pakistan. rhb ob. Club: Como.
ZITO, Filippo Emerico b 25.10.1967 Rome. rhb rm. Club: Cesena.
ZUPPIROLI, Valerio b 17.6.1974 Bologna. rhb rm. Club: Pianoro.

Batting	Year	M	I	NO	Runs	HS	Ave	100	50	Ct/St
Akhlaq Qureshi	1997	5	4	0	49	18	12.25	-	-	3
A.Amati	1997	5	4	0	24	13	6.00	-	-	1
M.B.M.da Costa	1997	2	1	1	2	2*	-	-	-	1
S.V.de Mel	1997	4	3	0	57	25	19.00	-	-	2
B.Giordano	1997	5	4	0	102	32	25.50	-	-	-
K.Kariyawasam	1997	4	3	0	18	13	6.00	-	-	4/3
R.Maggio	1997	3	1	0	3	3	3.00	-	-	1
Mohammad Razzaq	1997	4	3	0	48	26	16.00	-	-	1
T.Parisi	1997	1	1	0	0	0	0.00	-	-	1
A.Pezzi	1997	5	4	1	10	9	3.33	-	-	-
A.Pieri	1997	4	3	0	31	17	10.33	-	-	0/1
M.G.L.Rajapakse	1997	3	3	2	6	6*	6.00	-	-	-
Sajjad Ahmed	1997	3	3	1	18	8*	9.00	-	-	-
F.E.Zito	1997	2	2	0	7	7	3.50	-	-	1
V.Zuppiroli	1997	5	4	0	35	19	8.75	-	-	5

Bowling	Year	O	M	R	W	Ave	BB	4w
Akhlaq Qureshi	1997	45	5	171	10	17.10	3-30	-
A.Amati	1997	11	0	69	0	-	-	-
M.da Costa	1997	16	0	68	2	34.00	2-35	-
S.V.de Mel	1997	40	4	146	7	20.85	3-40	-
B.Giordano	1997	40	2	190	6	31.66	3-35	-
R.Maggio	1997	4	0	37	0	-	-	-
Mohammad Razzaq	1997	2	0	19	0	-	-	-
T.Parisi	1997	10	0	81	2	40.50	2-81	-
M.G.L.Rajapakse	1997	28.1	1	145	3	48.33	2-40	-
Sajjad Ahmed	1997	28.4	1	128	3	42.66	1-26	-
V.Zuppiroli	1997	4	0	30	2	15.00	2-30	-

Highest Totals

For:	142	v Scotland	Univ of Malaya	1997
Against:	282	by Hong Kong	Royal Selangor	1997

Highest Individual Innings

For:	32	B.Giordano	v Hong Kong	Royal Selangor	1997
Against:	102	M.R.Farcy	for Hong Kong	Royal Selangor	1997

Best Bowling Analysis

For:	3-30	Akhlaq Qureshi	v E & C Africa	Univ of Malaya	1997
Against:	4-20	I.R.Beven	for Scotland	Univ of Malaya	1997

Most in a Career

Runs:	102	(Ave 25.50)	B.Giordano	1997
Wickets:	10	(Ave 17.10)	Akhlaq Qureshi	1997
Matches:	5		five players	

Most in a Tournament

Runs:	102	(Ave 25.50)	B.Giordano	1997
Wickets:	10	(Ave 17.10)	Akhlaq Qureshi	1997

Record Wicket Partnerships

1st	14	V.Zuppiroli & A.Amati	v Scotland	Univ of Malaya	1997
2nd	53	V.Zuppiroli & B.Giordano	v Bermuda	Tenaga NSC	1997
3rd	26	B.Giordano & Akhlaq Qureshi	v P.N.G.	PKNS	1997
4th	31	Akhlaq Qureshi & Mohammad Razzaq	v Bermuda	Tenaga NSC	1997
	31	S.de Mel & Akhlaq Qureshi	v Scotland	Univ of Malaya	1997
5th	33	A.Amati & S.de Mel	v Hong Kong	Royal Selangor	1997
6th	61	Mohammad Razzaq & B.Giordano	v Scotland	Univ of Malaya	1997
7th	31	B.Giordano & F.Zito	v Hong Kong	Royal Selangor	1997
8th	3	K.Kariyawasam & Sajjad Ahmed	v P.N.G.	PKNS	1997
	3	Sajjad Ahmed & M.G.L.Rajapakse	v Bermuda	Tenaga NSC	1997
9th	19	B.Giordano & P.Pieri	v Scotland	Univ of Malaya	1997
10th	12	Sajjad Ahmed & M.da Costa	v Hong Kong	Royal Selangor	1997

KENYA

GUPTA, Sandeep Kumar b 7.4.1967 Nairobi. Rhb. Club: Nairobi Gymkhana.

KARIM, Asif Y. b 15.12.1963 Mombasa. rhb sla. Club: Jaffrey Sports Club. †

MODI, Hitesh S. b 13.10.1971 Kisumu. lhb ob. Club: Nairobi Gymkhana.

ODOYO, Thomas (Thomas Odoyo MIGAI) b 12.5.1978 Nairobi. rhb rmf. Club: Nairobi Gymkhana.

ODUMBE, Edward Olouch (known as "Tito") (shown in previous books as E.Tito and E.T.Odumbe). b 19.5.1965 Kendu-Bay. rhb rmf. Club: Aga Khan Sports Club.

ODUMBE, Maurice Omondi b 15.6.1969 Nairobi. rhb ob. Club: Aga Khan Sports Club.

ONYANGO, Lameck "Ngoche" b 22.9.1973 Nairobi. rhb rfm. Club: Swamibapa Sports Club.

OTIENO, Kennedy "Obuya" b 11.3.1972 Nairobi. rhb wkt. Club: Ruaraka Sports Club.
PATEL, Brijal b 14.11.1977 Nairobi. rhb sla. Club: Premier Club.
SUJI, Anthony b 5.2.1976. rhb rm.
SUJI, Martin A. b 2.6.1971 Nairobi. rhb rfm.
TIKOLO, Lazaro Openda "David" b 27.12.1964 Nairobi. rhb rm.
TIKOLO, Stephen Ogomji b 25.6.1971 Nairobi. rhb ob. Club: Swamibapa Sports Club. †

Batting	Year	M	I	NO	Runs	HS	Ave	100	50	Ct/St
S.K.Gupta	1990-1997	13	11	2	150	30*	16.66	-	-	2
A.Y.Karim	1986-1997	30	21	2	238	53	12.52	-	1	16
H.S.Modi	1997	8	5	1	68	49	17.00	-	-	2
T.Odoyo	1997	10	7	0	53	21	7.57	-	-	2
E.O.Odumbe	1986-1997	18	14	2	164	25	13.66	-	-	6
M.O.Odumbe	1990-1997	25	24	7	1173	158*	69.00	3	6	18
L.Onyango	1997	4	3	1	23	13	11.50	-	-	-
K.Otieno	1994-1997	19	18	2	360	52*	22.50	-	3	17/6
B.Patel	1997	8	-	-	-	-	-	-	-	2
A.Suji	1997	10	6	3	71	29*	23.66	-	-	1
M.A.Suji	1990-1997	20	5	3	45	14*	22.50	-	-	2
L.O.Tikolo	1990-1997	21	13	4	129	40*	14.33	-	-	5
S.O.Tikolo	1994-1997	19	19	4	719	147	47.93	1	5	10

Bowling	Year	O	M	R	W	Ave	BB	4w
A.Y.Karim	1986-1997	261.1	41	798	48	16.62	5-20	3
T.Odoyo	1997	49	7	147	8	18.37	3-22	-
M.O.Odumbe	1990-1997	165.1	17	566	20	28.30	3-36	-
B.Patel	1997	11	2	27	1	27.00	1-2	-
A.Suji	1997	23	4	96	5	19.20	3-38	-
M.A.Suji	1990-1997	155.5	19	508	34	14.94	5-7	2
L.O.Tikolo	1990-1997	79	12	308	9	34.22	1-4	-
S.O.Tikolo	1994-1997	108	20	404	19	21.26	4-10	2

Highest Totals
For:	318-5		v Bermuda	Aga Khan	1994
Against:	282-8		by U.A.E.	Ruaraka	1994

Highest Individual Innings
For:	158*	M.O.Odumbe	v Bermuda	Aga Khan	1994
Against:	108	C.Smith	for Bermuda	Aga Khan	1994

Best Bowling Analysis
For:	5-7	M.A.Suji	v U.S.A.	Univ of Malaya	1997
Against:	6-41	P-J.Bakker	for Netherlands	HCC, The Hague	1990

Most in a Career
Runs:	1173	(Ave 69.00)	M.O.Odumbe	1990-97
Wickets:	48	(Ave 16.62)	A.Y.Karim	1986-97
Matches:	30		A.Y.Karim	1986-97

Most in a Tournament
Runs:	493	(Ave 98.60)	M.O.Odumbe	1997
Wickets:	19	(Ave 8.26)	A.Y.Karim	1997

Record Wicket Partnerships
1st	78	D.Chudasama & Tariq Iqbal	v Israel	Premier	1994
2nd	116	D.Chudasama & M.O.Odumbe	v Bangladesh	Simba Union	1994
3rd	142	M.O.Odumbe & S.O.Tikolo	v Bermuda	Aga Khan	1994
4th	199	S.O.Tikolo & M.O.Odumbe	v Canada	Tenaga NSC	1997
5th	76	M.O.Odumbe & H.S.Modi	v Ireland	RRI	1997
6th	115	A.Y.Karim & M.Kanji	v Netherlands	HCC, The Hague	1990
7th	69	H.S.Mehta & Z.U.D.Sheikh	v P.N.G.	Tamworth	1982
8th	71	T.J.Tikolo & A.Y.Karim	v Bermuda	ACC, Amsterdam	1990
9th	34	T.J.Tikolo & M.A.Suji	v Namibia	Simba Union	1994
10th	32	E.T.Odumbe & B.Odumbe	v P.N.G.	HBS	1990

JEEVANDRAN, S Nair b 18.3.1974 Port Dickson. rhb ob.
MENON, Ramesh b 14.12.1963 Malaka. rhb ob.
MUNIANDY, Marimuthu A. b 28.2.1971 Ipoh, Perak. rf.
NAVARATNAM, Suresh b 7.10.1975 Kajang, Selangor. rhb rm.
RAJAH, Vivekananda Ranjit b 1.11.1969 Tanau, Sabah. rhb.
RAMADAS, Dinesh b 13.4.1967 Alor Setar, Kedah. rhb ob.
RAMADAS, Kunjiraman b 13.5.1970 Johor. wkt.
RAMADASS, Venu b 24.12.1977 Selangur D. E.
SAAT JALIL, Mohammad b 17.10.1963 Johor Bahru. wkt.
SEGERAN, Santhara Vello b 19.5.1972 Ipoh, Perak.
SELVARATNAM, Rohan Mark b 12.3.1974 Johore, Bahru.
SURESH SINGH b 27.9.1973 Labuan, Sabah. rhb rm.
TAN KIM HING, Abdullah Mohammad Firdaus b 25.10.1958 Rawang, Selangor. rhb sla.
WILLIAMS, Matthew Arthur b 31.12.1976 Sabah. rhb ob.

Batting	Year	M	I	NO	Runs	HS	Ave	100	50	Ct/St
S.N.Jeevandran	1997	7	7	1	44	16	7.33	-	-	-
R.Menon	1994-1997	13	13	1	188	49*	15.66	-	-	3
M.A.Muniandy	1990-1997	13	10	3	25	13*	3.57	-	-	1
S.Navaratnam	1994-1997	14	13	2	207	41	18.81	-	-	4
V.R.Rajah	1997	6	6	0	79	25	13.16	-	-	3
D.Ramadas	1994-1997	14	14	1	167	46*	12.84	-	-	1
K.Ramadas	1990-1997	17	15	1	104	23	7.42	-	-	14/4
V.Ramadass	1997	1	1	1	0	0*	-	-	-	-
Saat Jalil	1986-1997	14	14	1	161	53	12.38	-	1	6
S.V.Segeran	1994-1997	10	10	0	158	41	15.80	-	1	1
R.M.Selvaratnam	1994-1997	12	11	1	154	53*	15.40	-	1	2
Suresh Singh	1997	3	3	0	4	2	1.33	-	-	1
Tan Kim Hing	1982-1997	17	15	3	191	66*	13.40	-	1	5
M.A.Williams	1997	7	7	1	158	58	26.33	-	2	-

Bowling	Year	O	M	R	W	Ave	BB	4w
S.N.Jeevandran	1997	47.2	3	135	6	22.50	4-22	1
R.Menon	1994-1997	111.3	22	342	15	22.80	3-43	-
M.A.Muniandy	1990-1997	89	12	279	11	25.36	4-28	1
S.Navaratnam	1994-1997	55.5	7	232	14	16.57	3-41	-
D.Ramadas	1994-1997	98	14	315	14	22.50	3-24	-
V.Ramadass	1997	6	1	26	0	-	-	-
S.V.Segeran	1994-1997	0.3	0	9	0	-	-	-
R.M.Selvaratnam	1994-1997	60	5	228	11	20.72	2-9	-
Suresh Singh	1997	2	0	7	0	-	-	-
Tan Kim Hing	1982-1997	100.2	13	369	10	36.90	3-15	-
M.A.Williams	1997	1	0	11	0	-	-	-

Highest Totals
For:	253-4		v Gibraltar	Ngara	1994
Against:	348-9		by Bermuda	Wednesbury	1982

Highest Individual Innings
For:	112*	D.Tallalla	v Gibraltar	Ngara	1994
Against:	155*	R.E.Lifmann	for Netherlands	Redditch	1982

Best Bowling Analysis
For:	5-40	D.P.John	v Bangladesh	Moseley Ashfield	1986
Against:	5-2	E.G.James	for Bermuda	Wednesbury	1982

Most in a Career
Runs:	380	(Ave 29.23)	A.Stevens	1986-90
Wickets:	15	(Ave 22.80)	R.Menon	1994-97
Matches:	17		M.Harris Abu Bakar	1979-90
	17		K.Ramadas	1990-97

Most in a Tournament

Runs:	196	(Ave 28.00)	A.Stevens		1990
Wickets:	13	(Ave 12.46)	D.P.John		1986

Record Wicket Partnerships

1st	72	R.Chander & S.W.Hong	v E & C Africa	Hermes	1990
2nd	97	E.Seah & D.Tallalla	v Gibraltar	Ngara	1994
3rd	148	M.Saat Jalil & A.Stevens	v Argentina	Rood en Wit	1990
4th	60	S.Bell & V.Vijiyalingam	v Hong Kong	Hermes	1990
5th	95*	D.Tallalla & Tan Kim Hing	v Gibraltar	Ngara	1994
6th	41	A.Stevens & P.Balakrishnan	v Bangladesh	Moseley Ashfield	1986
7th	105*	D.Ramadas & R.M.Selvaratnam	v Israel	Ngara	1994
8th	44	M.A.Williams & D.Ramadas	v Argentina	RMC	1997
9th	62	Yazid Imran & L.J.Jing	v Bangladesh	Moseley Ashfield	1986
10th	32	D.Ramadas & M.A.Muniandy	v Singapore	RRI	1997

NAMIBIA

ACKERMAN, Barry Wayne b 1.9.1960 Alice.

BARNARD, Mark Robert b 3.11.1967 Vereeniging, South Africa.

COETZEE, David b 17.2.1975 Kuruman, South Africa.

KARG, Morne b 12.7.1977 Windhoek.

KEULDER, Daniel b 2.8.1973 Namibia.

KOTZE, Bjorn b 11.12.1978 Windhoek.

KOTZE, Deon b 12.9.1973 Windhoek.

MURGATROYD, Bryan Gavin b 19.10.1969 Walvis Baai.

SEAGER, Darren b 28.5.1976 Pietermaritzburg, South Africa.

STEVENSON, Ian James b 14.2.1961 South Africa.

THIRION, Jackie b 26.9.1965 Upington, South Africa.

VAN SCHOOR, Ian b 9.9.1965 Cape Town, South Africa.

VAN SCHOOR, Melt b 7.4.1967 Mowbray, South Africa. wkt.

VAN VUUREN, Rudolf b 20.9.1972 Windhoek.

Batting	Year	M	I	NO	Runs	HS	Ave	100	50	Ct/St
B.W.Ackerman	1994-1997	12	11	1	79	36*	7.90	-	-	2
M.R.Barnard	1994-1997	7	7	0	43	19	6.14	-	-	1
D.Coetzee	1997	5	4	0	18	12	4.50	-	-	2
M.Karg	1994-1997	12	11	1	209	51	20.90	-	2	5
D.Keulder	1994-1997	12	12	1	254	78	23.09	-	1	7
B.Kotze	1997	4	4	1	11	8*	3.66	-	-	3
D.Kotze	1994-1997	6	6	3	118	37	39.33	-	-	2
B.G.Murgatroyd	1994-1997	14	14	3	381	106	34.63	1	1	2
D.Seager	1997	3	3	0	15	8	5.00	-	-	1
I.J.Stevenson	1997	5	5	0	86	32	17.20	-	-	-
J.Thirion	1997	1	-	-	-	-	-	-	-	-
I.van Schoor	1994-1997	11	8	2	79	21*	13.16	-	-	2
M.van Schoor	1994-1997	14	11	3	133	32*	16.62	-	-	17/2
R.van Vuuren	1997	5	4	1	14	8	4.66	-	-	1

Bowling	Year	O	M	R	W	Ave	BB	4w
B.W.Ackerman	1994-1997	64.3	4	225	12	18.75	3-20	-
M.R.Barnard	1994-1997	55.3	7	143	6	23.83	3-18	-
D.Coetzee	1997	22	0	105	3	35.00	3-24	-
D.Keulder	1994-1997	36.5	8	112	6	18.66	2-19	-
B.Kotze	1997	12	0	63	0	-	-	-
D.Kotze	1994-1997	17	2	80	4	20.00	2-16	-
J.Thirion	1997	6	0	19	1	19.00	1-19	-
I.van Schoor	1994-1997	52.2	1	259	9	28.77	3-44	-
R.van Vuuren	1997	42.4	6	148	13	11.38	4-27	2

Highest Totals

For:	262-8		v Denmark	Premier	1994
Against:	264-8		by Canada	Kelab Aman	1997

Highest Individual Innings

For:	106	B.G.Murgatroyd	v Denmark	Premier	1994
Against:	125	M.Diwan	for Canada	Kelab Aman	1997

Best Bowling Analysis

For:	4-27	R.van Vuuren	v Malaysia	Tenaga NSC	1997
Against:	5-16	V.Pala	for P.N.G.	Univ of Malaya	1997

Most in a Career

Runs:	381	(Ave 34.63)	B.G.Murgatroyd	1994-97
Wickets:	19	(Ave 10.26)	B.G.Murgatroyd	1994-97
Matches:	14		B.G.Murgatroyd	1994-97
	14		M.van Schoor	1994-97

Most in a Tournament

Runs:	287	(Ave 47.83)	B.G.Murgatroyd	1994
Wickets:	19	(Ave 10.26)	B.G.Murgatroyd	1994

Record Wicket Partnerships

1st	50	A.Fallis & D.Keulder	v Fiji	Ngara	1994
2nd	81	I.J.Stevenson & D.Keulder	v Canada	Kelab Aman	1997
3rd	85	D.Fallis & B.G.Murgatroyd	v Denmark	Premier	1994
4th	152	B.G.Murgatroyd & M.Martins	v Israel	Impala	1994
5th	47	M.Martins & L.Louw	v Argentina	Impala	1994
	47	B.G.Murgatroyd & N.Martins	v Denmark	Premier	1994
6th	56	L.Louw & B.W.Ackerman	v Argentina	Impala	1994
7th	84	L.Louw & N.Curry	v P.N.G.	Jaffery	1994
8th	56*	E.Brits & M.van Schoor	v Argentina	Impala	1994
9th	34	B.W.Ackerman & D.Coetzee	v Netherlands	Tenaga NSC	1997
10th	23	I.Van Schoor & A.Smith	v Canada	Nairobi CG	1994

NETHERLANDS

CANTRELL, Peter Edward b 28.10.1962 Gunnedah, New South Wales, Australia. rhb ob. Clubs: Kampong (Utrecht), Queensland. †

DE LEEDE, Timotheus Bernardus Maria b 25.1.1968 Leidschendam. rhb rm. Club: Voorburg.

EDWARDS, Godfrey Leon b 7.4.1959 Rose Hall Village, Guyana. lhb lm. Club: Kampong (Utrecht).

GROOT, Tjade Heico b 22.7.1973 Amsterdam. rhb rm. Club: VRA (Amsterdam).

KHAN, Khan Asim b 14.2.1962 Lahore, Pakistan. rhb rm. Clubs: Kampong (Utrecht).

LEFEBVRE, Roland Phillippe b 7.2.1963 Rotterdam. rhb rmf. Clubs: Canterbury, Glamorgan CCC, Somerset CCC. †

NOTA, Marc Antoine Clemens b 11.5.1965 Voorburg. rhb ob. Club: Voorburg.

SCHOLTE, Reinout Hans b 10.8.1967 The Hague. rhb wkt. Club: HBS (The Hague).

SINGH, Ravi b 6.4.1974 New Delhi, India. rhb ob. Club: VRA (Amsterdam).

SMITS, Jeroen b 21.6.1972 The Hague. rhb wkt. Club: Haagschell (The Hague).

VAN DIJK, Steven b 23.8.1969 Rotterdam. rhb rm. Club: VOC (Rotterdam).

VAN NOORTWIJK, Klaas-Jan Jeroen b 10.7.1970 Rotterdam. rhb rm. Club: VOC (Rotterdam).

VAN OOSTEROM, Robert Frank b 16.10.1968 The Hague. rhb ob. Club: HBS (The Hague).

VAN TROOST, Adrianus Petrus b 2.10.1972 Schiedam. rhb rfm. Clubs: Somerset CCC, Griqualand West. †

ZUIDERENT, Bastiaan b 3.3.1977 Utrecht. rhb rm. VOC (Rotterdam).

ZULFIQAR AHMED b 23.2.1966 Sialkot. rhb ob. Club: Voorburg.

Batting	Year	M	I	NO	Runs	HS	Ave	100	50	Ct/St
P.E.Cantrell	1997	7	5	1	99	53*	24.75	-	1	7
T.B.M.de Leede	1990-1997	25	21	3	539	56*	29.94	-	4	10
G.L.Edwards	1990-1997	8	2	2	11	8*	-	-	-	-
T.H.Groot	1997	1	1	0	35	35	35.00	-	-	-
K.A.Khan	1997	7	3	1	72	48*	36.00	-	-	-
R.P.Lefebvre	1986-1997	34	29	6	688	109*	29.91	1	1	20
M.A.C.Nota	1997	5	2	0	7	4	3.50	-	-	1
R.H.Scholte	1990-1997	20	12	3	176	90*	19.55	-	1	21/3
R.Singh	1997	1	-	-	-	-	-	-	-	-
J.Smits	1994-1997	2	1	0	1	1	1.00	-	-	3
S.van Dijk	1997	4	2	2	6	5*	-	-	-	1
K-J.J.van Noortwijk	1997	6	3	1	55	24*	27.50	-	-	1
R.F.van Oosterom	1990-1997	25	18	1	292	64	17.17	-	1	9
A.P.van Troost	1990-1997	9	5	3	53	16*	26.50	-	-	1
B.Zuiderent	1997	7	5	2	82	38	27.33	-	-	2
Zulfiqar Ahmed	1997	6	2	0	28	27	14.00	-	-	2

Bowling	Year	O	M	R	W	Ave	BB	4w
P.E.Cantrell	1997	47	9	104	7	14.85	4-10	1
T.B.M.de Leede	1990-1997	78	8	279	15	18.60	2-10	-
G.L.Edwards	1990-1997	63	4	210	5	42.00	2-40	-
K.A.Khan	1997	57.1	7	195	19	10.26	7-9	3
R.P.Lefebvre	1986-1997	262.1	60	606	51	11.88	4-16	1
M.A.C.Nota	1997	19	3	56	2	28.00	1-20	-
R.Singh	1997	4	0	21	0	-	-	-
S.van Dijk	1997	24	8	77	5	15.40	3-35	-
A.P.van Troost	1997	79	7	226	13	17.38	3-11	-
B.Zuiderent	1997	1.4	0	20	0	-	-	-
Zulfiqar Ahmed	1997	10	0	50	0	-	-	-

Highest Totals
For:	425-4	v Israel	Old Silhillians	1986
Against:	251-8	by Kenya	Ruaraka	1994

Highest Individual Innings
For:	169*	R.Gomes	v Israel	Amsterdam	1990
Against:	95	S.O.Tikolo	for Kenya	Ruaraka	1994

Best Bowling Analysis
For:	7-9	K.A.Khan	v E & C Africa	RMC	1997
Against:	4-43	S.Sorensen	for Denmark	Hermes	1990

Most in a Career
Runs:	1040	(Ave 74.28)	N.E.Clarke	1990-94
Wickets:	51	(Ave 11.88)	R.P.Lefebvre	1986-97
Matches:	35		S.W.Lubbers	1979-94

Most in a Tournament
Runs:	523	(Ave 65.38)	N.E.Clarke	1990
Wickets:	21	(Ave 13.19)	P-J.Bakker	1986

Record Wicket Partnerships
1st	257	R.F.Schoonheim & R.E.Lifmann	v Malaysia	Redditch	1982
2nd	248	R.Gomes & N.E.Clarke	v Israel	Amsterdam	1990
3rd	135	R.Gomes & S.W.Lubbers	v Canada	Cheltenham	1986
4th	108	R.E.Lifmann & R.J.Elferink	v P.N.G.	Wolverhampton	1986
5th	117	R.Gomes & R.P.Lefebvre	v Denmark	Mitchell & Butler	1986
6th	116	R.P.Lefebvre & N.E.Clarke	v Argentina	Klein Zwitserland	1990
7th	67	S.W.Lubbers & R.J.Elferink	v Zimbabwe	Lord's	1986
8th	42	B.Kuijlman & H.F.Visée	v Hong Kong	Nairobi CG	1994
9th	29	S.W.Lubbers & A.P.van Troost	v Zimbabwe	HCC, The Hague	1990
10th	22	F.Jansen & P.Keukelaar	v U.A.E.	Nairobi CG	1994

AMINI, Charles. b 12.12.1964 Port Moresby rhb rm.
ARUA, Fred b 14.10.1967 Papua New Guinea. rhb rf.
GUADI, Toka b 19.5.1972 Port Moresby. lhb lm.
ILARAKI, Kosta b 3.1.1961 Kwikila. (shown in previous books as K.Ila). rhb rm.
IPI, Rarua Hitolo b 17.7.1973 Port Moresby. lhb rm.
KEVAU, Vai Boe b 4.5.1967 Port Moresby. rhb.
KILA, Wari. b 17.8.1965. rhb.
LEKA, Leka b 2.2.1965 Hood Lagoon (Keapara), Central Province. rhb.
MAHA, James b 30.6.1977 Port Moresby. lhb ob wkt.
MAHA, Navulani b 30.9.1974 Alukuni. lhb.
MOREA, Ipi b 7.5.1975 Port Moresby. rhb wkt.
OVIA, John b 26.7.1976 Port Moresby. rhb lb.
PALA, Vavine b 23.9.1955 Port Moresby. lhb lm.
RAKA, Tuku b 18.4.1963 Keapara. rhb rf.
VUIVAGI, Keimelo b 5.4.1976 Alewai Hula. lhb.

Batting	Year	M	I	NO	Runs	HS	Ave	100	50	Ct/St
C.Amini	1986-1997	24	22	2	508	97	25.40	-	4	5
F.Arua	1994-1997	13	9	6	16	9	5.33	-	-	3
T.Gaudi	1994-1997	9	4	1	9	3*	3.00	-	-	-
K.Ilaraki	1982-1997	19	14	3	140	34	12.72	-	-	5
R.H.Ipi	1997	4	4	0	59	29	14.75	-	-	1
V.B.Kevau	1997	4	4	0	49	32	12.25	-	-	1
W.Kila	1997	2	2	0	23	19	11.50	-	-	1
L.Leka	1994-1997	8	8	0	115	45	14.37	-	-	-
J.Maha	1997	4	4	0	46	18	11.50	-	-	3
N.Maha	1997	5	5	0	55	45	11.00	-	-	1
I.Morea	1997	5	4	0	49	38	12.25	-	-	5/1
J.Ovia	1997	5	5	0	168	94	33.60	-	2	2
V.Pala	1979-1997	27	22	5	471	101*	27.70	1	2	9
T.Raka	1986-1997	26	25	7	261	59*	14.50	-	1	4
K.Vuivagi	1997	4	4	0	32	29	8.00	-	-	1

Bowling	Year	O	M	R	W	Ave	BB	4w
C.Amini	1986-1997	121.2	9	521	22	23.68	5-19	2
F.Arua	1994-1997	113.2	11	341	26	13.11	5-31	3
T.Gaudi	1994-1997	69	9	237	12	19.75	4-23	1
K.Ilaraki	1982-1997	94.1	9	345	17	20.29	3-14	-
R.H.Ipi	1997	21	2	77	2	38.50	1-30	-
N.Maha	1997	26	4	87	2	43.50	1-20	-
J.Ovia	1997	4	0	20	0	-	-	-
V.Pala	1979-1997	225.1	41	658	33	19.93	5-16	2
T.Raka	1986-1997	246	27	870	34	25.58	4-27	1

Highest Totals
For:	455-9		v Gibraltar	Cannock	1986
Against:	356-5		by Canada	Walsall	1986

Highest Individual Innings
For:	162	B.Harry	v Israel	Worcester City	1986
Against:	164*	P.Prashad	for Canada	Walsall	1986

Best Bowling Analysis
For:	5-12	W.Maha	v Gibraltar	Cannock	1986
Against:	5-18	P-J.Bakker	for Netherlands	Wolverhampton	1986

Most in a Career
Runs:	644	(Ave 25.76)	W.Maha	1982-94
Wickets:	34	(Avc 25.28)	T.Raka	1986-97
Matches:	28		W.Maha	1982-94

Most in a Tournament

Runs:	338	(Ave 48.28)	B.Harry		1986
Wickets:	19	(Ave 10.52)	F.Arua		1994

Record Wicket Partnerships

1st	126	Karo Au & Tauna Vai	v Canada	Walsall	1986
2nd	205	C.Amini & B.Harry	v Gibraltar	Cannock	1986
3rd	159	B.Harry & W.Maha	v Israel	Worcester City	1986
4th	125	J.Ovia & C.Amini	v Italy	PKNS	1997
5th	120	C.Amini & Renagi Ila	v Hong Kong	Rood en Wit	1990
6th	98*	L.Oala & V.Pala	v Gibraltar	Jaffery	1994
7th	107	A.Leka & Raki Ila	v Bermuda	Nuneaton	1986
8th	86*	V.Pala & Guma Ravu	v Canada	Kenilworth	1982
9th	34*	T.Ao & T.Raka	v Fiji	Old Hill	1986
10th	36*	C.Amini & T.Raka	v Canada	Walsall	1986

SCOTLAND

ALLINGHAM, Michael James de Grey b 6.1.1965 Inverness. rhb rm. Club: George Heriot's School Former Pupils. †

BEVEN, Ian Robert b 27.11.1958 Hobart, Tasmania, Australia. lhb ob. Clubs: Grange, Tasmania. †

BLAIN, John Angus Rae b 4.1.1979 Edinburgh. rhb rfm. Clubs: George Heriot's School Former Pupils, Northamptonshire CCC. †

COWAN, David b 30.3.1964 St. Andrews. lhb rfm. Club: Freuchie. †

DAVIES, Alec George b 14.8.1962 Rawalpindi, Pakistan. rhb wkt. Clubs: Grange, Surrey CCC. †

GOURLAY, Scott b 8.1.1971 Kirkcaldy. rhb rm. Club: Freuchie.

KENNEDY, Stuart Robert b 9.1.1965 Paisley. rhb rm. Club: Ferguslie.

LOCKHART, Douglas Ross b 19.1.1976 Glasgow. rhb wkt. Club: Glasgow Academicals. †

LOCKIE, Bryn Gardner b 5.6.1968 Alloa. rhb. Club: Carlton. †

PHILIP, Ian Lindsay b 9.6.1958 Falkirk. rhb sla. Club: Stenhousemuir. †

SALMOND, George b 1.12.1969 Dundee. rhb rm. Club: Grange. †

SHERIDAN, Keith Lamont Paton b 26.3.1971 Bellshill. lhb sla. Club: Poloc. †

SMITH, Michael Jonathan b 30.3.1966 Edinburgh. rhb rm. Club: Aberdeenshire. †

TENNANT, Andrew McBlain b 17.2.1966 Ayr. lhb sla. Club: Prestwick. †

THOMSON, Kevin b 24.12.1971 Dundee. rhb rmf. Club: Aberdeenshire. †

WILLIAMSON, John Greig b 28.12.1968 Glasgow. rhb rm. Club: Clydesdale. †

Batting	Year	M	I	NO	Runs	HS	Ave	100	50	Ct/St
M.J.de G.Allingham										
	1997	5	3	1	71	35*	35.50	-	-	3
I.R.Beven	1997	7	4	0	19	10	4.75	-	-	1
J.A.R.Blain	1997	4	2	0	13	9	6.50	-	-	1
D.Cowan	1997	1	1	0	7	7	7.00	-	-	1
A.G.Davies	1997	8	5	1	74	24	18.50	-	-	12/2
S.Gourlay	1997	6	4	1	21	11*	7.00	-	-	1
S.R.Kennedy	1997	8	5	1	15	5	3.75	-	-	7
D.R.Lockhart	1997	5	5	0	74	21	14.80	-	-	4
B.G.Lockie	1997	6	5	1	114	58	28.50	-	1	2
I.L.Philip	1997	9	8	0	205	71	25.62	-	1	5
G.Salmond	1997	9	8	1	253	59	36.14	-	1	3
K.L.P.Sheridan	1997	8	3	2	9	6*	9.00	-	-	4
M.J.Smith	1997	8	7	0	161	67	23.00	-	1	4
A.M.Tennant	1997	1	1	1	3	3*	-	-	-	-
K.Thomson	1997	5	2	1	8	4*	8.00	-	-	4
J.G.Williamson	1997	9	8	2	171	42	28.50	-	-	3

Bowling	Year	O	M	R	W	Ave	BB	4w
M.J.de G.Allingham								
	1997	23	0	112	7	16.00	3-34	-
I.R.Beven	1997	65	10	183	17	10.76	4-20	2
J.A.R.Blain	1997	28	1	129	7	18.42	3-23	-

D.Cowan	1997	6.2	0	39	2	19.50	2-39	-
S.Gourlay	1997	41.2	4	145	8	18.12	3-26	-
S.R.Kennedy	1997	67.4	21	138	8	17.25	3-15	-
K.L.P.Sheridan	1997	62.1	7	180	12	15.00	4-34	1
A.M.Tennant	1997	6	0	24	1	24.00	1-24	-
K.Thomson	1997	30.4	3	136	6	22.66	3-37	-
J.G.Williamson	1997	46.3	4	187	10	18.70	3-26	-

Highest Totals
For:	273		v Italy	Univ of Malaya	1997
Against:	243-7		by Bangladesh	Tenaga NSC	1997

Highest Individual Innings
For:	71	I.L.Philip	v Italy	Univ of Malaya	1997
Against:	70	Khaled Mashud	for Bangladesh	Tenaga NSC	1997

Best Bowling Analysis
For:	4-20	I.Beven	v Italy	Univ of Malaya	1997
Against:	4-25	P.Jensen	for Denmark	RRI	1997

Most in a Career
Runs:	253	(Ave 36.14)	G.Salmond	1997
Wickets:	19	(Ave 9.63)	I.R.Beven	1997
Matches:	9		three players	

Most in a Tournament
Runs:	253	(Ave 36.14)	G.Salmond	1997
Wickets:	19	(Ave 9.63)	I.R.Beven	1997

Record Wicket Partnerships
1st	127	I.L.Philip & B.G.Lockie	v Italy	Univ of Malaya	1977
2nd	56	D.R.Lockhart & M.J.Smith	v Ireland	Tenaga NSC	1997
3rd	82	M.J.Smith & G.Salmond	v Hong Kong	RRI	1997
4th	71	G.Salmond & J.G.Williamson	v Bermuda	Royal Selangor	1997
5th	31	G.Salmond & J.G.Williamson	v Bangladesh	Tenaga NSC	1997
6th	69	G.Salmond & A.G.Davies	v Denmark	RRI	1997
7th	36*	M.J.de G.Allingham & A.G.Davies	v Hong Kong	RRI	1997
8th	10	M.J.de G.Allingham & S.R.Kennedy	v Ireland	Tenaga NSC	1997
9th	11*	K.Thomson & K.L.P.Sheridan	v Bermuda	Royal Selangor	1997
10th	12	K.L.P.Sheridan & I.R.Beven	v Denmark	RRI	1997

SINGAPORE

CHANDRAN, Ravi Thambinayagam b 17.8.1960 Colombo, Sri Lanka. (shown in previous books as T.Ravichandran). rhb sm. Club: Singapore CC.

CHELVATHURAI, Dinesh Jayaratnam b 21.6.1961 Sri Lanka. rhb ob. Club: Ceylon Sports Club (Singapore).

DASS, Abhijit b 2.4.1957 India. rhb rm. Club: Singapore Airlines.

DAVID, Roderick b 26.8.1963 Sydney, Australia. rhb rm. Club: Singapore Chinese Recreation Club.

DESHPANDE, Kiran Malhar b 19.12.1961 Thane, India. lhb lm. Club: Indian Association (Singapore).

GOH SWEE HENG b 3.3.1956 Singapore. rhb. Club: Singapore Recreation Club.

GUNNINGHAM, Charles J. F. b 12.8.1963 Bath, England. rhb ob wkt. Club: United World College.

MARTENS, Reginald S. R. b 2.9.1961 Singapore. rhb rm. Club: Singapore CC.

MOHAMED, Rasheed Thai Yar b 12.5.1958 Sri Lanka. rhb rm.

MURUTHI, Sreerangam b 31.5.1952 Singapore. rhb ob. Club: Singapore CC.

PATIL, Manoj b 15.11.1960 Indore, India. rhb rm. Singapore Airlines.

RAMADAS, Remesh Prasad b 25.10.1966 Singapore. rhb lbg. Club: Singapore Recreation Club.

RANGGI, Anthon Juda b 18.5.1965 Indonesia. rhb rm. Club: Singapore Airlines.
SITHAWALLA, Moiz Haider b 2.9.1971 Singapore. lhb lm. Club: Ceylon Sports Club (Singapore).
STONE, Jeremy H. b 17.10.1962 Australia. rhb rm wkt. Club: Singapore CC.
WILSON, Graham Stephen b 7.2.1962 England. rhb rm. Club: Singapore CC.

Batting	Year	M	I	NO	Runs	HS	Ave	100	50	Ct/St
R.T.Chandran	1990-1997	19	17	1	207	27	12.93	-	-	7
D.J.Chelvathurai	1997	4	4	2	43	23*	21.50	-	-	-
A.Dass	1986-1997	5	5	0	86	35	17.20	-	-	-
R.David	1997	5	4	1	22	11*	7.33	-	-	1
K.M.Deshpande	1997	4	4	0	103	60	25.75	-	1	2
Goh Swee Heng	1979-1997	15	15	2	152	53	11.69	-	1	6
C.J.F.Gunningham	1997	5	4	0	19	13	4.75	-	-	1
R.S.R.Martens	1997	7	6	1	20	9	4.00	-	-	2
R.T.Y.Mohamed	1994-1997	14	14	1	257	65	19.76	-	1	5
S.Muruthi	1979-1997	23	20	8	190	29*	15.83	-	-	13
M.Patil	1997	1	1	0	2	2	2.00	-	-	-
R.P.Ramadas	1997	2	2	0	3	3	1.50	-	-	-
A.J.Ranggi	1997	6	6	0	87	38	14.50	-	-	-
M.H.Sithawalla	1997	5	5	0	33	15	6.60	-	-	1
J.H.Stone	1997	6	5	1	27	11	6.75	-	-	8
G.S.Wilson	1997	7	7	1	104	50	17.33	-	1	2

Bowling	Year	O	M	R	W	Ave	BB	4w
D.J.Chelvathurai	1997	3.1	1	12	2	6.00	2-12	-
R.David	1997	28	5	119	4	29.75	3-19	-
K.M.Deshpande	1997	26	3	97	2	48.50	1-30	-
R.S.R.Martens	1997	56	3	239	11	21.72	3-30	-
R.T.Y.Mohamed	1994-1997	109	19	349	15	23.26	4-38	1
S.Muruthi	1979-1997	191.1	29	564	22	25.63	3-22	-
M.Patil	1997	2	0	12	0	-	-	-
R.P.Ramadas	1997	4.2	0	20	0	-	-	-
A.J.Ranggi	1997	1	0	8	0	-	-	-
G.S.Wilson	1997	59.4	8	216	13	16.61	4-25	1

Highest Totals
For:	231-6		v Gibraltar	Ruaraka	1994
Against:	291-7		by Bermuda	Klein Zwitserland	1990

Highest Individual Innings
For:	67	F.J.R.Martens	v Malaysia	Old Edwardians	1982
Against:	141	Imran Brohi	for E & C Africa	Nairobi CG	1994

Best Bowling Analysis
For:	5-39	R.Rajalingham	v Fiji	Solihull	1982
Against:	5-12	T.Gardner	for Canada	Impala	1994

Most in a Career
Runs:	257	(Ave 19.76)	R.T.Y.Mohamed	1994-97
Wickets:	22	(Ave 25.63)	S.Muruthi	1979-97
Matches:	23		S.Muruthi	1979-97

Most in a Tournament
Runs:	178	(Ave 44.50)	B.Balakrishnan	1990
Wickets:	13	(Ave 16.61)	G.S.Wilson	1997

Record Wicket Partnerships
1st	87	N.Amrasurya & J.Stevenson	v Gibraltar	Ruaraka	1994
2nd	59	F.J.R.Martens & S.Sethivail	v Malaysia	Old Edwardians	1982
3rd	82	A.J.Ranggi & K.M.Deshpande	v Israel	Victoria Institute	1997
4th	124	K.M.Deshpande & R.T.Y.Mohamed			
			v Gibraltar	Tenaga NSC	1997
5th	48	Goh Swee.Heng & R.T.Chandran	v West Africa	Simba Union	1994
6th	53	J.Stevenson & R.T.Chandran	v Namibia	Ngara	1994

7th	28*	B.Balakrishnan & T.E.Seal	v Malaysia	VRA, Amsterdam	1990
8th	27	R.T.Chandran & D.S.Chelvathurai			
			v Kenya	Royal Selangor	1997
9th	25	Imran Hamid Khwaja & T.E.Seal	v E & C Africa	Nairobi CG	1994
10th	24	R.David & S.Muruthi	v Gibraltar	Tenaga NSC	1997

UNITED ARAB EMIRATES

ADNAN MUSHTAQ Ahmed Syed b 11.4.1977 Dubai. rhb wkt. Culb: E.C.B.Colts.
AHMED NADEEM b 26.10.1976 Abu Dhabi. rhb rfm. Club: E.C.B.Colts.
ALI AKBAR RANA b 5.6.1959 Lahore, Pakistan. lhb wkt. Club: Emirates Bank International.
ARIF YOUSUF Al-Atfar Abdul Rehman b 1976 Ajman. rhb, rm. Club: Sharjah.
ARSHAD LAEEQ b 28.11.1970 Karachi, Pakistan. rhb rfm. †
ASIM SAEED, b 5.10.1979 Al Ain. rhb lm. Club: E.C.B.Colts.
AZHAR SAEED, Syed b 25.12.1968 Lahore, Pakistan. lhb sla. †
HYDER, Mohammed Ali b 5.5.1967 Delhi, India. rhb lb. Club: Air India (Dubai).
JAYAWARDENE, Basil Chandran b 29.12.1963 Colombo, Sri Lanka. rhb rfm. Club: Lanka
    Lions. †
MEHMOOD PIR BAKSH b 25.10.1976 Sharjah. rhb, sla. Club: E.C.B.Colts.
MOHAMMAD ATIF b 12.9.1982 Sharjah. rhb lb. Club: E.C.B.Colts.
MOHAMMAD TAUQEER Khan b 14.1.1972 Dubai. rhb ob. Club: E.C.B.Colts.
PERERA, Mailange Vijayananda b 11.6.1966 Colombo, Sri Lanka. rhb wkt. Club: Sharjah.
SAEED-AL-SAFFAR b 31.7.1968 Dubai. rhb lm. Club: Sharjah.
SALIM RAZA b 25.12.1964 Lahore, Pakistan. rhb ob. †
SHAHZAD ALTAF Hussain b 6.10.1957 Lahore, Pakistan. rhb rmf. †

Batting	Year	M	I	NO	Runs	HS	Ave	100	50	Ct/St
Adnan Mushtaq	1997	3	3	0	24	22	8.00	-	-	1
Ahmed Nadeem	1997	7	5	2	36	15*	12.00	-	-	2
Ali Akbar Rana	1994-1997	7	6	1	120	32	24.00	-	-	15/1
Arif Yousuf	1997	2	1	0	14	14	14.00	-	-	-
Arshad Laeeq	1994-1997	15	11	4	247	66	35.28	-	1	1
Asim Saeed	1997	7	7	0	56	21	8.00	-	-	1
Azhar Saeed	1994-1997	16	16	3	536	126*	41.23	1	3	4
M.Hyder	1994-1997	4	3	1	44	29*	22.00	-	-	-
B.Jayawardena	1997	1	-	-	-	-	-	-	-	-
Mehmood Pir Baksh	1997	3	2	0	8	6	4.00	-	-	1
Mohammad Atif	1997	6	2	1	3	2	3.00	-	-	1
Mohammed Tauqeer	1997	7	5	2	53	24	17.66	-	-	2
M.V.Perera	1997	4	4	1	64	32*	21.33	-	-	1/1
Saeed-al-Saffar	1997	7	5	1	37	24*	9.25	-	-	3
Salim Raza	1994-1997	15	14	4	426	78	42.60	-	3	6
Shahzad Altaf	1997	2	1	0	7	7	7.00	-	-	-

Bowling	Year	O	M	R	W	Ave	BB	4w
Ahmed Nadeem	1997	55.5	4	184	7	26.28	2-26	-
Arshad Laeeq	1994-1997	132	16	521	32	16.28	4-14	3
Asim Saeed	1997	25	3	90	4	22.50	2-25	-
Azhar Saeed	1994-1997	99.5	3	435	18	24.16	4-24	1
M.Hyder	1994-1997	14	1	48	2	24.00	2-20	-
B.Jayawardena	1997	6	1	26	0	-	-	-
Mohammad Atif	1997	21	2	80	3	26.66	2-31	-
Mohammed Tauqeer	1997	4	0	11	1	11.00	1-11	-
M.V.Perera	1997	10	1	40	2	20.00	1-6	-
Saeed-al-Saffar	1997	39	4	137	5	27.40	2-13	-
Salim Raza	1994-1997	120.2	14	436	16	27.25	4-23	1
Shahzad Altaf	1997	20	4	30	2	15.00	1-15	-

Highest Totals

For:	330-9		v Bermuda	Nairobi CG	1994
Against:	329-9		by Bermuda	Nairobi CG	1994

Highest Individual Innings

For:	126*	Azhar Saeed	v Canada	Aga Khan	1994
Against:	117*	M.J.Alam	for Bangladesh	Ngara	1994

Best Bowling Analysis

For:	4-14	Y.Samarasekera	v E & C Africa	Sir Ali Muslim	1994
	4-14	Arshad Laeeq	v West Africa	Royal Selangor	1997
Against:	4-81	M.A.Suji	for Kenya	Ruaraka	1994

Most in a Career

Runs:	536	(Ave 41.23)	Azhar Saeed	1994-97
Wickets:	32	(Ave 15.96)	Arshad Laeeq	1994-97
Matches:	16		Azhar Saeed	1994-97

Most in a Tournament

Runs:	370	(Ave 52.85)	Azhar Saeed	1994
Wickets:	17	(Ave 19.94)	Arshad Laeeq	1994

Highest Wicket Partnerships

1st	141	R.H.Poonawala & Azhar Saeed	v Kenya	Ruaraka	1994
2nd	134	Azhar Saeed & Arshad Laeeq	v Argentina	Victoria Institute	1997
3rd	78	S.M.Hussain & Mohammed Ishaq	v Ireland	Ruaraka	1994
4th	56	Ali Akbar Rana & Salim Raza	v U.S.A.	Victoria Institute	1997
5th	123*	M.Ishaq & Salim Raza	v Netherlands	Nairobi CG	1994
6th	72	Arshad Laeeq & Asim Saeed	v Denmark	Univ of Malaya	1997
7th	51*	Y.Samarasekera & Arshad Laeeq	v U.S.A.	Aga Khan	1994
8th	22	Arshad Laeeq & I.Abbasi	v Bermuda	Nairobi CG	1994
	22	Ahmed Nadeem & Mohammed Tauqueer			
			v Bermuda	Kelab Aman	1997
9th	47	Arshad Laeeq & S.M.Zarawani	v Bermuda	Nairobi CG	1994
10th	11*	Arshad Laeeq & S.Butt	v Bermuda	Nairobi CG	1994

UNITED STATES OF AMERICA

ABDUL NAZIR b 7.7.1973 Lahore, Pakistan.

ADAMS, Morris Compton b 29.3.1957 Barbuda, Antigua. lhb.

AIJAZ ALI b 20.6.1968 Pakistan.

AMIN, Zamin b 5.4.1963 Berbice, Guyana. rhb sla. Club: American Cricket Society (Commonwealth).

BACCHUS, Sheik Faoud Ahamul Fasiel b 31.1.1954 Georgetown, Guyana. rhb rm. Clubs: Guyana, Border, Western Province, West Indies, Canada. †

BENJAMIN, Reginald b 7.2.1961 Antigua.

DENNIS, Kenrick b 7.11.1966 Clarendon, Jamaica. †

DENNY, Raymond b 21.1.1963 Barbados. wkt. Club: Miami Caribbean CC (SFCA).

GRANT, Eyon b 3.3.1959 Georgetown, Guyana. †

KALLICHARRAN, Derrick Isaac b 4.4.1958 Guyana. lhb lb. Clubs: Everset Sports Club (EACA), Guyana. †

LACHMAN, Rudy b 19.10.1961 Guyana. lhb sla.

LEWIS, Edward Alexton b 25.10.1959 Antigua. lhb sla. †

NAZIR ISLAM b 7.7.1973 Lahore, Pakistan.

SINGH, Paul b 27.7.1965 Guyana. rhb rm. Club: Vikings CC (EACA).

SOHAIL ALVI

TEXEIRA, Albert Douglas b 7.1.1960 St Vincent, Grenadines. lhb sla wkt. Clubs: Cavaliers CC (Brooklyn), St. Vincent, Windward Islands.

Batting	Year	M	I	NO	Runs	HS	Ave	100	50	Ct/St
Abdul Nazir	1997	2	1	1	0	0*	-	-	-	-
M.C.Adams	1997	4	4	0	53	27	13.25	-	-	1
Aijaz Ali	1994-1997	10	7	2	91	44	18.20	-	-	-
Z.Amin	1990-1997	20	14	1	173	53	13.30	-	1	6
S.F.A.F.Bacchus	1997	7	7	2	223	100*	44.60	1	1	3
R.Benjamin	1990-1997	11	3	1	3	3	3.00	-	-	2
K.Dennis	1997	6	5	1	71	40	17.75	-	-	2
R.Denny	1994-1997	11	10	1	298	61	33.11	-	-	18/8
E.Grant	1997	6	3	2	21	17*	21.00	-	-	2
D.I.Kallicharran	1994-1997	14	11	3	228	60*	28.50	-	2	4
R.Lachman	1994-1997	7	6	1	167	75*	33.40	-	1	1
E.A.Lewis	1994-1997	11	11	1	251	68*	25.10	-	1	2
Nazir Islam	1997	5	4	0	13	9	3.25	-	-	1
P.Singh	1994-1997	10	9	1	297	69	37.12	-	3	8
Sohail Alvi	1997	1	1	0	24	24	24.00	-	-	1
A.D.Texeira	1994-1997	12	12	3	250	44*	27.77	-	-	3

Bowling	Year	O	M	R	W	Ave	BB	4w
Abdul Nazir	1997	14	0	66	2	33.00	1-12	-
Aijaz Ali	1994-1997	33	3	135	4	33.75	2-16	-
Z.Amin	1990-1997	173.5	20	546	32	17.06	5-20	2
S.F.A.F.Bacchus	1997	46	6	155	7	22.14	2-33	-
R.Benjamin	1990-1997	87.3	4	318	17	18.70	5-27	1
K.Dennis	1997	41	9	134	4	33.50	2-37	-
E.Grant	1997	38.1	6	127	5	25.40	2-8	-
D.I.Kallicharran	1994-1997	127.5	21	404	20	20.20	3-18	-
E.A.Lewis	1994-1997	77	4	122	6	20.33	2-26	-
Nazir Islam	1997	20	1	66	5	13.20	3-15	-

Highest Totals

For:	396-4		v Israel	Solihull Mun.	1986
Against:	332-4		by Zimbabwe	Moseley	1982

Highest Individual Innings

For:	143*	K.R.Khan	v Israel	Solihull Mun.	1986
Against:	135	D.L.Houghton	for Zimbabwe	Moseley	1982

Best Bowling Analysis

For:	5-17	K.R.Khan	v Wales	Olton	1979
Against:	5-7	M.A.Suji	for Kenya	Univ of Malaya	1997

Most in a Career

Runs:	623	(Ave 36.64)	K.R.Khan	1979-90
Wickets:	32	(Ave 17.06)	Z.Amin	1990-97
Matches:	21		K.R.Khan	1979-90

Most in a Tournament

Runs:	295	(Ave 49.16)	S.Shivnarine	1986
Wickets:	14	(Ave 9.85)	M.U.Prabhudus	1986

Record Wicket Partnerships

1st	116	N.S.Lashkari & H.Blackman	v Israel	Solihull Mun.	1986
2nd	83	P.Singh & R.Denny	v Gibraltar	RRI	1997
3rd	125*	S.Shivnarine & T.Foster	v Gibraltar	Aston Manor	1986
4th	118	N.S.Lashkari & K.R.Khan	v Fiji	Kenilworth W.	1986
5th	135*	K.R.Khan & K.Lorick	v Israel	Solihull Mun.	1986
6th	94	R.Lachman & D.I.Kallicharran	v Argentina	Sir Ali Muslim	1994
7th	81	D.I.Kallicharran & K.Dennis	v Singapore	PKNS	1997
8th	57*	T.Mills & J.C.Miller	v Bermuda	Stratford-u-Avon	1986
9th	31	K.Wedderburn & V.Stoute	v Zimbabwe	Quick (N)	1990
10th	26	D.I.Kallicharran & E.Grant	v Ireland	Tenaga NSC	1997

AGODO, Oghenokome Onoziakpezi b 10.3.1957 Warri, Delta State, Nigeria. wkt.
AHUCHOGU, Chuka b 10.2.1968 Port Harcourt, Nigeria.
ASIEDU, Kwasi b 17.3.1963 Koforidua Ghana.
CROOKS, Alfred b 27.7.1957 Banjul, Gambia.
FADAHUNSI, Seye b 16.10.1959 Ibadan, Nigeria.
IDOWU, Oladipupo b 28.8.1960 Ibadan, Nigeria.
KPUNDEH, Albert b 20.11.1969 Freetown, Sierra Leone. wkt.
KPUNDEH, Sahr b 8.6.1968 Freetown, Sierra Leone.
NTINU, Uche b 18.7.1965 Lagos, Nigeria.
NUTSUGAH, Edinam b 23.9.1956 Accra, Ghana.
OMOIGUI, J. b 28.9.1969 Edo State, Nigeria.
SAGOE, Kofi b 2.2.1962 Lagos, Nigeria.
TURAY, Serry b 23.10.1979 Freetown, Sierra Leone.
UKPONG, Okon E. b 21.8.1960 Lagos, Nigeria.
VANDERPUJE-ORGLE, P. Daniel b 25.5.1953 Accra, Ghana.
WILTSHIRE, George Idowu b 9.8.1960 Lagos, Nigeria.

Batting	Year	M	I	NO	Runs	HS	Ave	100	50	Ct/St
O.O.Agodo	1994-1997	11	11	1	114	42	11.40	-	-	5
C.Ahuchogu	1997	1	1	1	4	4*	-	-	-	-
K.Asiedu	1997	1	1	0	2	2	2.00	-	-	-
A.Crooks	1997	2	2	0	0	0	0.00	-	-	3
S.Fadahunsi	1997	8	6	1	17	6*	3.40	-	-	-
O.Idowu	1997	6	4	2	29	18*	14.50	-	-	1
A.Kpundeh	1994-1997	10	10	2	127	30	15.87	-	-	6/3
S.Kpundeh	1982-1997	13	13	1	98	27	8.16	-	-	6
U.Ntinu	1994-1997	11	10	0	106	46	10.60	-	-	3
E.Nutsugah	1990-1997	7	7	2	19	10	3.80	-	-	1
J.Omoigui	1997	8	8	2	122	32	20.33	-	-	3
K.Sagoe	1994-1997	15	15	0	128	21	8.53	-	-	6
S.Turay	1997	2	2	1	9	9*	9.00	-	-	-
O.E.Ukpong	1982-1997	18	18	1	329	106	19.35	1	1	5
P.D.Vanderpuje-Orgle	1994-1997	11	7	1	11	4	1.83	-	-	1
G.I.Wiltshire	1994-1997	13	13	2	190	37*	17.27	-	-	2

Bowling	Year	O	M	R	W	Ave	BB	4w
C.Ahuchogu	1997	7	0	30	1	30.00	1-30	-
S.Fadahunsi	1997	61.5	8	195	13	15.00	3-22	-
O.Idowu	1997	33.1	4	89	8	11.12	4-14	1
A.Kpundeh	1994-1997	7	0	27	0	-	-	-
S.Kpundeh	1982-1997	37.5	5	194	10	19.40	4-65	1
U.Ntinu	1994-1997	21	3	73	5	14.60	3-19	-
J.Omoigui	1997	1	0	4	1	4.00	1-4	-
O.E.Ukpong	1982-1997	81	6	330	12	27.50	3-23	-
P.D.Vanderpuje-Orgle	1994-1997	96.3	12	323	23	14.04	5-31	3

Highest Totals
For: 249 v Bermuda Olton 1982
Against: 355-8 by Hong Kong Sir Ali Muslim 1994

Highest Individual Innings
For: 106 O.E.Ukpong v Singapore Simba Union 1994
Against: 124 S.J.Brew for Hong Kong Sir Ali Muslim 1994

Best Bowling Analysis
For: 5-31 P.D.Vanderpuje-Orgle
v Israel RMC 1997
Against: 4-10 S.Henrikson for Denmark Premier 1994

Most in a Career

Runs:	329	(Ave 19.35)	O.E.Ukpong	1982-97
Wickets:	23	(Ave 14.04)	P.D.Vanderpuje-Orgle	1994-97
Matches:	15		K.Sagoe	1994-97

Most in a Tournament

Runs:	180	(Ave 60.00)	S.Elliott	1982
Wickets:	13	(Ave 15.00)	S.Fadahunsi	1997

Record Wicket Partnerships

1st	57	O.E.Ukpong & J.Onyechi	v Malaysia	Wroxeter	1982
2nd	118	J.Onyechi & S.Elliott	v Bermuda	Olton	1982
3rd	54	Kwesi Sague & O.E.Ukpong	v Singapore	Simba Union	1994
4th	47	O.E.Ukpong & D.Ovberedjo	v Bangladesh	Sandwell Park	1982
5th	91*	J.O.Elliott & T.Ayama	v E & C Africa	Premier	1994
6th	60	D.Ovberedjo & J.Gomez	v Gibraltar	Aga Khan	1994
	60	O.E.Ukpong & G.O.Wiltshire	v Singapore	Simba Union	1994
7th	49*	O.E.Ukpong & J.Omoigui	v Israel	RMC	1997
8th	69	S.Kpundeh & S.Elliott	v Bangladesh	Sandwell Park	1982
9th	22	O.O.Agodo & O.Idowu	v Gibraltar	Victoria Institute	1997
10th	13	T.Ayama & O.A.Akinyombo	v Fiji	Jaffery	1994
	13	O.Idowu & P.D.Vanderpuje-Orgle	v Gibraltar	Victoria Institute	1997
	13	S.Turay & S.Fadahunsi	v Bangladesh	PKNS	1997

Additions and Amendments to Previous Volumes

In general, changes of names or initials as more information has become available are not noted here.
Corrections to the 1979, 1982, 1986 book that were printed in the 1990, 1994 volume are not repeated here.
Corrections to career averages in previous volumes are not shown for players who appeared in the 1997 Trophy - updated career records are shown in this volume.

ICC Trophy Competitions 1979, 1982, 1986

p9	East Africa - add H.S.Mehta to team
p12	Bermuda - A.N.Other should be E.G.James
p26	Kenya - bowler was Z.U.D.Sheikh
P30	Zimbabwe team: †D.L.Houghton, J.G.Heron, K.M.Curran, A.J.Pycroft, *D.A.G.Fletcher, C.A.T.Hodgson, R.D.Brown, PP.W.E.Rawson, A.J.Traicos, V.R.Hogg, E.H.Hough
p40	Bermuda - W.A.Reid c C.A.C.Browne; L.Thomas c C.A.C.Browne
p41	Holland - A.de la Mar c C.A.C.Browne
p55	Zimbabwe - R.D.Brown c M.R.Roberts
p55	East Africa - P.M.Patel c J.Jensen
p88	Athar Ali ct 0; K.Z.Islam HS 15*
p89	E.G.James matches 12
p90	T.Burgess BB 4/10, 4i 3; E.G.James runs 281; A.Edwards mdns 17
p91	F.A.Dennis batting ave 28.66; I.F.Kirmani matches 11; M.G.Patel ct 5, st 0
p92	O.B.Andersen ct 1 st 0; N.Bindslev st 2; T.Hadersland HS 3*; B.Rossen ct 4 st 1 S.Thomsen HS 1*; T.Nielsen bowling and T.S.Nielsen bowling interchange
p93	B.K.Desai ave 1.00; A.N.Hasham ct 0; H.Patadia batting average 18.66 Y.Patel HS 8*
p94	A.Kumar overs 42.4; D.M.Patel bowling runs 269, ave 24.45
p95	S.V.Campbell HS 68*; M.I.Konrote ct 1; S.Misiki HS 19*; S.Sekinini ct 3 I.Suka HS 1; I.Veikauyaki ct 6, st 0; I.Vuli HS 31*; M.I.Konrote overs 61 T.Korocowiri bb 2/34
p96	C.M.Head matches 2; W.T.Scott ct 2
p98	S.W.Lubbers 50s 2; P-J.Bakker bowling runs 277, ave 3.19
p100	D.G.Greenwood bowling ave 18.33
p101	J.Kessel ct 1, st 2; V.E.Worrell overs 91.3
p102	Tariq Iqbal 50s 1; A.Karim matches 4 inns 3; A.S.Mehta ct 5 A.Rehman ct 5, st 3; S.Solanki matches 2 inns 2
p103	K.S.Mankoo bowling ave 16.50; A.Njuguna bowling runs 59, ave 11.80 J.C.Patel ct 4
p104	Chan Yow Choy ct 2; K.Kamalanathan batting 8-7-0-106-30-15.14 P.Banerji wkts 7, ave 49.85; S.Marimuthu BB 1/15; A.Stevens wkts 8, ave 20.12
p105	Taunao Vai ct 13; S.Malum batting ave 6.00
p106	Api Leka BB 1/13
p107	M.Rajalingham ct 0
p108	R.S.A.Jayasekera matches 1; S.A.Jayasinghe matches 3, ct 1, st 0
p109	K.R.Khan ct 9; N.S.Lashkari ct 2
p110	A.C.Ernest bowling ave 93.00; Hasib Khan overs 28.5
p111	J.T.Bell ct 2; S.Carey overs 12
p112	D.Ovberedjo ct 1
p113	R.D.Brown matches 13; K.M.Curran matches 8; D.A.G.Fletcher matches 8; J.G.Heron matches 8; C.A.T. Hodgson matches 8, V.R.Hogg matches 8 ct 2; E.J.Hough matches 5; A.J.Pycroft runs 444; P.W.E.Rawson matches 16 E.A.Brandes BB 5/37, 4i 3; V.R.Hogg bowling 60-10-151-10-15.10 E.J.Hough bowling 36-10-99-4-24.75; P.W.E.Rawson 156.3 overs

ICC Trophy Competitions 1990, 1994

Throughout	A.Njoroge of Kenya should be A.Njuguna E.Tito of Kenya should be E.T.Odumbe M.Orewa of Kenya should be Martin Odumbe D.Tikolo of Kenya should be L.Tikolo M.K.Sibtain of Kenya should be S.Kassamali
p14	Denmark v East & Central Africa - P.Jensen c D.M.Patel
p22	Denmark v U.S.A. - H.Blackman c J.Jensen

p23	Papua New Guinea v Holland - bowler is C.Amini
p54	U.A.E. v U.S.A. - add S.Khan to UAE team (did not bat)
p61	Bangladesh v U.S.A. - P.Singh c F.Ahmed
p64	Namibia v Israel - bowler is I.van Schoor
p68	Kenya v Hong Kong - L.H.Beaman c T.J.Tikolo
P72	Bangladesh v Hong Kong - M.A.Islam c Brewster b Brew
p79	Papua New Guinea v Namibia - T.Raka c sub (D.Kotze)
p90	Batsmen scoring 600 runs in a career - S.W.Lubbers 50s 5
	Bowlers taking 30 wickets in a career - A.Edwards maidens 28; E.A.Brandes 4wi 4; P.W.E.Rawson overs 156.3
	Bowlers taking 20 wickets in a tournament - P-J.Bakker runs 277, ave 13.19
p93	F.Ahmed ct 5; M.J.Alam ct 1 st 3; M.J.(Dulu) Alam ct 1
	M.J.(Dulu) Alam bowling 96.5-8-328-11-29.81-3/27-0
	M.A.Islam bowling 25-3-100-2-50.00-1/13-0; Mizanur Rahman overs 6
p94	D.Lewis ct 2; A.Edwards maidens 28
p96	R.Jayasekera batting average 17.50
p97	A.Butt NO 1, ave 31.30; J.Gregsen HS 53; S.Saddique HS 21*
p98	S.Dassu HS 0*; H.Davda ct 1; S.Naik ct 5; Janak Patel ct 4 st 5; H.Tejani ct 4
p102	S.W.Lubbers 50s 5
p104	K.Kumar 50s 1; T.Sawney ct 1
p105	C.J.Hoey matches 7
p106	G.Talkar ct 2
p108	Delete A.Njoroge - combine his figures with A.Njuguna
	A.Njuguna batting 17-10-3-113-43*-16.14-0-0-3
	A.Njuguna bowling 145-22-461-19-24.26-5/24-1
	Delete E.Tito - combine his figures with E.T.Odumbe
	Delete M.Orewa - combine his figures with Martin Odumbe
	Martin Odumbe batting 6-4-3-37-24-37.00-0-0-1
	Martin Odumbe bowling 40.3-6-170-6-28.33-3/21-0
	Delete D.Tikolo - combine his figures with L.Tikolo
	Delete M.K.Sibtain - combine his figures with S.Kassamali
	S.Kassamali batting 9-8-0-141-49-17.62-0-0-3
p109	R.Menon wickets 6, bowling ave 32.66; S.Menon bowling 6-0-30-1-30.00-1/15
p111	N.Alu batting 11-10-3-80-29-14.14-0-0-12
p112	O.Raka bowling 11-0-41-1-41.00-1/17-0
p113	T.Mohammed BB 4-38
p118	D.L.Houghton matches 24; A.J.Pycroft matches 20, runs 552, ave 50.18; G.W.Flower inns 7, ave 63.25; A.J.Traicos matches 23; E.A.Brandes 4wi 4